DESIGNING
INTERVENTIONS
FOR THE
HELPING
PROFESSIONS

Edwin J. Thomas

 SAGE PUBLICATIONS Beverly Hills London New Delhi

For information address:

SAGE Publications, Inc.
275 South Beverly Drive
Beverly Hills, California 90212

SAGE Publications India Pvt. Ltd.
C-236 Defence Colony
New Delhi 110 024, India

SAGE Publications Ltd
28 Banner Street
London EC1Y 8QE, England

Printed in the United States of America

Library of Congress Cataloging in Publication Data

Thomas, Edwin J. (Edwin John), 1927-
  Designing interventions for the helping professions.

  Includes bibliographical references.
  1. Counseling.   2. Helping behavior.   I. Title.
BF637.C6T49   1984   158'.3   84-3395
ISBN 0-8039-2300-7
ISBN 0-8039-2301-5 (pbk.)

FIRST PRINTING

Contents

Foreword by Richard H. Price 7

Preface 9

Part I: Introduction **13**
1: Contributions to Intervention Design 15

Part II: The Anatomy of the Helping Strategy **27**
2: Objectives, Targets, and Roles in Intervention 29
3: Assessment and Intervention Planning 42
4: Intervention Methods 53
5: Implementation, Maintenance, and Termination 66
6: Monitoring, Evaluation, and Follow-Up 74
7: Behavior Theory and Intervention Theory 84

Part III: Design and Development of Interventions **96**
8: What Makes for Good Intervention? 97
9: Generation Processes in Innovation 111
10: Analysis 139
11: Design 151
12: Development 169
13: Evaluation 191

Part IV: Selected Tools and Techniques   **215**

14: Information Retrieval and Review   217

15: Some Empirical Techniques   231

16: Some Analytic Techniques   243

17: Some Practice Techniques   263

Appendix A: The Design Specification Chart   281

References   291

About the Author   303

Foreword

Interventions are the core technologies of the helping professions. We first learn about interventions through our professional training, which passes them on in a variety of forms including theories, technologies, prescriptions, and case studies. But in our professional life, new problems and new tasks confront us with fresh challenges. Programs are needed to serve diverse client groups. Thus, we see programs being developed to serve the needs of widows, schoolchildren, executives under stress, single mothers, and numerous other groups. All too often, our professional training offers us no specific programs or interventions specifically designed to meet the needs of these client groups. Frequently our clients are not individuals, but agencies and organizations in the community that serve a diverse clientele. Interventions need to be implemented in hospital emergency rooms, police agencies, schools, factories, clinics, and social service agencies.

Many of us have tried to design interventions to meet these new challenges, and frequently we muddle through but find that we need a more systematic approach. We need tools for idea generation, for the retrieval of existing scientific information, for analysis of that information, for the design of interventions, and for their development and evaluation. To be sure, scattered references exist in the literature on the problem of the design of interventions, but until now there has been no single resource that draws together the best of this thinking in a single volume.

The need for such a volume is great because, in a real sense, everyone in the helping professions is a designer of interventions, not just the few social scientists currently identified with this enterprise. In our daily work, we are constantly serving in roles that call this need to our attention. Some of us serve as counselors or clinicians, others as supervisors, still others as evaluators, planners, or decision makers involved in creating programs to respond to client needs. And many of us are teachers who train those who will design and implement helping interventions in their own professional work in the future. Thus, in one role or another, all of us are concerned with the enterprise of intervention design.

It is ironic that now there exists a voluminous literature on the evaluation of programs, and yet little has been done to aid us systematically in program design in the first place. Professor Thomas's book begins to fill that enormous gap in the literature and to provide some balance between the enterprise of design and that of evaluation. This important book is a synthesis of many influential technologies including social research and development, program evaluation, experimental social innovation, planning, and more. It is more than a compilation of techniques. It is a road map to be followed in the development of new interventions.

While this is certainly a handbook for practitioners, it is also a text for those whom we teach. Our students will have to adapt their practices to a changing world with new client groups, needs, and problems. Thus, this is also a book for students and, of course, ultimately for those whom we wish to serve, our clients in the community.

—Richard H. Price

Preface

Along with most practitioners and many researchers in the diverse areas of human service, I have been involved in designing intervention methods for some time without the benefit of a methodology for doing so. My training in practice was helpful but it was oriented exclusively toward the provision of clinical service, and my training later as a behavioral scientist included conventional behavior science research methods that had little application to the analysis, design, and development of interventions. My work, and no doubt the work of many others, would have benefited from having had available a relevant methodology. I wrote this book to help meet this need and to stimulate further work in this area.

This book presents the concepts, logic, and methodology of intervention design for practitioners, administrators, and researchers whose task is evolving new human service interventions for purposes of remediation or prevention. The audience includes practitioners, administrators, and researchers as well as students in such fields as psychology, social work, public health, psychiatry, rehabilitation, behavioral medicine, nursing, education, and counseling, among others. The book clearly is intended to apply to designing and developing interventions for individuals, groups, and families, and most of the examples involve this level of intervention. Even so, much of the methodology should also apply more broadly to evolving intervention efforts for organizations, communities, and programs having statewide or national scope.

The book is organized into four sections. Part I presents an introduction and an overview of the need for and the main contemporary developments that make contributions to the emerging methodology of interventional design. This provides the context and orientation for the reader. Part II is addressed to explaining what gets designed and developed—namely, the components of the helping process. This part essentially provides the anatomy of the helping process. Part III consists of the criteria that apply to appraising interventions, the nature of the design and development process, and the phases of analysis, design, development, and evaluation. This part provides the basic concepts and methods of intervention design. Part IV presents relevant tools and techniques for reviewing and retrieving information, analysis, empirical inquiry, and practice—all as applied to design and development. These are the tools and techniques that may be applied in different phases and with other methods of design and development.

ACKNOWLEDGMENTS

This book was a long time in the making, and many helped in the process. Material was gathered off and on over many years while I carried out other responsibilities in teaching, practice, and research. I had the good fortune of being able to apply many of the ideas and methods in my current research on unilateral family therapy for alcohol abuse while we were also endeavoring to develop this mode of family therapy in the alcohol area. This research was funded by Grant 1 RO1 AA04163-01 of the Psychosocial Research Branch of the National Institute of Alcohol Abuse and Alcoholism. I was able to organize the material and to write the book through the time made available during 1981-1982 by a Senior Fulbright Award to conduct research and teach at LaTrobe University in Australia, an award that was concurrent with a sabbatical leave from the University of Michigan and a Visiting Professorship at LaTrobe University.

I wish to acknowledge the essential administrative support provided by Dr. Phillip Fellin, formerly dean, and Harold Johnson, current dean, of the University of Michigan School of Social Work. Herbert Bisno, Professor in the Department of Social Work at LaTrobe University, provided critical support during the period when I was in Australia. Selected chapters were read in draft form by Professor Donald Pilcher and Ann Pilcher, Dr. Norman Smith, Professor Walter Hancock, and Damodar Golhar—all of whom gave me useful feedback. Some of the advanced graduate students who participated actively with me in applying some of the concepts and methods described in the research on the unilateral approach included Cathleen Santa, Denise Bronson, Joanne Yaffe, and Daphna Oyserman.

Chapters 2-7 and 9 were read in draft form as part of a special seminar on intervention design I gave at LaTrobe University. The students who gave written and verbal feedback in this "field test" of the material were Colin Bray, Angela Gallipoli, Gina Giannoulis, Sandra Ginca, Aileen Halloran, Jonathan Halls, Peter McDonald, Bruce Middleton, Zena Pigden, Wendy Rollins, Debbie Sonin, Margaret Whelan, Kathleen Wooden, and Elfie Weiss. Many secretaries here and in Australia helped type the various drafts of the manuscript. Vivian A. Thomas typed the entire dictated draft and Carol Thurman and Therese McNeil in the main typed the first draft. Revisions for the final draft were prepared by Pauline Bush, Kathleen Cornell, Bonnie Kerschbaum, Millie Leavy, Roxanne Loy, Mary Martinowicz, Betty McLean, Ann Page, Doris Rauser, and Dottylou Sarff. I greatly appreciate the diligent and competent efforts of these secretaries as well as the administrative assistance provided by Carol Thurman and Shirley Anderson. Finally, I wish to acknowledge the support and guidance provided by Richard Price, the consulting editor for this volume.

DEDICATION

This book is dedicated to the new breed of practitioner and researcher who will also be competent in and comfortable with the world of design and development.

Part I

Introduction

Therapists and researchers regularly engage in creating new interventions. They have designed programs in such areas as weight control, health care, self-care, moods and depression, anxiety and stress management, sexual competence, marital harmony, child management, nondelinquent behavior, social, educational and employment skills, as well as occupational adjustment and success. Given currently available methods, what can practitioners and researchers bring to bear when designing such interventions? Their skills—although of great importance—are largely those involved in employing existing helping methods, rather than making new ones.

Behavioral science research methods are also very useful, especially in studying relevant human behavior, but such methods are capable only of providing assistance in generating new knowledge; and such knowledge, even if relevant to the intervention area, is insufficient in itself to design a new intervention. Judgment, creativity, and knowledge are important also, but at present it is uncertain how they can be used in the design. A new methodology is therefore needed—one that will assist practitioners and researchers to design and develop new methods of intervention.

There have been important changes in conceptions of practice and applied research, so that an intellectual climate now exists that is receptive to the introduction of a methodology of intervention design. Some of these changes are outlined in Chapter 1, where I also highlight some of their contributions to intervention design. Among such contributions are those of behavioral science research methods, applied research, study of the use of research, retrieval models from the literature that demonstrate how to generate intervention guidelines, program evaluation, experimental social innovation, action models, empirically oriented practice, how to plan interventions, and models of research and development. Some of the strengths and limitations of each of these contributions are presented along with directions for further work on intervention design. These directions provide the focus for the main themes of this book.

Contributions to
Intervention Design

Human service achieves its objectives in large part through its intervention methods, yet there is no methodology of intervention design. Despite this lack, human service practitioners and researchers regularly face problems for which solutions must be adopted. By one means or another, interventions must be developed. The problem, however, is that making interventions without a design methodology is like making bridges without mechanical engineering or creating computers without electrical engineering. It is handicapping, to say the least. The lack of a design methodology must inevitably restrict the interventions evolved to those that are more obvious, familiar, and comfortable and, more generally, to limit innovative options and retard the rate of intervention advancement. Without a framework of intervention design, the human service professions are deprived of a methodology by which they can be systematically and actively involved in generating the intervention methods so vital to their professional accomplishment.

The lack of a design methodology is made more acute by the continuing need for new interventions. In this modern era, interventions generally are used only briefly. One reason is that many of the interventions, when examined critically, would generally be judged as incomplete or not fully adequate otherwise, and deserving of alteration. Although some interventions have been shown to be more effective than others for certain objectives, the results of most outcome studies typically disclose some intervention shortcomings. Even in areas in which the intervention procedures are relatively well developed (e.g., token economies), there is considerable room for improvement, especially in achieving long-term change (e.g., Kazdin, 1977).

There are also frequent changes in resources, priorities, and social objectives that provide impetus for changing the goals, tasks, and methods of human service. Information that provides the basis for the development of new interventions pours forth unremittingly. Behavioral science research continues to yield abundant findings relevant to intervention. Developments in allied fields continue apace and cannot be ignored. The physical technology itself is blooming with innovations in such areas as electronics, audio and visual recording, and computers—most of which eventually have an impact on intervention methods. Interventions in human service will doubtless be subject to continuing and rapid change in the foreseeable future.

SOME REVELANT CONTRIBUTIONS

Although there currently exists no methodology of interventional design, several areas of research and practice make contributions to an emerging model of intervention design. Some of these are outlined below.

Behavioral Science Research Methods

The research methods of behavioral science are perhaps the single best set of methodological tools that most human service researchers currently have at their disposal. These tools have heretofore been the dominant methodology of research in areas related to human service. These are the research methods that most students learn and researchers employ in psychology, sociology, and the other behavioral and social sciences. If human service professionals are familiar with research methods, these are the methods they are most likely to know. These methods are, of course, best suited to developing knowledge of human behavior in the disciplines of behavioral science, in which research is directed toward the generation of facts, empirical relationships, and the testing of hypotheses and theories. The methodology of behavioral science research will no doubt continue to be a mainstay of research in human service that is oriented toward building knowledge of human behavior in contrast to that which is directed toward the development of human service interventions.

However, the major shortcoming of behavioral science research methods is that they contribute little to the actual process of generating intervention innovation (for further details, see Thomas, 1978b). In short there is no methodology of design and development for interventions. Even so, some of the component research methods of behavioral science have a place in intervention design. For example, the methods of conducting exploratory inquiries may be useful in the early stages of development, and methods of measurement and experimentation are especially valuable in evaluating innovations. Indeed, the entire field of evaluation research has been enriched immensely by the methodological contributions of behavioral science research methods.

Applied Research

In contrast to pure research, applied research in the behavioral and social sciences focuses largely on learning more about improving socially important behaviors or the conditions that affect those behaviors (e.g., see Deitz, 1978). Such research is generally conducted in the natural habitats of the client or clients and meets the usual requirements of research methodology. Applied behavior analysis, for example, has contributed many important principles and procedures of behavior change as well as a methodology of single-case experimentation appropriate for research in applied settings (e.g., see Baer, Wolf, & Risely, 1968; Hersen & Barlow, 1976).

A related approach to applied research is that of Azrin and his associates (e.g., Azrin, 1977) in which the focus is expressly on the creation of interventions that are intended to be effective. In evolving interventions, behavioral principles such as those of reinforcement are drawn on, as well as ideas from other sources, and interventions are evaluated using group as well as single-case experimental designs. Although there is dispute concerning whether such research can make contributions to fundamental principles of behavior (e.g., Birnbrauer, 1979; Deitz, 1978; Hayes, 1978), this type of applied research highlights the advantages of an outcome- or cure-oriented approach that draws eclectically on many sources of knowledge in generating interventions and on diverse research methodologies for their evaluation.

Study of Research Utilization

An important development, begun largely in the 1960s, was research on the utilization process itself. Havelock (1973) described this emerging discipline as "the science of knowledge utilization" (p. 3). Research centers for inquiry into the utilization of scientific knowledge were established, and there was a great deal written in the 1960s and 1970s on the utilization process. Phases in the utilization process have been isolated. For example, one school of thought identified by

Havelock (1973) is called the "social interaction perspective" in which primary emphasis is placed on the processes of diffusion and adoption of knowledge. Thus, given an innovation that is already available, such as a new practice procedure, the stages in this approach consist of having the potential recipients of the innovation become aware of the practice, interested in it, involved in its evaluation, and, subsequently, in its trial use and acceptance.

Another perspective identified by Havelock (1973) is that of research and development (R&D), the model of industry, engineering, and science. The four phases of this approach are research, development, diffusion, and adoption. They have been specified in different ways for nonengineering fields. For example, in their version of this model for the field of education, Guba and Clark (as cited in Havelock, 1973) describe the phases as follows: research, the objective of which is the advancement and extension of knowledge; development, which consists of the two subactivities of invention and design; diffusion, divided into the two subactivities of dissemination and demonstration; and adoption, in which there are the three subactivities of trial use, installation, and, finally, institutionalization. The social R&D perspective is relevant because it distinguishes a developmental phase in which a technological product is evolved and identifies a set of activities prior to this phase— in this case, research.

An important related development grew out of efforts, begun in many human service fields largely in the 1950s and 1960s, to use contributions from social and behavioral science. This was the effort to specify the criteria by which knowledge could be selected for use (e.g., content relevance, knowledge power and referent features; see, e.g., Gouldner, 1957; Thomas, 1964; Tripodi, Fellin, & Meyer, 1969; Zetterberg, 1965). Work in this area continued into the 1970s with extensions and refinements of the criteria (e.g., see Bloom, 1975; Fischer, 1978; Rothman, 1974; Tripodi, 1974).

Models to Retrieve Literature and
to Generate Intervention Guidelines

Several investigators (e.g., Bloom, 1975; Mullen, 1978; Rothman, 1974) evolved a methodology by which research findings may be reviewed critically and applied to the task of evolving intervention guidelines. The model of the research utilization process developed by Rothman (1974) is illustrative. This framework evolved in connection with research directed toward specifying action principles based on the findings of social science research. Attention was given in particular to the subprocesses and operations that appeared to be necessary in order to formulate the more general findings of social science and move from these to specific, operational action guidelines that would be useful in planning and organizing for social change.

Rothman proposed a sequence of stages and operations. For example, the findings from the literature of the basic research pool in social science are first retrieved, coded, and generalized. This leads to the formulation of consensus findings and generalizations for which translation and conversion into generalized application principles are required. These principles, in turn, are operationalized in the form of concrete and delimited application principles. Initial implementation and field testing follow that result in practice and policy outcomes, refined and elaborated application principles, and diffusion media. Finally, through wide diffusion, the application principles are put into broad practice with clients, consumers, or constituents. Rothman (1980) more recently conceived of these phases as aspects of corresponding phases of social R&D, to be described shortly.

Among the contributions of this approach to literature retrieval are the identification and elaboration of the extended series of phases and operational steps required to draw action guidelines from social and behavioral science, attention to the process of converting descriptive behavioral and social science generalizations to prescriptive guidelines for action, and the specification of guidelines amenable to empirical testing.

Program Evaluation

Evaluation research has grown rapidly in the last few years, and it is now a vigorous, multidisciplinary specialization (see Struening & Guttentag, 1975; Suchman, 1967; Weiss, 1972). Program evaluation has been described as "the systematic accumulation of facts for providing information about the achievement of program requisites and goals relative to efforts, effectiveness, and efficiency within any stage of program development" (Tripodi, Fellin, & Epstein, 1971, p. 12). Such evaluation is important because it provides for empirical appraisal of intervention efforts, generally to provide feedback to those responsible for the program and to sponsors.

Experimental Social Innovation

Related to program evaluation is what Fairweather (1967) called "experimental social innovation." In contrast to introducing a new program on a broad and more or less permanent basis without experimental evaluation or provision for disbanding the innovation if it is not successful, in this approach a social innovation is introduced tentatively and evaluated experimentally. Experimental social innovation can take the form of demonstrations or field experiments, well-established methods of introducing innovations on a trial basis combined with outcome evaluation (e.g., see Benn, 1981; Community Research Associates, 1953; French, 1953; Thomas, 1960; Weeks, 1958).

Implemented as part of a problem-solving process, there are three steps in experimental social innovation according to Tornatzky, Fergus, Avellar, Fairweather, and Fleischer (1980): (1) defining the social problem, (2) creating alternative models, and (3) creating an experimental test in which there is a true experimental comparison of the innovation with alternative programs or policies. Based in part the earlier work of Fairweather (1964), Tornatzky and associates compared the "community lodge," designed as an innovative living and working arrangement for the ex-mental patient, with control groups. Among the conclusions was that there were many benefits of the community lodge as compared with institutionalization or traditional aftercare programs. The advantage of experimental social innovation over customary change is that the innovation is implemented only on a limited and contingent basis, with its continuation depending obtaining on beneficial outcomes as experimentally determined.

Action Models

Social action research is instructive because it combines a practice objective, the formulation of an intervention, and a subsequent evaluation (see Argyris, 1970; Corey, 1954; French & Bell, 1973; Lewin, 1946). For example, the action model of Specht (1968) is addressed to activities practitioners may carry out in the process of social policy formulation. According to this model, the stages of policy formulation are as follows: (a) identification of the problem (e.g., case finding, recording, and discovery of gaps in service); (b) analysis (e.g., data gathering, analysis, and conceptualization); (c) informing the public (e.g., dramatization, public relations, and communications); (d) development of policy goals (e.g., creating strategy and carrying out program analysis); (e) building public support (e.g., developing leadership and achieving consensus); (f) legislation (e.g., drafting of legislation and the design of programs); (g) implementation and administration (e.g., program organization); and (h) evaluation and assessment (which, again, involves case finding, recording, discovering gaps in service, and gathering data). This approach is valuable because it recognizes the importance of analysis as an early effort in design and development. It is also useful because it tries to come to grips with how practice can contribute to the development of social technology—in this case, social policy.

Empirically Oriented Practice

Stimulated largely by the procedures followed in behavior therapy, applied behavior analysis, behavioral research, and efforts to establish closer relationships between clinical research and practice, there has been increasing interest in empirically oriented practice. Conceptions of the empirically and scientifically oriented helper have been articulated (see Barlow, 1981; Barlow, Hayes, & Nelson, 1984; Bloom, 1975; Briar, 1973; Fischer, 1978; Jayaratne & Levy, 1979; Marks, 1982; Thomas, 1975, 1977b; Tripodi & Epstein, 1978), and the specific contributions of such methodologies as single-case experimentation (see Bloom & Fischer, 1982; Fischer, 1978; Hayes, 1981; Howe, 1974; Jayaratne & Levy, 1979; Stuart, 1971; Thomas 1975, 1983), and other methods of measurement and quantitative evaluation have appeared (e.g., Bloom, 1975; Bloom & Block, 1977; Fischer, 1978; Marks, 1982; Nelson, 1981; Thomas, 1975; Tripodi & Epstein, 1980). In addition to its benefits for direct service to clients, developments in empirically oriented practice should substantially increase the likelihood that contributions to knowledge as well as to procedure will emanate from practice.

Intervention Planning

All therapists must formulate treatment plans that identify intervention methods appropriate for addressing particular client concerns. The fashioning of an intervention plan calls for consideration of suitable alternatives, given available methods, as well as new approaches that might be adopted to meet the problem in question. Although carried out with a particular client or clients for given service purposes, such planning is a limited form of design that can result in producing a novel intervention for cases of that type.

Experience and knowledge of the field are clearly essential in formulating a sound intervention plan. However, what is required to make a plan is not yet well articulated. Further, all too often planning is made within the confines of one's favored treatment perspective rather than being based on more diverse and comprehensive information relating to the area of intervention. Despite these limitations, however, the skills involved in planning interventions are also directly relevant in interventional design.

Models of Research and Development

There is increasing interest in new approaches to research in which at least some of the requirements of innovational design and development have a place. At this early point the approaches are known variously by such names as social R&D, programmatic research, problem-solving research, developmental research, technique-building research, and model development research. There is as yet no established name or model. However, most of the approaches contain significant departures from the conventional behavioral science model of research in which the objective is to make contributions to knowledge of human behavior.

One example is Rothman's (1980) recent approach to social R&D, a model that takes its principal concepts from industrial and scientific R&D but which is applied to the utilization of findings from social science. In this version of R&D, research, the first phase, takes the form of literature review and retrieval of findings from social science. Following this is a phase of conversion and design that results in pilot testing of the application concepts. In the phase of development, there is the main field testing and evaluation, following which there is a phase of diffusion of results. In addition to the methodology of retrieving and applying research findings already mentioned in connection with literature retrieval models, a further contribution of this approach is its conception of social R&D, an orientation that need not be restricted to literature review and application testing. For more detailed appraisal of this approach, the reader is referred to Patti (1981).

A variant of social R&D and program evaluation identified by Tripodi (1974) is called RDTE, or research, development, training, and evaluation. This model, in brief, consists of research on a significant aspect of practice, followed by selection of those features for purposes of training that are found to be empirically supported, and then a training program is developed and evaluated. The addition of an evaluation phase following development is important, a phase generally not formally recognized in most approaches to R&D.

Another model is the Program Development Model (PDM), proposed by Gottman and Markman (1978) for research in psychotherapy. In this framework there are the following steps: (a) selection of the target population; (b) design of the content of the program (to be based, for example, on empirical studies of responses indicative of competent and incompetent client performance in the area in question); (c) selection of the evaluation measurement network; (d) selection of modes of delivery; (e) testing the program's effectiveness; (f) assessing the successes and failures of the program; (g) systematic dismantling of the program (directed toward improving its efficiency); and (h) specification of the program's cost, benefits, and limitations. One of the advantages of PDM is its inclusion of empirical methods to assist in designing the content of the program of therapy (step b). As a means of isolating desirable target responses of clients to be included in the program, task analysis is employed in an endeavor to identify fundamental processes that distinguish competent from incompetent client performance in the content area of the program. This approach to evaluation also has the virtue of providing for relatively detailed appraisal of the psychotherapy program.

The model of developmental research I proposed (Thomas, 1978a, 1978b) is expressly directed toward the development of human service methodology. Developmental research is conceived as consisting of those methods by which the social technology of human service is analyzed, designed, created, and evaluated. In addition to knowledge from behavioral and social science, information necessary in innovation of human service methods is viewed as deriving from many other sources (e.g., scientific and allied technology, legal policy, practice, indigenous innovation, and professional and personal experience). In this approach, strong emphasis is placed on the generation processes by which information from basic sources is transformed into designs for innovation (for further details, see Thomas, 1980).

The phases of developmental research are analysis, development (which also includes design), and evaluation, each of which has its distinctive activities and steps. The phases of developmental research are viewed as the early and essential phases that come before the subsequent phases of utilization, which are those of diffusion and adoption. The full sequence of these phases—analysis, development, evaluation, diffusion, and adoption—with their constituent steps and conditions, is called developmental research and utilization (DR&U). In addition to evaluation, this model explicitly recognizes the importance of analysis, design, and development along with a number of constituent methods not currently contained in conventional research and practice methodologies. Although formulated more generally, the concepts and phases appear to be directly relevant to intervention design, as do the operational steps of this approach, which are not outlined here.

Although none of the developments outlined above represents a fully satisfactory approach to intervention design, each makes contributions that should be taken into consideration in further work in this area. In the approach presented in this book, many of the contributions outlined above will be drawn on as they apply to different aspects of intervention design.

FOCI FOR AN EMERGING METHODOLOGY

A methodology of intervention design should provide a systematic and orderly means by which design problems may be formulated and solved and the resulting innovations developed and evaluated. Such a methodology would serve the same function as any other methodology. While it could not guarantee success in every case or convert modest ability into creative genius, it should increase the chances of successful design when properly applied by those with appropriate background and training.

Enough prior work has been done to make it feasible to begin to formulate a methodology of intervention design. At this point there would appear to be three related priorities, each of which provides focus for further work in intervention design. The first is to identify what is to be designed—in this case, the particular components of the helping strategy that provide options that may be the objects of design. The second is to endeavor to identify and explicate the main phases and constituent activities of design and development. The third is to isolate and describe the particular tools and techniques that can assist practitioners and researchers in specific design tasks. These three priorities are the main subjects of this book, with one part of the book devoted to each. When taken together, the subjects embraced by these foci represent a provisional framework and some of the components of an emerging methodology of intervention design.

SUMMARY

1. Interventions in human service are subject to continuing and rapid change.

2. Human service achieves its objectives in large part through its interventions, yet there is no methodology of intervention design.

3. Without a design methodology, the human service professions are deprived of a means by which they can be involved systematically and actively in generating the intervention methods so vital to their professional accomplishment.

4. There are several areas of research and practice that make contributions to an emerging model of intervention design. These include behavioral science service methods, applied research, study of research utilization, models to retrieve literature and generate interventional guidelines, program evaluation, experimental social innovation, action models, empirically oriented practice, intervention planning, and models of research and development, such as social R&D and developmental research.

5. Although none of these contributions represents a fully satisfactory approach to intervention design, each should be taken into consideration in further work in this area.

6. Methodology of intervention design should provide a systematic and orderly means by which design problems may be formulated and solved and the resulting innovations developed and evaluated.

7. Enough work has been done to make it feasible to begin to formulate a methodology of intervention design.

8. Three priorities provide focus for further work in intervention design. These involve identification and description of the particular components of the helping strategy, the phases and constituent activities of design and development, and the tools and techniques to assist practitioners and researchers in specific design tasks.

9. The three priorities are the main themes for this book and, when taken together, the subjects embraced by these themes represent a provisional framework and some of the components of an emerging methodology of intervention design.

PART II

The Anatomy of the Helping Strategy

What is a helping strategy? Of what does it consist, and what are some of the significant variations? The purpose of the chapters in this part is to provide provisional answers to these questions in the context of intervention design. Because each component of a helping strategy may be the focus of design effort, emphasis in these chapters is on the features of design and possible variations that the practitioner-researcher should keep in mind in the design process. Although aspects of recommended practice are necessarily highlighted at various points, the intention here is that these recommendations be taken as illustrative rather than as definitive. What is recommended practice today may well be outmoded with new developments. In light of this, emphasis has been placed mainly on the nature of the component, its relationship to the overall helping strategy, and some of the issues that need to be considered in intervention design. It is thus that these chapters are not intended as guides to practice. The reader is referred to writings in his or her own field of human service for details of practice methodology.

A helping strategy may be defined as of one or more interventions directed toward given targets of intervention that is carried out with particular objectives and participants who perform given roles and who make use of specific adjuncts and props in certain contexts of helping. Further, the intervention involves such related procedures as assessment, implementation, maintenance, termination, monitoring, evaluation, and follow-up. Each element in this definition is a component that needs to be fleshed out in some detail in any mature helping strategy. This conception of the helping strategy is most relevant to direct intervention with individuals, couples, families, and groups, but because each component has its macro counterparts, it also has implications for the design and development of interventions for organizations, communities, and society. *A major purpose of intervention design is to provide a method by which the practitioner-researcher can specify and elaborate the helping strategy components that are the focus of design and development (D&D).*

The Anatomy of a Helping Strategy

Change Objectives
Targets of Intervention
Participants
    Target Persons
    Helping Persons
Roles
    Helping Person Roles
    Client Roles
Contexts of Helping
    Helping Situations
    Service Settings
Adjuncts and Props
Assessment Methods
Method of Planning Intervention
Intervention Methods
    Techniques of Intervention
    Program Format
Implementation Procedures
Maintenance Methods
Termination Procedures
Monitoring Methods
Evaluation Methods
Follow-Up Procedure
Behavior Theory
Intervention Theory

Objectives, Targets, and Roles in Intervention

An intervention is a planned intrusion into the life or environment of an individual, couple, family, or other target unit that is intended to bring about beneficial changes for the individuals or others involved. The intervention is usually but not necessarily given by a professional in one or another of the fields of human service in connection with some type of organized human service activity. The interventive action is the most conspicuous and central element in producing the desired outcomes of the helping effort, but it does not stand alone. It is, or should be, part of a helping strategy in which the other components help shape the interventive action and have an influence on the outcomes achieved. Beginning with this chapter and continuing through the chapters of this section, each of the components of a helping strategy is discussed in the context of intervention design.

CHANGE OBJECTIVES

Change objectives indicate the goals toward which the efforts of helping should be directed and can influence all components of the helping strategy. Some of the principal objectives relevant to intervention design are summarized in Table 2.1. These are the objectives of remediation, enhancement, competence, education, prevention, advocacy, resource provision, and social control. Every change effort generally has one primary change objective, and sometimes secondary objectives as well.

Each objective has a legitimate place in human service and has both strengths and limitations. Like all components of a helping strategy,

TABLE 2.1
Selected Change Objectives with Examples

Change Objective	What It Is	Examples
Remediation	Intervention directed toward altering a problem that is a source of difficulty for the client.	Providing assertive training for an unassertive young person, sex therapy for a young man with psychological impotence, or communication training for marital partners who disagree excessively.
Enhancement	Intervention directed toward improving functioning above an already satisfactory level.	Providing a sexual improvement program for marital partners whose sexual adjustment is already satisfactory to make the sexual satisfaction greater, or a parent training program for parents whose children do not have severe problems and who already handle most problems well.
Competence	Intervention directed toward strengthening the client's ability to handle not only an existing difficulty but also a variety of difficulties in a given area, including those that may rise in that area in the future.	By focusing on self-induced relaxation and cognitive coping, providing anxiety management training for individuals who experience disabling anxiety in a particular area and who also have other areas of anxiety, doing so in such a way as to strengthen the individual's ability to manage existing anxieties as well as anxiety-evoking situations that may come up later; training parents to handle any of a variety of child management difficulties that may be presented now and later.

Education	The presentation of information to facilitate understanding in an area of intervention.	Presenting information to the family of a substance abuser concerning, for example, the nature of the substance, its adverse effects, the typical course of addiction, possible ways in which the family members may cope with the ill effects of the substance abuse, and how they may assist in rehabilitation.
Prevention	Intervention directed toward eliminating potential difficulties before they arise or become sufficiently problematic to require remediation.	Training adolescent children in secondary school in conflict resolution, communication, and decision making to provide the participants with skills so that possible future discord in intimate relationships would be averted.
Advocacy	Speaking up for and taking other actions on behalf of the client to protect the client's rights and to pursue client interests.	Assisting the client to take legal action in connection with alleged discrimination; negotiating for the client to obtain more satisfactory housing.
Resource Provision	Provision of such resources as food, clothing, shelter, money, or medicine.	Giving food to the unemployed who have exhausted unemployment benefits; providing shelter to flood victims.
Social Control	Interventions directed toward protecting the clients and/or society, generally through provision of special residential arrangements.	Incarceration of legal offenders; establishing separate residential facilities for the mentally impaired, the aged, or those terminally ill.

ideally the change objective should be chosen carefully rather than taken as given. However, there are often practical considerations that dictate what the objective should be, leaving little choice for the practitioner-researcher. When choice exists, the objective most suitable to the problem should be chosen. Prerequisite conditions for that objective should be met and the intervention designed accordingly.

Of these objectives, remediation is the most common and widespread in human service intervention. Problems calling for remediation are generally conspicuous and pressing, and intervention methods directed toward remediation have been the best developed. Contemporary intervention has often been criticized because it does not focus sufficiently on the objectives of competence and prevention. As laudable as these objectives are, current methodology for these objectives is relatively undeveloped and few resources have been allocated to their achievement. Fortunately, attitudes are changing, and intervention methods focusing on competence and prevention are now beginning to receive the attention they deserve.

At the same time, however, the problems for which remediation is appropriate are likely to be with us for a long time. Even with much greater emphasis on competence and prevention than now exists, as long as there are problems pressing for solution, there will be the need for remedial intervention.

TARGETS OF INTERVENTION

The targets of intervention include the problem behavior itself, behavior incompatible with the problem behavior, and the conditions that control the problem behavior, including systems. These targets and illustrative subtypes are presented in Table 2.2. Targets are important because they are where intervention effort is directed. As will be highlighted below, the focus of intervention must be on the appropriate target, and should avoid leaving out relevant aspects or embracing more than is necessary. Through selecting the suitable target, the helper wishes to avoid intervention that causes needless distress for clients, risks relapse, only tangentially affects desired outcomes, and is likely to produce adverse side effects.

Problem Behavior

The most obvious and seemingly straightforward target of intervention is the problem behavior itself. This turns out to be more complex

TABLE 2.2
Varieties of Targets of Intervention

I. Problem Behavior
   A. Type (e.g., motoric, physiological, cognitive)
   B. Content domain (e.g., sexual, affectional, social skills, values, gender, emotional, marital, family, parent-child, school performance, work performance)
II. Incompatible Behavior
   A. Pro-social counterpart of the problem behavior (e.g., in-seat behavior instead of out-of-seat behavior in the classroom, assertive responding instead of unassertive responding, relaxed responding instead of anxiety)
   B. Other incompatible behavior (e.g., any other behavior instead of self-abuse, any verbal response instead of mutism)
III. Controlling Conditions and Systems
   A. Alter specific controlling conditions (e.g., remove particular conditions maintaining or instigating the problem behavior)
   B. Alter immediate system in which problem behavior is embedded (e.g., change family of alcohol-abusing family member)
   C. Alter larger system or systems in which problem behavior is embedded (e.g., change community and society to alter patterns of drinking beverage alcohol)
IV. The Environment

than it appears at first because different facets of behavior may be addressed. Thus, in the case of a phobia, the practitioner may focus on the motoric aspect of responding (e.g., avoidance of the feared object), the physiological (e.g., emotional sweating), the cognitive (e.g. irrational beliefs about the feared object), or various combinations of these. Each focus makes an assumption about the appropriate facet of behavior to target, an assumption that should be justifiable for the particular individuals who receive the intervention.

It is sometimes assumed that if you change one aspect of responding, other aspects will change accordingly. For instance, by changing the cognitive aspect of behavior somehow changes will also occur in the physiological and motoric. Perhaps, but not necessarily. It is risky to assume that response changes of any type necessarily promote other response changes. Indeed, there is some evidence that only under certain conditions will changes in responding in one response channel be related to responding in other areas (Borkevec, Weerts, & Bernstein, 1977; Hodgson & Rachman, 1974; Lang, 1968). It is safest for all concerned to design interventions around alteration of responding for each channel or area of response for which change is desired.

Another assumption sometimes made by interventionists is that it is sufficient to focus intervention on alteration of the problem behavior without giving attention to other possible targets, such as incompatible behavior or the controlling conditions for the problem behavior. As will be highlighted below, intervention focused only on the problem behavior itself is generally too narrow.

Turning now to the content domain for the problem behavior, there may be many areas of content, as Table 2.2 indicates. Although such domain labels are arbitrary to some extent, they are important in planning interventions because the practitioner inevitably intervenes in a particular area with given target behaviors. Identification of the content domain helps focus the practitioner-researcher on what is known about the behavior in question and on what the practical and theoretical problems are likely to be. In general, the more specific the content domain, the better.

Incompatible Behavior

Providing relaxation training for an anxiety-ridden patient would illustrate targeting responses incompatible with anxiety—in this case, profound muscular relaxation. Interventions should generally be focused not only on reducing problem behavior but on accelerating desirable responding. When designing interventions for incompatible behavior, one should focus on increasing the prosocial counterpart of the problem behavior, a means of simultaneously increasing precisely what is desirable while doing so at the expense of the undesirable. For example, incentives to assist Mary to stay in her seat when she shouldn't be running around the classroom, if successful, will increase in-seat behavior directly at the expense of out-of-seat behavior. Some behaviors, as in this example, are clearly incompatible because they involve essentially all other behavior except that which is problematic, whereas other behaviors are less inclusive and may be insufficiently incompatible. When intervening on incompatible behavior, it is essential that the clinician-researcher determine the extent to which the behavior alleged to be incompatible is in fact mutually exclusive in regard to the problem behavior in question.

Controlling Conditions and Systems

The purpose of altering the controlling conditions for the problem behavior is to try to remove or otherwise modify the causal conditions that brought the problem behavior into existence or maintain it.

Consider Mr. Jones, who drinks excessively because of the stress placed on him in his work. To remove the stress, changes may be made in Mr. Jones's pattern of work, in his superior's behavior toward him, and in his lifestyle. Altering specific controlling conditions is often an efficient and direct method of changing behavior, and, whatever else is done, this is generally highly desirable. Interventions designed to address controlling conditions should have a better chance of being effective and of yielding results that last longer than those that focus only on the target behavior.

Another way to alter controlling conditions is to direct intervention toward the immediate system in which the problem behavior is embedded. In the case of an alcohol abuser whose family members instigate and maintain the excessive drinking, intervention could be focused on changing the family system of which the abuser is a member. Intervention of this type is consistent with what is advocated by most family systems theorists. However, in such interventions, the controlling conditions in the family need to be specified and addressed precisely, otherwise the alcohol problem could remain, whatever else is changed in the family.

The interventionist also has the option, in principle, of designing change in the larger system in which the problem behavior is embedded. In the case of alcohol abuse, programs could be designed to change patterns of drinking alcohol in the community and in society at large. Such programs could be remedial as well as preventive.

The Environment

The arrangements of light, space, walls, floors, and other objects of the more immediate environment can also be the object of D&D, but with emphasis now on how the impact of the environment may facilitate change objectives of a helping strategy. For example, in Risely's (1982) research on living environments for dependent people, high-engagement toys were used to increase the amount of social play as opposed to isolate play for children in a residential facility, and tables of specific sizes were used to stimulate social conversation.

PARTICIPANTS

Target Persons

Whereas intervention in treatment ordinarily involves a particular individual or family, the target persons in intervention design embrace a cohort of individuals, families, or groups who are to be the target persons of the resulting intervention. At more embracing levels of intervention, the targets typically involve organizations, communities, cities, states, or societies.

Helping Persons

At least four types of helping persons need to be considered in intervention design. The first are the *professional helpers*, members of such human service fields as social work, psychology, psychiatry, education, nursing, rehabilitation, and counseling. Because such helping persons often face the same or very similar problems, interventions can often be designed broadly so that members of a variety of helping professions can use them. In any case, when designing interventions for given helping persons, limitations and strengths or professional training and background need to be taken into account.

A second type of helping person is the *mediator*, such as a friend, family member, or relative who has direct contact with the client and who can function in a quasi-rehabilitative capacity under the guidance of the helping person. Mediators, when capable of performing mediation tasks, can greatly extend the reach of the intervention and should be used whenever possible. Mediator tasks can include data gathering for assessment purposes, participation in planning with the helping person, and the implementation and monitoring of intervention once instituted.

The third type of helping person is the *client*, functioning in work with the helper. Although the primary target of change, the client can be called on to assume many responsibilities in a program, depending on its focus and client capability. If clients lack the skills to carry out the requisite functions, it is clearly inappropriate to design interventions that presuppose such skills. In any case, however, the design should stress increasing these skills so that as intervention progresses and maintenance is planned, client strengths can be drawn on systematically to assist in the intervention and sustain the gains achieved.

The fourth type of helping person is the *layperson* functioning to provide assistance through a self-help group or otherwise. In the case of the self-help group, such as Al-anon, Alcoholics Anonymous, or Parents Anonymous, the autonomy and anonymity of the group generally preclude direct involvement of the interventionist or design of the self-help group itself. Even so, existing self-help groups can often be used as part of a larger intervention scheme, and, as such, are subject to planning and inclusion in the design.

ROLES

Helping Person Roles

What roles are most relevant to intervention activities? Fischer (1978) described four roles that have wide applicability across fields of human service. The first is the *clinician-behavior changer*, who provides advice, counsel, therapy, behavior change, and crisis intervention. The second is the *consultant-educator*, who provides teaching, consultation, interpretation, and supervision. The third is the *broker-advocate*, who provides material aid, mediation-liaison, referral, resource location, problem identification, and aggressive representation of client's rights. The fourth is the *researcher-evaluator*, who gathers data in the course of intervention for purposes of research and/or evaluation. To these can be added a fifth, the *caretaker-caregiver*, who cares for the needs and/or safety of those who cannot care for themselves or who are a danger to others. The activities associated with each of these are clearly different and, within the confines of any role, may be defined in different ways. Although there are other roles in human service,[1] these five are those most likely to embrace the activities directly involved in intervention.

The role or combination of roles most appropriate for the intervention must be selected with consideration given to how the roles and their constituent activities facilitate achieving the intervention objective. Thus, if the goal of the intervention is to change some aspect of behavior, as it very frequently is, then the role of clinician-behavior changer would be most appropriate. If the goal is to inform and educate, then the role of consultant-educator would be most applicable. A mismatch of role and objective must be avoided, or the functions and activities required by the intended objective will not be performed, those carried out instead may foster other objectives, and the participants may experience needless conflict and stress.

The role of research-evaluator will increasingly be one carried out by helping persons and intervention designers. By combining the role of researcher-evaluator with one of those directly involving intervention, rich opportunities are afforded to enhance practice as well as research and evaluation. It must be recognized, however, that the requisites of service and research are different (e.g., see Kratchowill & Piersel, 1983; Thomas, 1978c) and these may pose conflicts that require resolution.

If the role of researcher-evaluator is to be combined with one or more roles involving practice more directly, the roles must be structured so as to minimize potential conflict and interference while also making possible the achievement of the intended objectives.

Client Roles

There are also at least five client roles that may be identified. Each of these is a client counterpart role to that described above for the helping person. Thus, for the clinician-behavior changer role of the helping person, there is the client counterpart role of *changee*, a central feature of which is some willingness to cooperate and change in response to the intervention of the helping person. For the consultant-educator role of helping person there is the counterpart role of *learner*, an important feature of which is the client's willingness to expose himself or herself to the information and advice of the helping person. For the broker-advocate role of helping person there is the client counterpart of *claimant*, an important feature of which is willingness to make known one's claim and/or needs for which assistance is desired. For the research-evaluation role of the helping person there is the counterpart of *subject*, a central feature of which is willingness to submit to the research or evaluation activities involved. For the caretaker-caregiver role of helping person there is the client role of *resident*, central features of which are inability to care for one's own needs and/or the need for safety and protection.

The client roles may be carried out by the client in relatively pure form or may be blended in various combinations, either at particular points in the interventive process or throughout. Further, each client role may vary in the extent to which there is involvement, participation, and collaboration of the target person.

It is essential that there be some correspondence between the role(s) of the helping person and the role(s) of the target person. In addition to interfering with the role functions, departures from the complementary pairing given above could present such difficulties as role strain or conflict for those involved (e.g., see Goode, 1960; Rosen, 1972; Thomas and Biddle, 1967). Not only should the client role be congruent with that of the helping person, both types of role need to be consistent with the desired change objectives.

CONTEXTS OF HELPING

Helping Situations

Situations of helping may be carried out in the office, home, school, and community, among others. One or more helping situations should be chosen that are appropriate for the intervention objective and the environment in which behaviors of the target persons are to be carried out. If the objective of the intervention is to effect changes in little Harold's behavior at school, the school would clearly be the appropriate helping situation; likewise, if the treatment arena involves the home, then the home is generally the ideal treatment setting. Many intervention activities may be legitimately carried out in the office, particularly those for which the changes involved may be successfully transacted or rehearsed in the office situation or, by means of instructions and other instigations, in situations outside the office. Even so, however, if the arena of intended change is in the natural environment, it is generally preferable to have that as the primary helping situation, using the office setting in addition on a limited basis or not at all.

Service Setting

The setting of service may involve public or private auspices, the later sometimes providing greater flexibility and opportunity for intervention innovation, given availability of funds. Further, the settings may be open, closed, or transitional. Each of these also defines opportunities and places limits on what may be planned and carried out in intervention. For example, closed settings, such as residential institutions, can limit the intervention that may be carried out in the natural environment. Transitional settings such as halfway houses often allow intervention to be carried out in the residential facility as well as in the community. Open settings, such as community mental health agencies, allow intervention to be carried out in the helping person's office, in the open community, or both. Thus, settings are environments for living and/or change that are themselves subject to D&D.

ADJUNCTS AND PROPS

The activities of helping are carried out with such common adjunctive equipment and props as rooms, furniture, and lighting as well as specialized devices such as timers, counters, audio and video equipment, calculators, computers, biofeedback equipment, and breathalyzers, among many others. The availability of such gear, where appropriate, can often make the difference between successful and unsuccessful intervention.

SUMMARY

1. Change objectives provide critical focus and direction for the helping strategy and include such objectives as remediation, enhancement, competence, education, prevention, advocacy, resource provision, and social control.

2. Targets of intervention include the target behavior itself, behavior incompatible with the problem behavior, and the conditions that control the problem behavior, including systems.

3. On selecting the target of intervention, intervention must focus on the appropriate target and should not exclude relevant aspects or embrace more than is necessary.

4. It is generally insufficient to focus intervention only on alteration of the problem behavior without giving attention to other possible targets, such as behavior incompatible with the problem behavior, controlling conditions of the problem behavior, systems within which the behavior occurs, as well as the environment.

5. Among the target persons who may be participants in intervention are individuals, families, or groups as well as larger social units, such as organizations or communities.

6. Among the helping persons who may participate in the intervention are professional helpers, mediators, clients when functioning in work with the helper, and laypersons.

7. Among the roles of helping persons relevant to interventional design are those of the clinician-behavior changer, consultant-educator, broker-advocate, researcher-evaluator, and caretaker-caregiver.

8. For each helping person role there is a counterpart role for the client, including the client roles of changee, learner, claimant, subject, and resident.

9. Roles must be appropriate for the intended change objectives and should be structured so as to achieve complementarity between those of the helping person and the client.

10. Contexts of helping include various helping situations, such as the office, home, school, and community, and should be chosen in light of the intervention objective and the environment in which the behaviors of the target persons are to be carried out.

11. Almost all intervention relies on the use of selected adjuncts and props, some of which are essential for the conduct and success of the intervention.

12. Contexts of helping include open, closed, or transitional settings; these, in turn, may be private or publicly funded.

13. Each service setting defines opportunities as well as places limits on what may be carried out in intervention.

NOTE

1. There are also the roles of assessor (e.g., gathering assessment data for purposes of assessment, testing, diagnosis), data manager (for decision-making purposes), community planner, and administrator.

Assessment and
Intervention Planning

A major component of helping strategies consists of assessment methods. This chapter discusses assessment methods and the related topic of intervention planning.

ASSESSMENT METHODS

As it relates to the objectives of the intervention, assessment facilitates the gathering and processing of selected data. When designing a helping strategy, it is difficult to ignore assessment methods. Indeed, even when the main focus in development is on intervention methods themselves, appropriate assessment methods must generally also be addressed. In some cases, of course, the assessment methods themselves are the primary or only focus of D&D. In any case, the aspects of assessment addressed in design may be limited, such as a particular assessment instrument, or extensive and complex, including an entire approach to assessment for an area of treatment.

In formulating assessment methods, the researcher-practitioner needs to make decisions concerning the purposes and content of assessment; what sources of data, response channels, measurement, and indicators to employ; who should conduct the assessment; how much data to obtain; the length of assessment, when and where assessment is to be conducted; and how data are to be obtained and handled. Table 3.1 presents an overview of the major areas potentially implicated in an approach to assessment. Each area is discussed briefly below, again in the context of intervention design. No effort will be made here to review the now large and technical literature on assessment, psychometrics, and measurement, all of which are beyond the scope of the present discussion. Readers interested in details of assessment methods themselves and how to conduct assessment are referred to other sources (e.g., Barlow, 1981; Ciminero, Calhoun, & Adams, 1977; Cone & Hawkins, 1977; Gelfand & Hartmann, 1975; Haynes, 1978; Hersen & Bellack, 1976; Keefe, Kopel, & Gordon, 1978; Mash & Terdal, 1976; Nay, 1979; McReynolds, 1978).

Purposes

The information gathered in assessment should relate to the assessment purposes, and these goals, in turn, should relate to the intervention objective. Except for the objective of research, each of the purposes outlined in part I of Table 3.1 can be implicated in a typical assessment. Further, all except research generally relate to the objective of case disposition. Only certain data, however, relate to the purposes of assessment, and one task in design is to determine what information the assessment method is to yield.

Some descriptive information is inevitably required in assessment so that the practitioner can become conversant with the essential facts of the case (e.g., age, sex, primary concerns, current living situation). Such descriptive information can relate to any or all of the content areas given in part II of the table. Descriptive data are important and can be the major type of data gathered. Although prediction is rarely a formal or exclusive objective of assessment, practitioners in most treatment areas need some predictive information. They often need to be able to predict certain serious eventualities (e.g., mental breakdown, family violence) and outcomes directly related to case management (e.g., the likely course of the client's difficulty and the benefits that the client might gain from a given intervention). Each area of prediction calls for gathering predictive information.

Classification in one form or another (e.g., psychiatric diagnosis) may be an integral component of assessment or may be relevant only in instances where certain types of disorder, such as frank mental illness or severe substance abuse, become evident. Because of uncertainties of classification systems, problems of misclassification, stigmatic labeling, and unjust consequences of classification, in recent years many have moved away from strict classification in most areas of assessment. However, there are often relevant categories into which problems, individuals, or families may fall that bear on conduct of the intervention for which some provisional classification may be appropriate. In general, classification should be done sparingly and advisedly, should

TABLE 3.1
**Overview of Major Areas Potentially Implicated in
an Approach to Assessment**

I. Purposes
  A. Description (e.g., what client concerns are)
  B. Prediction (e.g., whether there are indications of potential suicide)
  C. Classification (e.g., whether client is alcoholic)
  D. Monitoring and evaluation (e.g., to determine whether intervention is effective)
  E. Case disposition (e.g., what the intervention plan should be)
  F. Research (e.g., to contribute to knowledge about a type of client)
II. Content
  A. Problems and strengths
  B. Existing level of functioning
  C. Behavioral repertoire
  D. Motivation for treatment
  E. Etiology of problems (originating and maintaining conditions)
  F. Disposition to change
  G. Behavioral resources including self-control
  H. Personality factors
  I. Family history
  J. Developmental history
  K. Situational factors
  L. Environmental factors
  M. Social roles
  N. Sociocultural background
III. Sources of Data
  A. Interviews
  B. Schedules and checklists
  C. Observation
  D. Electromechanical and physiological devices
  E. Records
IV. Response Channels
  A. Overt-behavioral
  B. Cognitive-symbolic
  C. Physiological-somatic
V. Response Measurement
  A. Frequency (number of discrete responses)
  B. Duration (longevity of response in time)
  C. Magnitude (intensity of response)
  D. Latency (time between a given response and the onset of a relevant stimulus)
VI. Response Indicators
  A. Sign (indirect indicator of the phenomenon measured—e.g., a behavioral indicator of brain damage) versus sample (direct indicator of the phenomenon measured)
  B. Global versus specific
VII. Who Conducts Assessment
  A. Human assessors
    1. The interventionist himself or herself
    2. An outside specialist in assessment
    3. The target person herself or himself
    4. A mediator (e.g., a parent for a child)
    5. A volunteer
  B. Nonhuman assessors (e.g., a computer)

(Continued)

TABLE 3.1 Continued

VIII. Amount of Data to Obtain
  A. Restricted amount (e.g., "narrow band")
  B. Large amount (e.g., "broad band")
IX. Length of Assessment
  A. Short term (e.g., up to 2-3 hours)
  B. Long term (e.g., many hours or days)
X. When Assessment Is Conducted
  A. Antecedent to intervention
  B. Concurrent with intervention
  C. After intervention
  D. Before, during, and after intervention
XI. Where Assessment Is Conducted
  A. Naturalistic settings
  B. Analogue situations
XII. How Data Are Obtained
  A. Single versus multiple data sources
  B. Single versus multiple response channels
  C. Single versus multiple data gatherers
  D. Individualized versus nonindividualized assessment
  E. Standardized versus nonstandardized measurement
  F. Experimental versus nonexperimental methods
XIII. Data-Handling Factors
  A. Storage (e.g., human memory, narrative records, checklists, numerical representation, computer memory, audiotape, videotape)
  B. Retrieval (recovery procedures)
  C. Array and display (e.g., case record, card summary, test profile, graph, numerical display, TV monitor, audio speaker, mechanical counter, oscilloscope, digital panel meter)
  D. Processing (e.g., data representation, data reduction, statistical analyses)
  E. Appraisal (e.g., determining adequacy and relevance of data and, when appropriate, the reliability and validity of data)

relate clearly to intervention objectives, and should be done so that multidimensional complexity is captured, categories are not rigid, classifications can be easily changed, labeling is avoided, and client rights are protected if there are possible adverse consequences of certain classifications.

Interest has increased in recent years in gathering data for purposes of monitoring and evaluation. Such information helps to determine how the intervention is progressing and what its outcomes are. This topic is discussed in greater detail in Chapter 6.

Research in assessment broadens the scope of assessment to include data relevant to the research objectives. When also pursuing research objectives, it is important that the practitioner-researcher be clear about what objectives are being served by the data gathered and to keep the amount of data obtained within bounds.

Content

All areas of content given in part II of Table 3.1 can be relevant to an intervention. However, the specific information needed in each content area necessarily varies from one intervention area to another. What is known clinically and scientifically about the area of behavior in question often will also dictate what informational content is relevant.

Sources of Data

The practitioner-researcher generally has a choice of many sources of data to be used in assessment. The interview has been relied on most frequently and generally for good reason. However, schedules and checklists, observation, electromechanical and physiological devices, and archival records also are often appropriate, and should generally be used more frequently than they have been. Because each source of data reflects reality in its own way and has its own particular advantages and disadvantages, drawing on more than one source in assessing the same phenomenon is highly desirable. Such multimethod measurement provides a type of convergent validity inasmuch as that which is valid in the data gathered from each source makes a contribution to the overall validity of measurement and helps to offset the limitations of a different source.

Response Channels

What aspect of behavior should be taken as the primary feature of interest? There is increasing recognition that there may be distinctive response channels, such as the overt-behavioral, cognitive-symbolic, and physiological-somatic (e.g., see Bandura, 1969; Hodgson & Rachman, 1974; Lang, 1968). In this view, response channels should be selected in recognition of the appropriate channel, given the behavior of interest. Thus, if physical violence is the behavior, then the overt-behavioral channel would be appropriate, whereas if the rational and irrational thinking of an individual were of primary concern, then the cognitive-symbolic would be most relevant. Despite the particular importance of a given channel for specific behaviors of interest, the stream of behavior involves all three channels. Depressive behavior, for example, could be represented in the overt-behavioral channel as retarded motor action, in the cognitive-symbolic as worry and self-deprecating statements, and in the physiological-somatic as dysphoric mood and loss of appetite and libido. When behavior of interest can be represented as implicating all three response channels, methods of assessment should embrace response indicators for all channels.

Response Measurement

Relevant responses in assessment should be measured by one or more of the measurement methods of frequency, duration, magnitude, or latency. Each has its place, depending on the nature of the response and what is most relevant. For example, frequency is most appropriate when responses are discrete and countable (e.g., instances of head banging); duration when the response is either on or off and its duration is most germane (e.g., time spent sleeping); magnitude for responses that range in intensity, such as anxiety or other emotional responses; and latency when the time interval between a given response and the onset of a relevant stimulus is foremost (e.g., time between exposure to erotic stimulation and erotic response). Further, some responses are best represented by more than one type of measurement.

Response Indicators

Responses may be measured as samples or signs. As a sample, the behavior in question is measured directly, as in the case of timing a child's out-of-seat behavior in the classroom. As a sign, the behavior is measured indirectly, taking the measured indicator as a sign of the behavior (e.g., using a verbal response of the client as an indicator of possible brain damage, cognitive process, or emotional state). When behavior is measured as a sample, its most important feature is how adequate the sample is in relation to the information needed. When measured as a sign, one prefers to have a valid and reliable indicator. When possible, it is generally preferable to obtain response indicators as samples of behavior because the use of signs, when there are behaviors that can be sampled, is indirect and uncertain.

Response indicators may also involve global or specific representations. Specific indicators tend to be more accurate representations of what is characterized, particularly for those phenomena capable of relatively unambiguous and precise denotation. When this is not feasible or when a general, summary measure is desired, a global indicator may be appropriate. In addition, such response indicators as relevance, sensitivity, and unobtrusiveness are also pertinent (e.g., see Jayaratne & Levy, 1979).

Who Conducts Assessment

Most assessments are carried out by human assessors, mainly the practitioner. This is simplest and most direct when the information obtained from the interventionist is adequate for the assessment. For certain purposes, however, it is desirable to separate the function of intervention from that of assessment, particularly when having an outside specialist carry out the assessment would increase the likelihood of obtaining unbiased data. Although humans should continue to be centrally involved in assessment in the foreseeable future, no doubt there will be increasing use of automated and computer-assisted methods of assessment (e.g., see Angle, Ray, Hay, & Ellinwood, 1977; Thomas & Walter, 1973).

Amount of Data to Obtain

The ideal amount of data is obviously just enough to make the needed decisions in planning, conducting, and evaluating the intervention. How much is just enough depends on what is involved in the intervention decisions in a given case and varies considerably from one intervention to the next.

There are those who advocate gathering only a restricted amount of information over a "narrow band." This can be justified when relatively little information is required for the decisions or the penalties of not obtaining sufficient information in assessment are not large. At the other extreme are those who advocate obtaining a large amount of information over a "broad band." This practice can be justified in the early stages of development when little is known about what is relevant, when research objectives are combined with those of service, or when the treatment area requires a large amount of information. Clearly, the inefficiency and cost entailed in obtaining a large amount of assessment data must be offset by the anticipated gains.

Length of Assessment

As has been highlighted, the main factor that should determine the length of assessment is the amount of information needed to conduct intervention competently. This suggests that arbitrarily brief or comprehensive assessment may be too short or too long, depending on how much information is yielded and needed. Clearly, an open-ended assessment allows the practitioner to take the time to gather the needed information.

When Assessment Is Conducted

When time permits, most assessment is carried out before the intervention, thus making it possible to conduct intervention in light of the information revealed in the assessment. The disadvantage of carrying out assessment concurrent with or after intervention is that it may not help shape the intervention process, although it may be useful otherwise. Some information may be obtained concurrent with intervention that still serves to held guide treatment. In general, the more that is known about an area of intervention, the easier it is to try to complete an assessment prior to the intervention.

Where Assessment Is Conducted

Assessment conducted in the natural settings in which the behavior of interest occurs, such as the home, school, and community, is preferable to analogue situations to the extent that the naturalistic settings are more validly representative. Naturalistic settings need not always be validly representative, depending on the effects of biasing influences on assessment conducted in them; likewise, analogue situations need not be artificial or yield invalid data (e.g., see Kazdin, 1978b; McFall, 1977). In general, however, when biasing influences are minimal, the naturalistic setting is ordinarily the most valid setting for gathering assessment data.

How Data Are Obtained

As indicated in part XII of Table 3.1, there are different approaches to the gathering of data. Consider first the data sources, response channels, and data gatherers. Too often assessment information is obtained from a single data gatherer, such as the practitioner, drawing on essentially one source of data, such as the interview. Further, such data are often restricted to self-reports, which might not systematically embrace diverse response channels (e.g., the overt-behavioral, cognitive-symbolic, and physiological-somatic). To (a) protect the assessor against limitations of a particular source, response channel, or data gatherer, (b) provide augmented data, and (c) increase the validity of measurement, it is higly desirable to employ multiple data sources, response channels, and data gatherers in the assessment process.

Individualized assessment is vital in clinical work because it can capture the distinctive characteristics and conditions applicable to each individual or family. Individualized assessment may be carried out by tailoring the areas and instruments of assessment to the individual needs of the case. In contrast, standardized measurement involves a set of instruments having known reliabilities and validities that is administered in essentially the same way to all participants. An advantage of standardized measurement is that the data gathered may be compared with the information obtained by others using the same instruments, thus offering the promise of contributing to the body of knowledge in that area.

Standardization, however, is not entirely compatible with individualized assessment inasmuch as individualization requires a distinctive rather than a standardized set of assessment instruments or when the areas to be assessed in a given case are those for which suitable assessment instruments do not yet exist. One solution to this dilemma consists of dividing the assessment into two components, one that is standardized and the other that is not. In the standardized segment, established instruments that are relevant can be given in the same way to all participants; in the nonstandardized portion, individualized assessment involving diverse instruments and areas of content can be carried out in keeping with the practice objectives.

The last issue here is whether the methods are experimental or nonexperimental. Most assessment methodology is essentially nonexperimental wherein the data gathered are essentially correlational— that is, there is no intentional manipulation of some variables to determine their possible effects on others. The problem is that, not infrequently, clients are unable to provide information that would be adequate for purposes of inferring cause-effect relations. And there are some events clients have never or rarely experienced that, if systematically introduced and their effects observed, would yield critical information. A good case can thus be made for the selective use of experimental methods for purposes of obtaining assessment data. One way to do this is through the "assessment probe," a miniexperiment in which the clinician-researcher intervenes in the client's life situation, prior to beginning intervention proper, to obtain assessment information that would not otherwise be readily available. (More details in the assessment probe are presented in Chapter 17.)

Data-Handling Factors

A large and diverse technology exists for handling assessment data, as part XIII of Table 3.2 suggests. The challenge in design is to devise the storage, retrieval, array and display, processing, and appraisal of assessment data so that all functions can be handled accurately, quickly, and economically. Although all or most aspects are mediated by humans, data handling is greatly facilitated by the availability of a large variety of mechanical, electric, and electronic equipment as well as processes of analyzing and processing data. Increasingly, data handling will be accomplished by more sophisticated methods, particularly those that involve electromechanical devices and computers.

METHOD OF PLANNING INTERVENTION

The intervention plan consists of a proposed intervention applicable to given target behaviors to be carried out with selected participants carrying out their role responsibilities in particular ways. The activities that need to be performed to plan intervention consist of (a) information review and appraisal, including review of the assessment data, (b) generation and evaluation of interventional alternatives, and (c) selection of the most appropriate intervention or group of interventions for the plan.

SUMMARY

1. The design of interventions often includes assessment. Indeed, in some cases, the principal focus of design is on one or another aspect of the assessment methodology.

2. The purposes of assessment for intervention include case disposition and monitoring and evaluation, along with description, prediction, classification, and, in specialized instances, research.

3. Information in assessment typically needs to be gathered for a broad range of content, each area of which needs to be specified in the design process.

4. In addition to the commonly used interview, other sources of data useful in assessment include schedules and checklists, observation, electromechanical and physiological devices, and archival records.

5. Diverse response channels may be drawn on when gathering assessment data, each of which needs to be selected on the basis of the assessment area of interest.

6. In deciding how data are to be handled, attention must be given in design to such issues as the extent to which assessment involves methods that are individualized, standardized, and experimental.

7. In addition, decisions also need to be made in regard to the following:

(a) what methods to use to measure responses (e.g., frequency, duration);
(b) response indicators (e.g., signs versus samples and specific versus global representation);
(c) who conducts assessment (e.g., human versus nonhuman methods);
(d) the amount of data to be used in assessment;
(e) when assessments are conducted (e.g., before or during intervention);
(f) where assessment is conducted (e.g., natural versus analogue situations); and
(g) how data are handled in regard to such matters as storage retrieval, array and display, processing, and appraisal.

Intervention Methods

Intervention methods are the backbone in the anatomy of the helping process, for it is largely by means of these methods that helping objectives are achieved. The central effort in intervention design is generally devoted to the intervention methods. An intervention method is conceived here as comprising two components: one or more intervention technique and a program format. Here the practitioner-researcher encounters a large and potentially bewildering array of alternatives for which decisions are required. There are numerous techniques as well as many program formats. An overview of some of these is presented below.

TECHNIQUES OF INTERVENTION

In highlighting the importance of technique in the context of psychotherapy, Strupp said, "Techniques are of course the core and *raison d'etre* of modern psychotherapy" (1978, p. 11). As viewed here, the intervention technique is a recognized and distinctive set of helping activities that relate to a particular intervention objective. Consider systematic desensitization, widely used to alleviate anxiety and phobias. This technique has traditionally involved at least three separate components. The first consists of making a hierarchy of stimuli representing anxiety-eliciting scenes for the particular area of anxiety being worked with. The second involves providing training in a response incompatible with anxiety, such as deep muscle relaxation. The third entails systematic presentation of the anxiety-eliciting scenes, each time evoking the response incompatible with anxiety (e.g., inducing deep relaxation prior to introducing each scene in the hierarchy and progressing up the hierarchy from the least to the most anxiety-eliciting scene). Although there are variations, systematic desensitization is frequently the major and sometimes the only technique employed to alleviate anxiety.

Among the more common techniques in interpersonal helping are ventilation, interpretation, confrontation, universalization, catharsis, cognitive restructuring, contracting, and positive reinforcement. There are also more obscure techniques such as imagery training, primal screaming, consciousness raising, habit reversal, and covert extinction. In psychotherapy alone there are at least 250 different approaches (Corsini, 1981), and each approach has its own set of preferred techniques. Considering human service fields in general, there must be many hundreds of techniques, to say nothing of the many new techniques that are continuously being evolved.

The technique is generally the minimal set of intervention activities needed to accomplish an intended intervention objective. Although often capable in principle of being disassembled, as in the case of the component features of systematic desensitization, the components of techniques are typically used together rather than separately. This quality, plus the close partnering of the constituent activities in relation to a given intervention objective, imbue the technique with a unitary quality. Techniques are often employed with others in a program (e.g., use of systematic desensitization, *in vivo* desensitization, and cognitive restructuring to alleviate anxiety).

Accelerative and Decelerative Techniques

Many intervention techniques are largely accelerative or decelerative in their application. The accelerative technique is intended to increase desirable responding, whereas the decelerative technique is intended to decrease undesirable responding. Providing reinforcement in the form of praise to a child for doing his or her homework is illustrative of an accelerative technique. An example of a decelerative technique is prescribing the symptom, a form of paradoxical intention, to endeavor to decrease symptomatic behavior.

Many techniques, however, may be applied to accelerate some behaviors and decelerate others. Differential reinforcement, for example, is typically employed to reinforce desirable responding and to withhold reinforcement for undesirable responding. Training procedures of habit reversal are intended to reduce the undesirable habit, such as stuttering or compulsive self-stimulation, while simultaneously serving to increase a desirable response. Further, many techniques do not readily lend themselves to classification as being either mainly decelerative or accelerative because they may be used either way, depending on one's objective. Therapist instructions, for example, may be employed to increase assertive responding of the client and also to decrease undesirable social behaviors, such as failure to stand up for one's rights.

Experience in behavior change provides the basis for several provisional generalizations about the advantages and disadvantages of these types of techniques. The generalizations are tentative and subject to exceptions, as are all those here. The first is that, all things considered, accelerative techniques are preferred over the decelerative. For example, if Johnny fails to do his homework regularly, positive reinforcement for doing the homework would be preferred over some form of punishment for not doing homework. There are often negative effects of using a decelerative technique—for example, undesirable emotional reactions along with associating the therapist and the situation of intervention with unpleasant and aversive consequences. Further, deceleration alone need not and often does not bring about a simultaneous increase in the desired responding.

The preference for accelerative techniques over the decelerative is easy to endorse when the accelerative technique works. However, accelerative techniques are not always sufficiently powerful by themselves. There are difficult situations of behavior change in which even the strongest and best accelerative techniques may be ineffective. When an accelerative technique does not bring about a sufficient increase in the desirable responding, the therapist should consider applying a decelerative technique to the undesirable responding to strengthen the effect. For example, in addition to earning special privileges for doing his homework, Johnny could lose selected privileges for failing to do his homework. A combination of an accelerative technique to increase desirable responding with a decelerative technique to decrease the related undesirable responding can be much stronger than the use of either alone. This dual approach is the preferred alternative in situations in which either type of technique by itself would bring uncertain or unsatisfactory results.

Further, an accelerative technique successfully applied to a given behavior can be expected to have a certain beneficial effect only on that behavior and its polar opposite. Thus, if Johnny increases his homework because an accelerative technique has applied, this will clearly decrease his time when not engaging in homework—but it will not necessarily have any effect, for example, on how much Johnny watches TV. Some practitioners have presumed, incorrectly, that by increasing one behavior, another problem—not necessarily directly related—will also be changed. Such a happy result cannot be depended on except under special circumstances. Thus, in this example, excessive TV watching may be "accelerated out" only in the unusual instance in which the accelerative technique increases homework behavior so much that there is essentially no time left for anything else, including watching TV. Other problem behaviors, such as Johnny's excessive TV watching, that may coexist with the primary target behavior, need to be addressed on their own terms with separately applied techniques. For instance, Johnny could receive special privileges for doing his homework as well as for watching television for no more than a stipulated, reasonable period of time each day. While it is always possible that the use of a single accelerative technique will bring about bonus changes, the interventionist should not expect such changes unless prior research or practice experience provides a clear basis for anticipating such additional changes.

PROGRAM FORMAT

Intervention is typically carried out with a given assembly of intervention components applied to one or more target behaviors. Called a program here, this assembly of intervention elements consists of one or more intervention technique. Programs may vary greatly in format depending on such factors as their scope, number of interventions, order of intervention, strength of intervention, degree of individualization, longevity, and structure. Each of these is discussed below.

Scope of Program

Programs may range from those with broad focus on many behaviors and/or persons to those with more restricted focus on only selected or a few behaviors and persons. An example of a program with relatively broad scope is the community reinforcement approach to alcoholism of Hunt and Azrin (1973). In addition to the drinking behavior of the abuser, this program contains interventions for marital relationships, the abuser's work behavior, leisure-time activities, and the friends he or she keeps. Most programs in the alcohol area are not as broad. Some focus largely on the drinking behavior itself; others, in addition, address the drinker's personal difficulties and, sometimes, family factors.

In general, the scope of intervention has widened considerably through the years. Intervention was restricted largely to the problem behavior itself in earlier years, but now there is increasing recognition that the scope of intervention should include not only the target behavior but the incompatible behavior as well, significant controlling conditions relating to the problem behavior as well as aspects of the system and environment within which the behaviors in question are played out. In general, broad programs have the potential of achieving larger and longer lasting changes than narrow programs.

But even so, a program's scope should be appropriately broad or narrow, as the case may be. If too broad, program effort will be dissipated and more time and effort will be invested than is necessary. So-called shotgun programs that throw in "everything but the kitchen sink" must be evaluated in terms of whether the benefits achieved are worth the added cost. A program that is too restricted, in contrast, runs the risk of excluding significant conditions, behaviors, or persons required for an effective outcome.

Number of Interventions

Some programs contain few interventions; others, a great many. The former mental patient just released from hospital may receive only support from his helping person or may also receive vocational training, education for reentry into noninstitutional living, and training in social skills, problem solving, and cognitive restructuring, among others. Given the state of the art, it is a rare program that can succeed with one or a few techniques. Although the number of techniques need not always be large to be effective, there should be a sufficient number of appropriate techniques to do the job. Intervention components chosen must be compatible and complementary among themselves, and this, combined with considerations of appropriateness, places an upper limit on the number that can sensibly and practically be included in any program.

Sequence

Program sequences may be uniform, branching, or variable. In the uniform sequence, clients progress through a fixed set of program phases. In the early stages of the development of unilateral family therapy for alcohol abuse, all the cooperative spouses of uncooperative alcohol abusers went through three fixed phases of treatment (Thomas & Santa, 1982). The first phase focused on individual coping of the cooperative spouse, the second on strengthening family functioning through that spouse, and the third on facilitation of sobriety of the abuser through working with the cooperative spouse as a mediator.

Individualized intervention was provided in each phase. The only departure from uniformity in phase progression was that some spouses went through the phases more rapidly, and, when not a priority, a phase could be passed over and the spouse moved on to the next.

In Miller's (1975) child training program, all parents whose children have difficulties progress through a branching sequence of phases. First is an educational phase during which the participants read a manual on child management. If this helps sufficiently to alleviate the problems, participants do not progress further. But if problems persist, parents move on to the second phase, discrimination training. In this they are taught, for example, how to recognize appropriate responding of their children, and when and how to reinforce such behavior. If this does not succeed, participants then move on to the next phase. If desirable behaviors need acceleration, parents are then taught how to make contingency contracts with their children and also how to design and implement motivation systems using points and tokens. Again, if this succeeds, further progress does not ensue. However, if undesirable behaviors need deceleration, parents are trained in how to use time-out-from reinforcement and other forms of punishment for undesirable responding. If this succeeds, program activity stops. But if problems persist, the participants then move into a fifth phase, called parent counseling, in which individualized treatment is given with focus particularly on the difficulties that have not been responsive in earlier phases.

Variable phases allow for a high degree of individualization, with each client or family progressing through the most suitable sequence. For example, in a variable sequence for child management, one set of parents might receive education and bibliotherapy and contingency contracting, another discrimination training alone, a third training in time-out procedures, and still another individualized parent counseling first followed by discrimination training and then contingency contracting.

Each type of sequence makes important assumptions. For example, sequences of ordered phases presuppose that each phase should come before the next. In the first example above, each phase was assumed to be important in itself and a facilitating condition for moving forward. In the second example, each phase was assumed to be the probable minimal intervention needed at that point. Uniform and branching programs presuppose that a good deal is known about what the proper sequence should be. Variable sequences make the assumption that there is sufficient diversity or complexity of client condition to justify highly diverse sequencing, and also may be particularly suitable when little is known about what the proper sequence should be.

There are advantages to programs that have relatively fixed sequences inasmuch as time for assessment may be reduced, the phases are chosen so that each has a high likelihood of being successful, and the interventionists can specialize in what each phase requires. However, uniformly sequenced programs can be inefficient to the extent that differential assessment would make it possible to place clients directly in the most appropriate type of intervention, thus sparing clients the trouble of having to go through unnecessary phases. Variable sequencing obviously allows for the greatest flexibility and individual tailoring. It generally presupposes careful individualized assessment and a relatively high level of expertness on the part of the helping person.

In the early stages of development, the use of a uniform sequence allows the development of assessment and intervention procedures to take place in the intervention area of each phase, thus being sure to cover each area. Later, but still before mature interventions have been evolved, the variable sequence has the advantage of focusing development on what is central in each case, with consideration given to identifying the conditions under which one as opposed to another focus of intervention should be pursued. The final type of sequence for a program for routine practice should be based on the results of careful design and development.

Strength of Intervention

Intervention programs and their components vary along the dimension of strength—that is, in their ability to bring about change. To keep it simple for illustrative purposes, consider what a parent might do to provide incentive for a ten-year-old child to carry out household chores. Let us assume further that a monetary incentive was appropriate and that the amount required to have a satisfactory level of chores completed was $4.00 per week, $.50 higher than the child's present allowance. Providing $4.00 per week for the completion of chores would then be "just enough" to get the job done. Or, to be on the safe side, let us say the parents gave the child $6.00, in which case we might say that it was "plenty". However, if the parents gave the child $12.00 per week, that would be "too much." Likewise, were the parents to give the child $3.50 and this did not produce all the chores, then this would be "not enough." In this example, just enough will produce the behavior but with little margin of safety, whereas plenty, although somewhat more costly, provides that margin. Although not as easily orderable on a scale of amount, all interventions in principle have a given level of strength that must be considered in relationship to what is required to bring about the desired change in behavior. The strength should be at least just enough, if not plenty.

Interventions that are too strong may be overly costly and also may produce undesirable side effects. Weak interventions obviously do not do the job sufficiently well and are wasteful. What defines sufficient intervention strength depends very much on the difficulty of changing the behavior, countervailing influences, and how competently the intervention may be carried out. In the early stages of intervention development, it is justifiable to err, if one must, on the side of plenty when too little is known to make more finely tuned determinations. As more is learned, however, the interventions can be set at sufficient and appropriate strength.

Individualization

In the fixed, nonindividualized program, everyone receives the same thing in essentially the same way. An important disadvantage of the standardized program is that by treating everyone in the same way, individuals may be given more or different interventions than they need. However, when it has been well designed to meet the needs of the typical participant and participants are carefully selected to ensure the appropriateness of the program, the standardized program can be most efficient and economical without necessarily being less effective.

Because it allows for flexibility and tailoring to conditions particularly applicable to the individual, the individualized program has the potential advantage of being uniformly most effective. Such a program is typically more costly and time consuming than the standardized program. Some of the benefits of individualization and standardization can be achieved with a standardized program that allows for individualization under given conditions. In any event, the individualized program is generally most appropriate in the early stages of development when the types of interventions and the conditions under which they should be employed are still evolving. If standard programs are desired, they can often be developed on the basis of prior experiences and design with individualized programs.

Longevity

Programs vary in the length of time required to carry them out— some requiring one or a few sessions, as in crisis intervention; others spanning many sessions, in some cases years. How long is long enough? Change is typically easier to achieve for some cases than others, and generally large individual differences in responsiveness to change efforts need to be taken into account. In any case, for any given area of intervention, there is clearly a lower limit of time below which desirable outcomes will not be forthcoming. And above a certain duration, subsequent time devoted to achieving change may yield very little in return for the added time and effort. Comparative studies of brief and unlimited therapies have shown essentially no difference in results (Butcher & Koss, 1978), thus suggesting the value of relatively brief, time-limited treatment. Even so, however, when little is known about how long intervention in a given area should take, it is clearly wise to leave enough time to carry out the intervention competently. Time may be employed as needed or may be fixed, providing it is not too brief. Time can always be extended to allow for further intervention.

Structure

One way or another, programs provide a framework within which the intervention task is accomplished. Although other factors are important, program and interventions are the principal means by which change is accomplished. A program may be structured as "tight" or "loose." The extent to which a program is tight or loose depends on the following: (a) the explicitness of the agreement between practitioner and clients to work in a given area; (b) the specificity of program directives and instructions concerning what behaviors are to be carried out; (c) how closely the implementation and outcomes of the program are monitored; and (d) whether there are consequences for the client for program compliance and noncompliance. Each of these aspects can be tightly or loosely specified, thus yielding many patterns of tightness or looseness.

With the consent and cooperation of the marital partners, a tight program in the area of marital counseling might involve the following: (a) a written understanding between the marital partners and the therapist concerning exactly what area was to be addressed (e.g., marital communication); (b) provision of specific directives by the practitioner concerning what the partner behavior should be at various points in the program, supplementing these with written instructions; (c) program monitoring based on daily records kept by marital partners of program compliance and consequences, with the records reviewed every few days by the practitioner; and (d) progress through the program being strictly contingent on successful completion of earlier steps combined with praise for such progress and mild therapist disapproval of failure to comply with the regimen. A loose structure for this same couple might involve (a) a general, unwritten understanding that personal and marital difficulties were to be worked on; (b) program guidance given in the form of occasional mild suggestions or selected approval of given lines of behavior already being pursued; (c) no formal record keeping in the monitoring, with occasional questions by the practitioner to get some idea about what is going on; and (d) no consequences for failure to carry out program requirements and progress through the program without necessary completion of earlier stages.

The advantage of a tight program is that it facilitates program compliance, thus increasing the likelihood that the program will be given an opportunity to perform its good works. Being highly focused, the tight program also tends to be relatively efficient and can bring about the fastest change. Such a program, however, presupposes a high degree of client cooperation and that satisfactory progress would not be likely to be made without tight structure. The loose program, in contrast, can be inefficient and can result in aimless wandering, often with little benefit to the participants. Looseness of program has the advantage, however, of allowing for great flexibility and, in any case, may be especially suited to work with resistive, uncooperative, and unmotivated clients, clients with high maturation and capability of appropriate self-direction, participants who must exercise a high degree of control over the process of change, and those for whom a tight program otherwise would not work.

In the early stages of development, it is generally difficult to justify a tight program in all respects. The program that lends itself best to being structured strictly benefits from considerable prior development and evaluation and is known to have a given, satisfactory level of effectiveness, when implemented properly. Some looseness—especially in the early stages of development—allows for flexibility and exploration that would otherwise not be possible. As development progresses and more is learned about the intervention domain, greater structure can be placed on the program.

There is an important qualification to the above comments concerning the matter of risk. When there is some risk to the client or others associated with noncompliance, a much tighter program may be required. For example, if one were developing a program to have patients adhere to a medical regimen with life-saving benefits, some program strictness would be desirable. Because of the risk, certain areas of crisis intervention, child abuse, substance abuse, self-destructive behavior, and marital violence could justifiably be more rather than less tightly structured, even when work is in the early stages of development.

INTERVENTION FOR GENERALIZED CHANGE

Intervention that results in persisting change for clients in the diverse situations in which change is desired has long been a goal of the various fields of human service. The goal has been elusive, however, largely because very little is known about how to intervene for long-lasting change. In recent years, there has been increasing recognition that maintenance is also important and worthy of attention in its own right. This has resulted in the development of intervention methods that, to some extent, are different from and are introduced separately from intervention methods used to achieve desired outcomes in the first place. However, if intervention methods were capable from the outset of yielding long-term, generalized benefits, the need to employ special methods for maintenance and generalization following initial intervention would be reduced or eliminated. In addition to programming for generalization following successful change, interventions should ideally be designed in the first place to facilitate generalization.

The problem is that what little is known about generalization has been applied largely to programming for generalization following intervention, not to designing interventions for initial use. Even so, some of what is known about programming for generalization is relevant to the design of interventions, as the discussion of maintenance in the next chapter should make clear. A few additional observations are in order. Interventions that are artificial or synthetic should be avoided when more natural counterparts are available. For example, parental praise, if potentially effective, would be preferable to imposing a special token system that first requires introduction from outside the family, withdrawal following successful change, and then a maintenance program to assure longevity of change. In general, intervention given by mediators who are indigenous members of the client's natural environment would be preferable to those implemented by outsiders; and intervention drawing on client capabilities of self-control would be preferable to interventions introduced from outside. In contrast to the office or other analogue situation, the natural environment would generally be preferable as the setting for intervention.

SUMMARY

1. Intervention methods are the backbone of the anatomy of the helping process and are generally central in intervention design.

2. An intervention method is composed of one or more intervention techniques and a program format.

3. The intervention technique is a recognized and distinctive set of helping activities that relate to a particular interventional objective. Although often consisting of separate components, the elements of an intervention technique are typically used together rather than separately.

4. Many intervention techniques are largely accelerative or decelerative in their application; some may be both accelerative or decelerative; and a few are difficult to classify in these terms.

5. The accelerative technique is intended to increase desirable responding and, all things considered, is preferred over the decelerative.

6. The decelerative technique is intended to decrease undesirable responding, can incur negative side effects, and generally should be employed only when an accelerative technique would be insufficient by itself to produce the desired changes.

7. If it is necessary to use a decelerative technique, it is generally desirable also to employ an accelerative technique to endeavor to increase desirable responding.

8. A combination of an accelerative technique to increase desirable responding with a decelerative technique to decrease the related undesirable responding can be much stronger than the use of either alone.

9. If given behaviors are the objects of change, those behaviors and conditions relating to them generally should be the direct targets of intervention. Beneficial incidental changes in nontarget behaviors do accompany interventions, but their occurrence cannot be depended on unless they, too, are made direct targets of change.

10. Intervention is typically carried out in a program format in which a given assembly of intervention components is applied to one or more target behaviors.

11. When designing the format for the program, the practitioner-researcher must give attention to such factors as the appropriate scope of intervention; the numbers, order, strength, and longevity of interventions; and the degree of individualization and program structure.

12. There is increasing recognition that the scope of intervention in a program should include more than the target behavior itself—for

example, the controlling conditions for the behavior and related system and environmental influences.

13. Although the variety of techniques need not always be large to be effective, there should be a sufficient number of appropriate techniques to accomplish the intervention objective.

14. Program sequences of interventions may be uniform, branching, or variable, each of which has its advantages and disadvantages and involves important assumptions about behavior involved in the intervention process.

15. The strength of intervention should be neither too weak nor too strong; rather, it should be sufficiently potent to achieve the intervention objective.

16. When determining the extent to which the program should be individualized or standardized, attention needs to be given to such factors as the appropriateness of the program for the individuals involved, the cost in time and effort, and program benefits for clients.

17. While there are advantages to time-limited interventions, the time allowed for intervention should certainly be enough to carry out the intervention competently.

18. Programs may be structured as tight or loose, each of which has advantages and disadvantages depending on the characteristics of the participating clients, the degree of risk in the event of program noncompliance, and the stage of development of the interventions.

19. To increase the likelihood that interventions will yield long-term, generalized benefits, ideally interventions should be designed at the outset to facilitate generalization. For example, interventions that draw on strengths and resources of the client, of mediators, and of conditions prevailing in the natural environment may facilitate generalized change.

Implementation, Maintenance,
and Termination

Implementation, maintenance, and termination are critical components of a helping strategy because they are concerned with practitioner activity when the intervention is introduced and afterwards. Despite their importance in the ultimate fate of the intervention effort, they have received relatively little attention as compared with other aspects of the helping strategy, such as the intervention methods. This chapter covers some of the practitioner activities and issues applicable to this important segment of the helping process.

IMPLEMENTATION PROCEDURES

From the point of introducing the intervention to the eventual achievement of the desired changes, the intervener carries out many activities to implement the program. Some of the areas of implementation are outlined below.

Areas of Implementation

(1) Introducing the Intervention. The intervention must be introduced to the client, using procedures appropriate for the client and situation. Among possible activities here are the presentation of the intervention to the client, along with an explanation of and rationale for the program, obtaining his or her consent and cooperation, establishing a working agreement, and carrying out the initial activities required to start.

(2) Achieving Appropriate Program Involvement. Introducing a program is one thing and achieving suitable participant involvement is another. Appropriate client involvement generally calls for the client to carry out at least some requisite behavior. Compliance with program requirements is generally needed to achieve program objectives. To determine whether there is appropriate program involvement and compliance, it is necessary for the practitioner to monitor the behavior required by the program. Referred to as "adherence" in the health fields, such compliance cannot generally be determined without introducing specific monitoring procedures, such as those discussed in Chapter 6.

(3) Monitoring Target Behavior. It is also essential that target behavior be monitored along with program compliance. Such monitoring makes it possible to determine whether the intended objectives of the program are being achieved and what possible courses of action are called for. For example, if the desired changes are occurring and the client is adhering to the program, this suggests that the program is achieving its intended objectives and should be continued. However, if the desired changes are being achieved but the client is not adhering to the program, this indicates that there may be other factors producing the desired changes. If there is no positive change combined with no program adherence, this outcome suggests that the intervener should make program compliance a first priority.

(4) Reevaluating and Readjusting the Intervention Program. Depending on the outcome of the monitoring and the efforts in previous steps, it may be necessary to reevaluate and readjust the intervention program. In extreme cases, the program may need to be completely modified. This can necessitate further assessment. More typically, however, needed adjustments can be made without returning to earlier phases of the helping process. Even when the desired changes are occurring and there is proper program adherence, there is often need for fine-tuning and for making minor adjustments to improve the operation of the program.

(5) Sustaining Change. It is important that change be sustained sufficiently to allow for habituation and adjustment to the change and for stabilization of new behavior patterns. Weeks and months can be required to bring about sustained induction or change prior to entering a maintenance phase. Although it is difficult at this point to say how long a program should be continued to be sure that stabilized changes have been achieved, one rule of thumb is to continue the program for at least two months following achievement of the desired changes before considering maintenance.

Session Management

The frequency and number of sessions may vary considerably during intervention, depending on such factors as program needs and progress. Many programs are too complex to be introduced all at once and have to be introduced gradually, session by session. In any case, once initiated, programs require careful monitoring and periodic adjustment, as indicated above. From the onset, time should be set aside in each session—usually at first—to review client activity and any data that have been collected to determine if everything is progressing properly.

Program Structure and Management

It is in implementation that the degree of tightness or looseness of the program becomes a reality. The dimensions of program tightness or looseness, described earlier, now need to be put into operation. The structure that is implemented must be consistent with what is appropriate for the client and what has been planned for the intervention. Client response to the program should be determined and such factors as the match between client response and program requirements, possible client resistance, and countervailing conditions that may interfere with the smooth running of the program need to be considered and addressed.

Rather than being left out or haphazardly initiated, the approach to implementation should be included in intervention plans and should also be considered in the design and development of intervention.

MAINTENANCE AND GENERALIZATION METHODS

It is one thing to achieve change in intervention, still another to have that change persist following the intervention. That which brings about the initial change is not necessarily that which achieves persistence of the change. For instance, a weight reduction program consisting of such procedures as reduced caloric intake, regular meals, slow eating, and self-monitoring of these changes may achieve the initial reduction in weight, but the weight losses may be sustained later by a still different pattern consisting of moderate eating, regular exercise, and fear of losing physical attractiveness to a new-found lover. The persistence of change after the intervention program has stopped generally calls for special procedures.

What is referred to as maintenance of change by many practitioners and authors (e.g., Bandura, 1969) would be referred to as generalization by most applied behavior analysts. For example, the concept of generalization as proposed by Stokes and Baer (1977) includes persistence through time as one aspect of generalization. These authors define generalization as follows: "Generalization will be considered to be the occurrence of relevant behavior under different, non-training conditions (i.e., across subjects, settings, people, behaviors, and/or time) without the scheduling of the same events in these conditions as had been scheduled in the training conditions" (1977, p. 350). The interventionist would like changes to transfer to situations, people, or behaviors not included specifically in the intervention program and, further, would like such changes to persist in time. The term "generalization" will be used as indicated in the definition above and the more specific term "maintenance" will be employed to refer to the persistence of change following intervention.

Stokes and Baer pointed out that the methodology of generalization has been neglected and that applied researchers have tended not to program generalization but rather to expect passively that generalization will occur on its own. They point out further that whereas the training of response discrimination was understood as an active process for which there were widely used procedures, generalization was viewed more as a passive process not requiring active intervention. On the basis of their review of 270 applied behavior analysis studies relevant to generalization and a central core of some 120 studies contributing directly to the technology of generalization, these authors concluded that although there was no recognized technology of programming generalization, there was an implicit technology of generalization. Stokes and Baer (1977) evolved nine categories of generalization method, given below.

(1) *Train and Hope*: There is no active programming of generalization but, should it occur, it is most welcome.

(2) *Sequential Modification*: Determining whether generalization is or is not present and, if absent or deficient, procedures are initiated to accomplish the desired changes by systematic, sequential modification in every nongeneralized condition, (i.e., across responses, subjects, settings, or therapists). In effect, modification is sequentially applied as necessary to all of the contexts, settings, or behaviors for which generalization is desired.

(3) *Introduce to Natural Maintaining Contingencies*: This method consists to a large extent of providing intervention for behaviors that will normally

be maintained in the natural environment and introducing the individual to that environment so that the natural maintaining conditions can take effect. As Stokes and Baer prescribe: "Look for a response that enters a natural community; in particular, teach subjects to cue their potential natural communities to reinforce their desirable behaviors" (1977, p. 364).

(4) *Train Sufficient Exemplars*: "If the result of teaching one exemplar of a generalizable lesson is merely the mastery of the exemplar taught, with no generalization beyond it, then the obvious route to generalization is to teach another exemplar of the same generalization lesson, and then another, and then another, and so on until the induction is formed (i.e., until generalization occurs sufficiently to satisfy the problem posed)" (Stokes & Baer, 1977, p. 355)

(5) *Train "To Generalize:"* "If generalization is considered as a response itself, then a reinforcement contingency may be placed upon it, the same as with any other operant" (p. 362). As the authors further state: "When generalizations occur, reinforce at least some of them at least sometimes, as if 'to generalize' were an operant response class" (p. 364).

(6) *Train Loosely*: In this approach "teaching is conducted with relatively little control over the stimuli presented and the correct responses allowed, so as to maximize sampling of relevant dimensions for transfer to other forms of the behavior" (p. 355). As the authors further state: "Loosen [interventional] control over the stimuli and responses involved in training; in particular, train different examples concurrently, and vary instructions, S^Ds, social reinforcers and backup reinforcers" (p. 364).

(7) *Use Indiscriminable Contingencies*: "If contingencies of reinforcement or punishment, or the setting events that mark the presence or absence of those contingencies, are made indiscriminable, then generalization may well be observed" (p. 358). The authors further recommend the following: "Make unclear the limits of training contingencies; in particular, conceal, when possible, the point at which those contingencies stop operating, possibly by delayed reinforcement" (p. 364).

(8) *Program Common Stimuli*: "If it is supposed that generalization will occur, if only there are sufficient stimulus components occurring in common in both the training and generalization settings, then a reasonably practical technique is to guarantee that common and salient stimuli will be present in both" (p. 360). Stokes and Baer further recommend the following: "Use stimuli that are likely to be found in generalization settings and training settings as well; in particular, use peers as tutors" (p. 364).

(9) *Mediated Generalization*: Mediated generalization "requires establishing a response [a 'mediating stimulus'] as part of the new learning that is likely to be utilized in other problems as well, and will constitute sufficient commonality between the original learning and the new problem to result in generalization. The most commonly used mediator

is language, apparently" (p. 361). The mediating stimulus becomes discriminative of the responses desired in the generalization of other responses.

It is clear that the practitioner-researcher has many options when planning and designing programs for maintenance and generalization, although these are not yet well developed. All the methods given above are relevant to the initial formulation of the intervention as well as to programming for generalization later. The challenge in planning and design is to evolve an approach to intervention that has the ability from the outset to produce generalized change, thus eliminating the need first to program the change then its maintenance. When this is not possible, maintenance and generalization must be programmed following intervention, doing so on the basis of what was learned following the intervention about what needs to be considered in the program.

The methods of achieving generalization presented above rely on programming change for an individual such that desired responding will occur relatively autonomously after the individual no longer has exposure to the program. There are also other methods applicable to maintaining behavior changes following intervention that do not presuppose the ability to program an autonomous change. As indicated in Table 5.1, these are essentially all prosthetic inasmuch as without them, the desired persistence of responding could decrease or disappear. Because of limitations of client ability to respond or lack of feasibility otherwise, these more prosthetic methods of maintenance may be the only means by which longevity and generalization of intervention changes may be achieved.

When separate programs of maintenance must be designed, the practitioner-researcher must carry out an intervening set of activities to make this possible. There should generally be a limited empirical evaluation of the extent of generalization (a "generalization probe") to find out about what has and has not generalized. Additional assessment data may also need to be gathered at this point, and a plan for maintenance needs to be formulated, implemented, monitored, and evaluated.

TERMINATION

Termination refers of course to those activities that occur at the end of the helping process, ideally following successful intervention. There are at least two ways in which termination points may be established. In the first, the ending point is worked out in advance, generally in

TABLE 5.1
Other Types of Maintenance

Periodic "booster" sessions of intervention (e.g.,
   returning to see the
   therapist periodically for additional treatment)
Continuous intervention (e.g., seeing a therapist weekly
   for all of one's life)
Human prosthetic (e.g., relying on a "buddy" from a
   self-help group for
   former alcoholics to prevent relapses into
   heavy drinking)*
Nonhuman prosthetic (e.g., use of a wrist watch alarm signal to provide
a
   cuing signal concerning when to leave for appoint
   ments for an individual who otherwise would be
   chronically late)*
Drug control (e.g., use of antabuse by the former
   alcoholic to prevent return to drinking)

*For further details on the use of behavior prosthetics, the reader is
referred to Lindsley (1964).

connection with a fixed term of intervention covering either a given period of time, number of sessions, or degree of progress. Although such termination often has the advantage of mobilizing participants to work harder to finish, sometimes important work remains when the ending point arrives. The second method is more open ended: Termination occurs when it seems appropriate. In either case, an important disengagement sometimes can be emotionally difficult for clients (and also practitioners), particularly when strong attachments have been established. It is generally desirable to phase out the helping process gradually, to prepare the client in advance for each step, and to move at a pace responsive to the needs and concerns of the client. Termination should be designed so that the disengagement is smooth and the client is prepared properly for getting along independently and for sustaining the progress made.

SUMMARY

1. Implementation of an intervention calls for carrying out a number of activities, such as introducing the intervention to the client or clients, achieving appropriate program involvement, monitoring target behavior, reevaluating and readjusting the intervention program, and sustaining change.

2. Additional activities of implementation consist of structuring and managing the sessions and the program.

3. Introduction of maintenance and generalization following the intervention is directed toward endeavoring to ensure that the gains achieved in intervention generalize to situations, people, or behaviors not included specifically in the intervention program and persist through time following the intervention.

4. Although the methodology of generalization is relatively undeveloped as compared with that of direct intervention, methods are emerging. Among these are sequential modification, introduction to natural maintaining contingencies, training of sufficient exemplars, loose training, use of indiscriminable contingencies, the programming of common stimuli, mediated generalization, and training "to generalize."

5. There are also methods of maintaining and generalizing changes following intervention that do not presuppose the ability to program an autonomous change. These methods are largely prosthetic and include periodic booster sessions, continuous intervention, the use of human and nonhuman prosthetics, and drug control.

6. Occurring at the end of the helping process, termination involves those activities that relate to phasing out the helping process, disengagement of the participants, and the preparation of clients for getting along independently and for maintaining the benefits of intervention.

Monitoring, Evaluation, and Follow-Up

The activities of monitoring, evaluation, and follow-up provide essential feedback to the practitioner so that practice activities may be adjusted accordingly. The feedback afforded by these activities offers the promise of making practice more self-correcting and accountable than it typically has been in the past. Although discussed separately in this chapter because they relate to data-gathering methodology, the topics of monitoring, evaluation, and follow-up are intimately related to the practice activities of implementation, maintenance, and termination discussed in Chapter 5. This chapter should be read as a companion to Chapter 5.

MONITORING

Monitoring consists of gathering and evaluating data during the process of intervention to follow the progress of intervention. It is important because the information provides a basis for ongoing review and adjustment of the helping effort. Such monitoring is not always systematic and quantitative and much of it is informal and qualitative, considering the many types of information relevant to intervention. Practice models differ considerably in terms of the areas to be monitored and in how systematic and rigorous the monitoring needs to be.

Although generally less extensive than the data gathered in assessment, the information gathered in monitoring consists at least in part of some data gathered during assessment—for example, information about the level of the problem behavior and possibly related conditions.

Monitoring generally also embraces many other responses, events, and conditions that bear on the success of the intervention, only some of which are now being recorded systematically in most monitoring efforts.

Central to monitoring is information directly relevant to guiding the course of intervention. Thus, by monitoring the behavior or conditions that are the focus of intervention, it is possible to determine whether there has been improvement, deterioration, or no change. By monitoring other potentially correlated responses, it is possible to find out whether the intervention is associated with adverse side effects or coincidental benefits. It is also important to monitor the success with which an intervention is implemented, otherwise it would not be known whether the intervention was carried out as intended. Information such as that illustrated above helps the practitioner-researcher determine whether the program should be continued as it is or changed. Data central to intervention management should ideally be monitored systematically and quantitatively.

When setting up the monitoring, the interventionist faces many of the same decisions as those involved in an approach to assessment. For example, decisions need to be made in monitoring in regard to the sources of data, response channels, response measurement, response indicators, who conducts assessment, and how data are obtained and handled. The reader is referred to Chapter 3 for further discussion of these decision areas.

Monitoring is also ordinarily carried out for purposes of ongoing evaluation of practice and, in this regard, may be thought of as an aspect of the larger topic of outcome evaluation, discussed below.

OUTCOME EVALUATION

Some method of evaluation is part of every helping strategy, whether the evaluation is implicit or explicit, systematic or nonsystematic. The discussion here is restricted to evaluation as a component of a helping strategy rather than evaluation more broadly conceived as a phase of intervention design. The latter subject is discussed in Chapter 13.

Steps in Evaluation for Practice

If evaluation is systematically conducted as part of practice, it should include a series of ordered activities. Among these are the following:

(a) The evaluation objective must be established (e.g., to evaluate the effectiveness of the intervention for service purposes).

(b) The practice objectives need to be made clear, specific and measurable.

(c) The indicators of success or failure need to be isolated.

(d) These indicators should be measured where possible before, during, and after intervention (although the level of precision in measurement may be less than that required for research purposes).

(e) A suitable design for evaluation must be selected and implemented.

(f) The evaluation data must be gathered, analyzed, and appraised in light of the service objectives.

(g) The interventionist should take appropriate action, thus adjusting practice to what has been learned in the evaluation.

When evolving an approach to evaluation appropriate to a helping strategy, the practitioner faces many decisions similar to those implicated in assessment. However, assessment is broader in scope and, as viewed here, serves mainly to assist in the planning and formulation of intervention, whereas evaluation as it involves service is largely restricted to the gathering and appraisal of data relating to service outcomes. An overview of selected areas implicated in an approach to outcome evaluation is given in Table 6.1. The discussion below is organized around the topics presented in the table.

Purposes

A major decision is whether to focus evaluation exclusively on service outcomes or to include a research objective. The purpose of service is to achieve change for clients or help them otherwise and thereby improve some aspect of human well-being. Outcome evaluation of such service consists largely of determining the extent to which the criterion of change has been achieved. Research, in contrast, has the more general objective of making a contribution to knowledge of human behavior.

The purposes of evaluation have direct implications for the role of the interventionist. There has been increasing interest in recent years in extending the role of the helping person from that of practitioner to that of practitioner-researcher (e.g., see Barlow, 1981; Barlow, Hayes, & Nelson, 1984; Bloom, 1975; Bloom & Fischer, 1982; Briar, 1973; Fischer, 1978; Jayaratne & Levy, 1979; Marks, 1982; Schinke, 1983; Thomas, 1975, 1977b; Tripodi & Epstein, 1978, 1980). Such an extended role clearly adds an objective of research to evaluation. Although desirable in principle, adding a research objective to practice

TABLE 6.1
**Overview of Selected Areas Implicated in an Approach to
Outcome Evaluation**

I. Purposes
  A. Service outcome
  B. Service outcome and research
II. What Is Evaluated
  A. Effectiveness
  B. Efficiency
  C. Cost
III. Methods of Evaluation
  A. Nonexperimental
  B. Experimental
      1. Single-subject experimental designs
      2. Between-subjects experimental designs
IV. Measurement
  A. Sources of data (see Table 3.1)
  B. Response channels (see Table 3.1)
  C. Response measurement (see Table 3.1)
  D. Response indicators (see Table 3.1)
V. Who Conducts Evaluation (see Table 3.1)
VI. When Evaluation Is Conducted
  A. Concurrent with intervention
  B. Concurrent with intervention and in follow-up
      afterward
VIII. How Data Are Obtained (see Table 3.1)
IX. Data-Handling Factors (see Table 3.1)
X. Appraisal Criteria
  A. Clinical significance
  B. Statistical significance

is not without possible complications. For example, the methodological requirements of research are typically more rigorous and demanding than those necessary for service evaluation for practice purposes. Although many of the methodological requirements of research may be blended compatibly with the activities of service, there are differences between the requisites of research and service, and some of these may pose conflicts and strains (see Kratochwill & Piersal, 1983; Thomas, 1978c, 1983).

By setting clear priorities, it is often possible to avoid potential conflicts between the requirements of service and research. For example, if the primary objective in service evaluation is to evaluate the service for practice purposes and less to meet goals of research, then any potential conflict may be resolved by being sure that service is not interfered with. Likewise, if the research objective is foremost, then any potential conflicts between service and research in the outcome evaluation may be resolved by making the requirements of the research foremost.

Any endeavor to include an explicit research objective in service evaluation involves methodological considerations that are beyond the scope of the present discussion. For additional details, the reader is referred to standard texts on behavioral and social science research and to Chapter 13 on evaluation as a phase of interventional D&D.

What Is Evaluated

Another major decision in outcome evaluation involves what is to be evaluated. There are at least three alternatives: effectiveness, efficiency, or cost. Each of these deserves further comment.

Effectiveness

With regard to effectiveness, the question is, "What are the benefits of the service?" Practice objectives may or may not be achieved and there may or may not be other gains from the intervention. Evaluation of practice effectiveness is fundamental because if the intervention does not measure up to expectations of clients, practitioners, and outside observers, then the intervention should clearly be reconsidered or modified.

Efficiency

There is increasing interest in efficiency as well as effectiveness. Efficiency may be monitored and evaluated by keeping records of the amount of time the interventionist and others devote to the practice effort, the results of which may then be compared with effectiveness achieved and costs incurred. Efficiency is important because an intervention may not necessarily be more effective than its competitor, but it may take less time. Likewise, a highly effective intervention may take an excessive amount of time.

Cost

There is also increasing interest in the costs of intervention and these may be reckoned in at least three ways. In the first, the total costs of the helping effort may be calculated. Such costs may be expressed, for example, as the cost per case. In the second, costs may be determined in relationship to effectiveness, thus yielding a cost-effectiveness measure. For example, in a weight reduction program, the cost per pound of weight loss may be calculated. In the third, the benefits of the intervention are calculated and compared with the costs, thus yielding a cost-benefit ratio. Although highly desirable in principle, cost-benefit analyses are often not straightforward to carry out because of the difficulty in quantifying in monetary terms the benefits of intervention, such as personal satisfaction, the quality of family relationships, and personal adjustment. To the extent that benefits may be determined monetarily, however, the cost-benefit analysis provides a very useful measure of outcome.

Methods of Evaluation

Evaluation by nonexperimental means does not require the imposition of an experimental design but, rather, charts outcome and possibly other relevant data throughout the course of intervention. An important advantage of nonexperimental evaluation is that it can generally be carried out with little or no threat to service. It has the disadvantage, however, of generally providing less rigorous and less convincing evidence of change. Most practitioners are particularly interested in knowing whether the gross outcomes of their interventions with clients are beneficial, and typically have less interest in causal questions regarding outcome for which experimental methods would be suitable. The evaluation of gross effectiveness can often be carried out successfully with experimental manipulation and design. Such evaluation calls for measurement of outcome before, during, and after intervention, and the results are evaluated for significance by visual or statistical methods. Among the available methodologies for service evaluation are time-series analyses (see Glass, Willson, & Gottman, 1975; Jones, Vaught, Weinrott, 1977; McCain & McCleary, 1979), methods of measuring goal attainment (see Kiresuk & Sherman, 1968), and other statistical procedures (see Kazdin, 1976).

Experimental evaluation can be conducted with single-case experiments or with group experimental designs. Single-case experiments are particularly applicable to practice evaluation because single cases, families, or groups are the units dealt with. Single-case experiments are experiments conducted with single cases or, in some instances, several cases, generally using the subject as his or her own control. For example, in the simple A-B-A-B design for a client, there is first a baseline period (A), during which the preintervention level of responding is measured, followed by intervention (B), during which the effects of the intervention are measured, then return to baseline (A), and reinstitution of the intervention (B). Other single-case experimental designs are summarized in Table 13.1. Single-case experiments have been widely used in behavioral research and in applied behavior analysis (e.g., see Hersen & Barlow, 1976; Kazdin, 1973; Leitenberg, 1973) and have been advocated for use in empirically based practice (e.g., Barlow et al., 1984; Bloom & Fischer, 1982; Browning & Stover, 1971; Fischer, 1978; Hayes, 1981; Jayaratne & Levy, 1979; Mahoney, 1978; Risley, 1969; and Thomas, 1975).

A major decision faced by the interventionist is whether to employ single-case experimental methods in the service evaluation. Single-case experimentation calls for meeting the methodological requirements for the research design, and there is experimental manipulation of some variables or conditions while holding others constant. The main advantage of employing a single-case experimental design is that it provides the possibility of determining more rigorously whether the intervention may be regarded as accounting for the changes observed. In contrast, evaluation by nonexperimental methods allows its users to draw conclusions only about whether given effects were observed, not what may have caused the effects.

Because of the need to meet the methodological requirements of the research design, the use of single-case experimentation for purposes of service evaluation may cause problems. There are differences between single-subject research and service in regard to objectives, criteria of change, independent variables, types and sequences of change, target responses, and the role of researcher and practitioner. Because of such differences, there may be conflicts between the requirements of the design and of service. Adherence to the strict requirements of single-case experimentation may in some cases present threats to service, and the requirements of service, in contrast, may pose threats to the rigor of the experimentation. Practitioner-researchers who wish to employ single-case experimental designs need to be alert to ways to minimize such threats.

Service can also be evaluated using between-groups experimental designs that include an experimental group and one or more control groups (for example, see Azrin, 1977; Campbell & Stanley, 1966; Kratochwill, 1978). Some of these designs are summarized in Table 13.2. Quasi-experimental and true between-groups experimental designs have advantages over nonexperimental methods in regard to drawing conclusions about possible causal conditions. But again, however, the use of such methods may interfere with service. Further, such experimentation is generally more costly and time consuming than evaluation by nonexperimental methods.

Measurement and Other Topics

The issues of measurement in evaluation involve such matters as sources of data, response channels, and response measurement and indicators. These issues are very similar to those encountered in assessment; the reader is referred to Chapter 3, where these topics are discussed. The reader is also referred to that chapter for discussion of who conducts evaluation, how much data to obtain, how data are obtained, and data-handling factors, since these issues also relate to evaluation.

When Evaluation Is Conducted

Evaluation that embraces the current intervention activity as well as follow-up is most desirable inasmuch as it is more complete than evaluation that occurs only after the intervention or that omits follow-up.

Appraisal Criteria

Criteria for determining change in service evaluation can be criteria of the clients (e.g., their desired level of success in child management), of others (e.g., the achievement of success in child management consistent with norms in the community), or of the practitioners (e.g., carrying out child management to a level of success satisfactory to the helping person). Appraisal of such changes may be by visual inspection of the data (e.g., see Parsonson & Baer, 1978), by statistical criteria (see Kazdin, 1976), or some combination. Actually, these criteria are themselves subject to design and development inasmuch as they are an integral part of service evaluation. Nonstatistical and clinical criteria, including practices of "eyeballing" data to determine change, can often be subjective and of questionable reliability, whereas statistical criteria often do not coincide with service criteria of progress, all too frequently entail statistical assumptions that are hard to satisfy, and entail laborious calculation. Statistical and clinical criteria can often be combined such that the advantages of both can be retained.

FOLLOW-UP

Although not yet routinely included in most helping strategies, follow-up is important because it provides information concerning the longevity of change and what additional assistance may be needed. How long after termination should the follow-up be carried out? Practitioner-researchers differ in their recommendations and there would appear to be no uniformly satisfactory solution.

Long-term follow-up has the advantage of being a relatively demanding test because it provides information concerning the extent to which the changes have endured in the face of the changing conditions that generally accompany the passage of time. If changes persist over a long period, such follow-up information can be most valuable. However, failure to observe sustained change over the long term can be interpreted many ways. Indeed, some researchers have contended that failure to sustain long-term change should be expected to the extent that intervening conditions could alter the behaviors addressed. Although less demanding, short-term follow-up is fairer inasmuch as the conditions prevailing at the follow-up may be similar to those that were present at termination. Short-term results, then, tend to be less equivocal. Although positive change in short-term follow-up may not indicate as much as positive change for long-term follow-up, negative change in the short run clearly reflects adversely on the ability of the intervention to provide sustained change.

Because each contributes in a way that the other does not, it is ideal to have both short-term and long-term follow-up. The follow-up periods could occur, for example, every three or six months over the course of one to two years. This approach may provide more information than is required, but it is the safest course to follow until more is known concerning the likely course of change for the different areas of intervention.

SUMMARY

1. By obtaining selected data during the process of intervention, monitoring provides a basis for ongoing review and adjustment of the helping effort.

2. Monitoring generally includes many responses, events, and conditions that bear on the success of the intervention, but currently not all this information is monitored systematically and quantitatively.

3. Data central to intervention management ideally should be monitored systematically and quantitatively.

4. It is particularly important to monitor the behavior or conditions that are the focus of intervention and the success with which the intervention is implemented because this information is directly relevant to guiding the course of intervention.

5. Some method of evaluation that also includes monitoring is part of every helping strategy.

6. When conducted systematically as part of practice, evaluation includes a series of ordered activities that range from the specification of evaluation objectives to the adjustment of practice activities in light of what has been learned in the evaluation.

7. The decisions faced in evaluation are similar to those implicated in assessment except that, typically, the data gathered in evaluation are less extensive than those obtained in assessment.

8. The purposes of evaluation in practice may include service outcome and/or research.

9. Methods of evaluation of practice that also involve research objectives should be designed to avoid potential conflicts between the objectives of service and research.

10. Outcomes evaluated include effectiveness, efficiency, and/or cost, each of which may contribute valuable information for appraising the helping effort.

11. Methods of evaluation may include those that do not involve the imposition of an experimental design, but such evaluation generally is less rigorous than that which calls for the use of an experimental design.

12. Single-case experimentation is particularly applicable to practice evaluation, but it must be employed prudently and carefully if potential conflicts between the requirements of service and the methodological requirements of the research design are to be minimized or avoided.

13. Group experimental designs may also be employed in practice evaluation, particularly quasi-experimental designs.

14. The decisions required in outcome evaluation include many of the same issues that need to be addressed in assessment. Among these are decisions concerning the method of measurement, who conducts evaluation, how much data to obtain, when evaluation is conducted, how data are to be handled, and criteria for appraising the outcomes.

15. Follow-up data should be obtained to learn about the longevity of change in the short as well as the long term.

Behavior Theory and
Intervention Theory

A helping strategy is guided and shaped by two different types of theory, behavior and intervention theory. Behavior theory is addressed to understanding the behavior of clients and others affected by the intervention. Intervention theory, in contrast, is directed toward understanding and prescribing the behavior of the helping person and the activities involved in the helping process. Although still not widely accepted, this distinction between types of theory is beginning to be recognized (e.g., see Fischer, 1978; Greenwood, 1955; Mullen, 1981). The distinction is important because each type of theory has its functions and occupies an essential place in a helping strategy.

BEHAVIOR THEORY

What Behavior Theory Is

All helping strategies have a behavior theory, although it is often underlying rather than explicit or complete. Behavior theory embraces overt behavior as well as thinking, feeling, and states of being. In contemporary helping strategies the behavior theory might be identified as Freudian, neo-Freudian, behavioral, cognitive, cognitive-behavioral, personalistic, problem solving, humanistic, social psychological, psychobiological, transactional, or family systems, among others.

Behavior theories consist of an interrelated set of concepts, hypotheses, empirical generalizations, and basic assumptions to account for the behavior of clients and others affected by the helping effort. An example of a portion of behavior theory is given in Cameo 7.1. As it applies to a helping strategy, behavior theory serves the functions of defining what is important to intervention and what one should look for, of prediction of selected outcomes, and of explanation and interpretation of relevant behavior and conditions. By these means behavior theory makes it possible for helping persons to interpret assessment information and make the behavioral assumptions necessary for intervention.

Behavior theory embraces a broad range of content. More specifically, it serves to define the problems and strengths for individuals and families, the role of personality factors and what specific characteristics of personality may be important, the relevance of one's behavioral repertoire, the role of motivation as well as what particular aspects of motivation are important, the role of the individual's disposition to change, what aspects of the existing level of functioning are important and have prognostic relevance for the future, what factors are important in etiology including the weight that should be given to events of early development as well as to the contemporary environment, the importance of the family in the origin and change of difficulties, and the relevance of situational and environmental factors in contemporary human behavior.

Behavior theory in a helping process shares many similarities with its counterparts in pure behavioral science. Both are behavior theories consisting of concepts, hypotheses, empirical generalizations, and basic assumptions; both serve to facilitate interpretation and explanation and the prediction of relevant behavioral events, and to focus attention on what is considered important. Both draw on a body of prior research

---

Cameo 7.1
Some Behavioral Assumptions Made About Encounter Groups

1. (Assumption) An *encounter group* can generate a "psychological climate of *safety*."
2. (Hypothesis) If a person feels *safe* within an encounter group, then he or she will exhibit *freedom* of expression.
3. (Hypothesis) If a person exhibits *freedom* of expression, then he or she will provide genuine *communication* to others.
4. (Hypothesis) If a person genuinely *communicates* his or her ideas and feelings to others, then others will return genuine *feedback*.
5. (Hypothesis) If a person receives genuine *feedback*, then this will lead to *self-knowledge*.

From Bloom (1975, p. 78), based on Rogers (1970).

and theory in the behavioral and social sciences and related fields. However, there are several important differences.

First, behavior theory as employed in a helping process can be and often is less pure and more eclectic than its academic counterpart. Second, it is typically restricted to client behavior and the behavior of others affected by the helping process rather than being more general. Third, it has an applied, utilitarian function—a technological function, to use Mullen's (1981) term—inasmuch as its use is instrumental in achieving objectives of the helping strategy. This utilitarian function is paramount in a helping strategy for if the behavior theory provides vague concepts or incorrect assumptions, interpretations, or predictions, the related activities of practice will be jeopardized and service objectives threatened.

Some Selection Criteria

Because of the importance of behavior theory in human service, writers have attempted to identify the qualities of a good theory. Criteria have been proposed for assessing research, evaluating theories, and selecting knowledge from behavioral science (see Fischer, 1978; Gouldner, 1957; Mullen, 1981; Rothman, 1974; Thomas, 1967; Tripodi et al., 1969; Zetterberg, 1965). Examination of these criteria suggests that there are at least two sets. The first set applies to all behavior theory, whether used in a helping strategy or not, and includes such conventional criteria for evaluating theories as their verifiability, logical power, consistency, parsimony, coherence, and generality. These criteria are also important in behavior theory in a helping strategy, but the second set is particularly relevant. This set contains criteria that relate to the extent to which the theory is utilitarian and practical for use in a helping process. Among the criteria here are the following:

Content Relevance: Does the content embrace the appropriate target persons, behaviors, and related behavioral and social conditions?

Content Inclusiveness: Does the behavior theory embrace the relevant independent and dependent variables pertaining to the behavioral domain of the intervention?

Knowledge Validity: Have the propositions of the behavior theory been corroborated in appropriate research?

Knowledge Power: Are the variables of the theory capable of accounting for a large portion of the behavior to be explained or predicted?

Knowledge Engineerability: Are the real-world referents of the knowledge capable of being successfully implemented because the indicators are identifiable, accessible, manipulable, potent, economically feasible, and ethically suitable to manipulate?

For additional discussion of these and other criteria, the reader is referred to Thomas (1964, 1967) and others (Fischer, 1978; Gouldner, 1967; Mullen, 1981; Rothman, 1974; Tripodi et al., 1969; Zetterberg, 1965).

Many helping strategies begin with a strong commitment to a given behavior theory, as if the behavior theory itself were a given—even a doctrine—not to be questioned. Adoption of a given behavior theory is fine if it is the appropriate one—for example, it is one that most adequately meets criteria such as those outlined above. It is best in intervention design to view the behavior theory as a component of helping strategy that is itself subject in large measure to design and development. For example, the elements of behavior theory may be screened, selected, refined, explored, evolved, applied, and appraised in the D&D process. All of this, of course, is short of actually conducting formal research on the theory, an activity more appropriately carried out as part of behavioral science research.

INTERVENTION THEORY

Intervention theory consists of the concepts, informational content, assumptions, values, and prescriptions that serve to guide the practice activity of a helping strategy. The practice activities embraced by the intervention theory can include everything from the initial stages of contact through termination. Most writings on approaches to professional helping include a great deal of intervention theory, although common practices and "practice wisdom" in most approaches generally have not yet been codified and written. It is mainly through written or unwritten intervention theory that a helping strategy becomes known and implemented.

A few early statements aside (e.g., Fischer, 1978; Greenwood, 1955; Mullen, 1981), not much has been written on the nature of intervention theory, despite its importance. Unlike behavior or scientific theory, much of intervention theory is value oriented and prescriptive, serving to prescribe the relevant activities of helping. But intervention theory also serves to describe the relevant activities of helping; thus, it also has descriptive content. I offer the following components of intervention theory as a provisional framework to be expanded or modified as more work is done in this area.

Concepts

An important portion of descriptive knowledge appears in the form of concepts, such as "reframing," "victim," "identified patient," "relationship," "system," "patient," "system boundary" and "reinforcement." Concepts serve to identify what is important in helping and provide a vocabulary for describing and communicating about the helping process.

Informational Content

Descriptive knowledge also involves informational content about such constituent functions of helping as assessment and intervention, as well as all other components of a helping strategy. Without the informational content, the practitioner would not know the options of a helping strategy and what is typically done.

Assumptions about Helping Behavior

Still another type of descriptive knowledge in intervention theory involves assumptions about helping behavior. For example, if a brief assessment is advocated, assumptions are made about the amount and type of information the practitioner needs in order to get the job done. If client contacts are purposefully time-limited, assumptions are made about the possible beneficial effects of the time limits on the behavior of those involved.

Assumptions provide rationale for helping behavior and enable the users of the helping method and others to evaluate the validity of the assumptions. Assumptions may be evaluated on the basis of one's prior practice experience, the research of others, and, where possible, especially conducted empirical inquiry. Like all behavioral assumptions, these assumptions can be tested when made explicit and operational. Empirical examination and corroboration of the major assumptions involving helping behavior open up the exciting prospect of developing an empirical basis for this important aspect of intervention theory.

Values

As beliefs concerning what is desirable, values enter directly or indirectly at most points into a helping strategy. As Bergin (1980) put it in his persuasive essay on psychotherapy and religious values, *"Thesis 1: Values are an inevitable and pervasive part of psychotherapy"* (p. 97). Values are an important component of intervention theory because they chart the moral direction of helping. Being more pervasive than any intervention theory, values help to locate the intervention approach in the larger social-cultural context of which it is a part.

Intervention theories make a statement one way or another concerning such value-related matters as confidentiality, the right to treatment, individualization, and the self-determination and ethical treatment of clients. Indeed, implicit in every intervention are value assumptions. Accepting any person into therapy, as Szasz (1960) has repeatedly pointed out, validates the idea that a problem exists. If a behavior (e.g., cigarette smoking) is defined as a problem, this is undesirable by some value (smoking is harmful to health, and health is valued). If a behavior is defined positively rather than as a problem, then the desirable behavior is that which is valued. Change of problem behavior is "good," whereas failure to change is not. Also implicit in the intervention act are value assumptions that it is appropriate to intervene in situations of this type, that the intervention employed is appropriate, and that the interventionist is a suitable agent of intervention.

Consider treatment of a homosexual to change the individual's sexual identity and preference to that of heterosexuality. Not long ago, treatment of this type was fairly common and not likely to be questioned. In recent years, however, there has been increasing recognition that the values involved in such intervention are arguable or, indeed, untenable. In DSM-III (American Psychiatric Association, 1980), homosexuality in and of itself is no longer defined as a sexual deviation. Advocates of the rights of homosexuals would contend that it is a misuse of intervention to employ it to change gender preference, that interventionists have no business trying to change homosexual behavior unless, at best, special conditions are met, and that, in any case, a preferred alternative would be to try to assist the homosexual individual to be more accepting of his or her own sexual identity and preference.

As Bergin (1980) further indicated: *"Thesis 5: In light of the foregoing, it would be honest and ethical to acknowledge that we are implementing our own value systems via our professional work and to be more explicit about what we believe while also respecting the value systems of others*" (p. 101). More generally, values should be made explicit so that they may be more readily scrutinized, disputed, rationalized, explicated, modified, extended, and realized.

As an important basis of all prescription in the intervention theory, values relate to and are fundamental to practice principles, practice guidelines, and codes for ethical treatment of clients, each of which is discussed below.

Practice Principles

Practice principles are general statements that prescribe a broad range of helping activities. Consider the following examples: The client has the right under voluntary conditions to determine whether or not he or she receives help; consent to participate in intervention should be obtained from voluntary clients; "start where the client is"; "form a good working relationship with clients"; "treat every client or family individually"; and never use punishment with residents of the institution unless less aversive and intrusive interventions have been tried first and found ineffective and proper human subjects protections have been observed.

Practice Guidelines

When sufficiently well developed and articulated, prescriptive knowledge often takes the form of practice guidelines. Being more specific than practice principles, such guidelines often relate to one or more practice principle. The directives of such guidelines may apply to recurrent practitioner activities, such as maintaining a therapeutic relationship and sustaining a viable working understanding with the client, as well as such nonrecurrent activities as those that occur in stepwise fashion or occur intermittently or episodically (e.g., crises). When properly developed, practice guidelines can serve to organize practitioner activity in a focused, sequential, systematic fashion. As an illustration of practice guidelines, steps of a case management procedure are given in Cameo 7.2.

Code of Ethics

In a mature intervention theory there should be an ethical code. Such a code necessarily embodies values of the intervention theory and represents some values in concrete, operational terms. As with practice guidelines, an ethical code provides for clearer direction of and

---

Cameo 7.2
Steps of a Case Management Procedure

The behavioral case management procedure developed for the open setting was called PAMBOS, an acronym for Procedure for the Assessment and Modification of Behavior in Open Settings. Selected steps from PAMBOS are given below. These are based on an extension and elaboration of my prior work with various colleagues (Thomas, Carter, & Gambrill, 1970, Gambrill, Thomas, & Carter, 1971; Thomas & Carter, 1971; Thomas, Abrams, & Johnson, 1971). The 15 ordered procedural steps are listed below with a brief description of the practice activity involved.

(1) Inventory of problem areas. The inventory consists of client descriptions of presenting problems, as well as the more conspicuous problems the therapist discerns in the interview.

(2) Problem selection and contract. The therapist and client reach a verbal (or written) agreement concerning which of the problems, including those the worker has noted also, is most in need of attention first.

(3) Commitment to cooperate. The client is asked to agree to cooperate fully in those activities integral to the procedure, such as in providing full, accurate information during assessment, in complying with requests and recommendations made during the modification program, and in maintaining regular contact at the appointed times.

(4) Specification of focal behavior. Samples and instances of the behavioral components of the problem behavior and desirable alternatives are obtained through the interview, reports of others, and, when possible, observation of the behavior itself as it occurs in the natural environment.

(5) Baseline of focal behavior. Assessment of the frequency, magnitude, duration, or latency of the focal behavior is obtained prior to embarking on intervention.

(6) Identification of probable controlling conditions. Specific information is obtained concerning the events that occur just before, during, and after the emission of problem behavior.

(7) Assessment of environmental and behavioral resources. Requisite information is sought concerning such environmental and behavioral resources as potential mediators (e.g., family members or friends, potential reinforcers or potential aversive conditions that, if appropriate, might be made use of in modification).

(8) Specification of behavioral objectives. The therapist specifies the terminal behavioral repertoire of the client as well as appropriate successive approximations to the desired terminal behavior.

(9) Formulation of a modification plan. The therapist selects an appropriate behavioral role to adopt during modification (such as an instigator of modification rather than as a direct intervenor) and selects particular modification techniques most suitable to use in achieving the behavioral objectives.

(10) Execution of the modification plan. Interventions are carried out consistent with the modification objectives and the contract made with the client.

(11) Monitoring the outcomes of intervention. Changes that occur in the problem behavior and in pro-social alternatives are monitored using the same measures as those employed for the baseline (i.e., frequency, duration, etc.).

(12) Formulation of a maintenance plan. The therapist formulates a plan to maintain the behavior following successful modification of the behavior.

(13) Execution of a maintenance plan. The maintenance plan is implemented to maintain the behavior in the natural environment.

(14) Monitoring the outcomes of maintenance. The outcomes of maintenance, such as reduction of problem behavior or acceleration of pro-social alternatives, are monitored using the same measures as employed in the monitoring of modification and in the baseline.

(15) Follow-up. At a suitable point in time following the introduction of the maintenance regimen, follow-up is undertaken using measures commensurate with those used in prior monitoring.

Adapted from Thomas and Walter (1973, pp. 194-195).

accountability for practitioner helping behavior than would otherwise be the case. As an illustration of an ethical code, Cameo 7.3 summarizes some of the ethical issues for the human services, along with related questions that suggest guidelines for appropriate practitioner behavior.

The development of the components of intervention theory described above should go hand in hand with the evolution of the intervention itself.

SUMMARY

1. Behavior theory in a helping strategy is addressed to understanding the behavior of clients and others affected by the intervention.

2. Behavior theories consist of such components as concepts, hypotheses, empirical generalizations, and basic assumptions to account for the behavior of clients and others affected by the helping effort.

3. In addition to providing focus on behavior relevant to the helping process, behavior theory facilitates the prediction, explanation, and interpretation of pertinent behavior and conditions.

4. In contrast to theory in pure behavioral science, with which it shares many similarities, behavior theory in a helping strategy is

---

Cameo 7.3
Selected Ethical Issues for Human Services

A. Have the goals of treatment been adequately considered?
   1. To ensure that the goals are explicit, are they written?
   2. Has the client's understanding of the goals been assured by having the client restate them orally or in writing?
   3. Have the therapist and client agreed on the goals of therapy?
   4. Will serving the client's interests be contrary to the interests of other persons?
   5. Will serving the client's immediate interests be contrary to the client's long-term interest?
B. Has the choice of treatment methods been adequately considered?
   1. Does the published literature show the procedure to be the best one available for that problem?
   2. If no literature exists regarding the treatment method, is the method consistent with generally accepted practice?
   3. Has the client been told of alternative procedures that might be preferred by the client on the basis of significant differences in discomfort, treatment time, cost, or degree of demonstrated effectiveness?
   4. If a treatment procedure is publicly, legally, or professionally controversial, has formal professional consultation been obtained, has the reaction of the affected segment of the public been adequately considered, and have the alternative treatment methods been more closely reexamined and reconsidered?
C. Is the client's participation voluntary?
   1. Have possible sources of coercion on the client's participation been considered?
   2. If treatment is legally mandated, has the available range of treatments and therapists been offered?
   3. Can the client withdraw from treatment without a penalty or financial loss that exceeds actual clinical costs?
D. When another person or an agency is empowered to arrange for therapy, have the interests of the subordinated client been sufficiently considered?
   1. Has the subordinated client been informed of the treatment objectives and participated in the choice of treatment procedures?
   2. Where the subordinated client's competence to decide is limited, have the client as well as the guardian participated in the treatment discussions to the extent that the client's abilities permit?
   3. If the interests of the subordinated person and the superordinate persons or agency conflict, have attempts been made to reduce the conflict by dealing with both interests?
E. Has the adequacy of treatment been evaluated?
   1. Have quantitative measures of the problem and its progress been obtained?
   2. Have the measures of the problem and its progress been made available to the client during treatment?

F. Has the confidentiality of the treatment relationship been protected?
1. Has the client been told who has access to the records?
2. Are records available only to authorized persons?
G. Does the therapist refer the clients to other therapists when necessary?
1. If treatment is unsuccessful, is the client referred to other therapists?
2. Has the client been told that if dissatisfied with the treatment, referral will be made?
H. Is the therapist qualified to provide treatment?
1. Has the therapist had training or experience in treating problems like the client's?
2. If deficits exist in the therapist's qualifications, has the client been informed?
3. If the therapist is not adequately qualified, is the client referred to other therapists, or has supervision by a qualified therapist been provided? Is the client informed of the supervisory relation?
4. If the treatment is administered by mediators, have the mediators been adequately supervised by a qualified therapist?

From Association for the Advancement of Behavior Therapy (1977). Reprinted by permission.

generally more applied and utilitarian, among other important differences.

5. When selecting behavior theory potentially applicable in human service, there are two sets of criteria. One applies to all behavior theory and includes such criteria as verifiability, coherence, and generality. The other relates to how utilitarian the theory would be in the helping process and includes such criteria as content relevance, content inclusiveness, knowledge validity, knowledge power, and knowledge engineerability.

6. Behavior theory, like other components of a helping strategy, in large measure is subject to design and development.

7. In contrast to behavior theory, intervention theory is directed toward understanding and prescribing the behavior of the helping person and the activities involved in the helping process.

8. Descriptive knowledge in intervention theory includes concepts that provide a vocabulary for describing and communicating about the helping process, informational content about the constituent functions of the helping strategy, and assumptions about human behavior.

9. Values are an important part of intervention theory inasmuch as they chart the moral direction of the helping effort and relate intimately to what the theory prescribes as desirable.

10. Values relate the helping strategy to the larger sociocultural fabric of which it is a part and should be made explicit to facilitate careful appraisal.

11. Deriving in part from the values, the prescriptive content of intervention theory includes such components as practice principles, practice guidelines, and ethical codes.

PART III

Design and Development of Interventions

Practitioners and researchers cannot be expected to be actively engaged in generating intervention innovations unless they have a relevant methodology. As was indicated in Chapter 1, a new approach is needed that is applicable to the main activities and conditions in the design and development of human service interventions. The objective of Part III is to present some of the basic concepts, processes, phases, and activities of D&D applicable to intervention innovation. Intended as a working model, this approach is a framework composed of working conceptions and emerging methods to assist practitioners and researchers in planning, designing, developing, and evaluating new intervention methods.

Criteria applicable to appraising the quality of intervention innovation are given in Chapter 8. Here, standards for appraising the objective capability, procedural adequacy, ethical suitability, and usability of innovations are offered, along with several, more specialized criteria.

The sources of basic information for intervention innovation are described in Chapter 9, along with the generation processes by which such information is transformed into information directly useful in the process of D&D. More specifically, five generation processes are presented, each of which is applicable to the transformation of one or more sources of information. The role of "creativity" and particularly of systematic problem solving in D&D are covered as well.

What Makes for
Good Intervention?

Criteria for appraising human service interventions are needed to help human service professionals in the planning and selection of intervention for use in practice and in the design and development of new human service interventions. Such appraisal criteria should eventually foster the development of improved interventions.

CRITERIA FOR ASSESSING
HUMAN SERVICE INTERVENTIONS

No general set of assessment criteria has yet been formulated for assessing human service interventions.[1] However, several sets of more specialized appraisal criteria have been proposed. For example, Miller (1973) formulated a code of priorities for assessing psychotechnology, Schwitzgebel (1976) identified variables relevant to the design of behavioral and psychotechnological apparatuses, and Fawcett, Matthews, and Fletcher (1980) identified dimensions relevant to a contextually appropriate community technology. Selected contributions from these and other authors will be drawn on in the formulation below. The assessment criteria have been grouped into four general categories: objective capability, procedural adequacy, ethical suitability, and usability. These criteria as well as several types of specialized criteria are given below.

Objective Capability

Objective capability refers to the ability of the intervention to accomplish what it was intended to achieve. There are two aspects of objective capability, as given below.

Effectiveness

An effective intervention is one that produces the desired outcomes for those with whom it is employed. Evaluation of effectiveness is now widely recognized as highly desirable in the development of innovations. Effectiveness was identified by Fawcett et al. (1980) as the first of several characteristics of contextually appropriate technology; and Miller (1970), referring to effectiveness as validity, made this criterion the first priority in his code for assessing psychotechnology. Whatever else it may have to recommend it, an intervention that is not effective is essentially useless.

Efficiency

An efficient intervention is one that can be implemented without excessive effort or investment of time. Even if an intervention is effective, it may be inefficient and hence have limited usefulness. Likewise, an intervention that is equally effective with others may be so superior in efficiency as to make it preferable to its competitors.

Adequacy of the Intervention Procedure

Adequacy refers to aspects of the intervention procedure considered as a practical guide to action. An intervention procedure should have a valid basis, and be relatively complete, specific, correct, and behavior guiding.

Validity of the Basis

Interventions are based on many sources of information, and these sources may be valid or invalid. Intervention procedures with a valid basis are justifiable and credible and should have a greater likelihood of being effective than procedures lacking a valid basis. What is considered valid, however, depends on the source of information, and there are many sources of information potentially relevant to D&D. For example, research as a basis would be considered invalid if it consisted of invalid and unreliable measurement. Scientific or allied technology would be considered invalid if that technology were poorly designed and developed in its field of origin. Legal policy would be considered invalid if it were an aspect of policy that was in great dispute or in disrepute. Indigenous innovation would be considered invalid if it were of questionable effectiveness. Practice would be considered invalid if it were not directly relevant to the area of intervention and carried out competently by those involved. Professional and personal experience would be considered invalid if it were unrelated to the area of intervention. The relevance of each of these sources of information to D&D will be highlighted more fully in Chapter 9. An important aspect of design, as subsequent chapters will indicate, is to select sources of information that contain valid information and are relevant to the innovation problem.

Completeness

Baer, Wolf, and Risley (1968) identified "technological" as one of the six dimensions of applied behavior analysis. As these authors defined it, " 'technological' here means simply that the techniques making up a particular behavioral application are completely identified and described" (p. 95). Further, they indicated that "procedural descriptions require considerable detail about all possible contingencies of procedure" (p. 95). These authors went on to indicate that the best rule of thumb for judging a procedural description as being technological is "to ask whether a typically trained reader could replicate the procedure well enough to produce the same results, given only a reading of the description" (p. 95).

An important aspect of being technological is completeness. To be complete a procedure should embrace at least the following: (a) the areas of behavior that should be carried out to accomplish a given intervention objective; (b) the person to engage in the interventive behavior; (c) the target person, or clientele, to be affected by the intervention procedure; and (d) the conditions under which the interventions are to be carried out. If a map left out entire areas, such as states, it would not be inclusive. Likewise, a procedure would not be complete if it left out areas of content that should be included.

In his description of what a behavioral system model should accomplish in education, Zifferblatt (1973) described what a complete procedure would include for this area:

A behavioral system model should: (a) have the capability of representing all interrelationships between different contingencies (e.g., reading, math, social behavior), (b) specify all interrelated context or setting contingencies (home, library, classroom, etc.), (c) specify all operations (contingency arrangements) required to generate and maintain behavior (e.g., time, media, teacher behavior, cost), and (d) describe the progress of flow of activities in conducting the program. Thus, the model must take into consideration all learning objectives, all settings, all operations, and all progress towards the goal(s) of the program. (p. 335)

Specificity

Another aspect of a technological description is specificity. To be specific an intervention procedure should denote precisely the relevant details involved in the domain of the procedure. The directives given should be explicit enough so that an appropriately trained practitioner who was unfamiliar with the procedure could read the description of the desired interventive behaviors, if it were in written form, and the desired interventive behaviors would not be ambiguous. To return to the example of the map, if its directions for getting from one city to the next were not detailed concretely, it would be nonspecific in that regard.

Failure to describe the independent variable explicitly in research poses a threat to the external validity of the inquiry (Campbell & Stanley, 1966; Kratochwill, 1978). Likewise, the lack of explicitness of procedures in human service raises analogous questions about the replicability and generalizability of the interventions to which the procedures relate. More generally, when practice procedures are not specific or complete, doubts may be raised about whether such procedures may be evaluated informatively and about the accountability of the human service to which the procedures relate. Although undesirable, defects of completeness and specificity generally may be remedied by further trial use and developmental testing, as is described more fully in Chapter 11.

Correctness

To be correct, a procedure should direct the behavior of its user in the appropriate manner, given what is known about that intervention domain. If the procedure directed the practitioner to confront the client at an unsuitable time or in an unsatisfactory way, this would be incorrect; or if the procedure directed the practitioner to engage in behaviors that were intended to increase the anxiety of the client when research on this subject indicated that this would be counterproductive, this would be incorrect. Returning again to the example of the map, if its directions for going from city X took one instead to village Y, it would thus be incorrect. Defects of correctness may be remedied by altering the procedure so that it is made consistent with what is known about the intervention domain.

Behavior Guiding

As a primary means of directing practitioner behavior, the procedure should contain the appropriate instructions for producing the intended practitioner behaviors. A procedure is behavior guiding to the extent that the behaviors of its user are consistent with those specified by the procedure.

The concept of behavior guiding is similar to the idea of procedural reliability as proposed by Billingsley, White, and Munson (1980). With focus on the reliability of experimental procedures used in research, these authors indicated that the concept of procedural reliability "is broader in scope than an examination of independent variable manipulation. Rather, it refers to the degree to which all variables (whether presumed to remain constant or manipulated in some fashion) occur in accordance with the experimental plan" (p. 231). In an illustrative study, these researchers examined the extent to which participating teachers administered programs consistently in terms of program specification and found that there was sufficient inconsistency to pose a threat to both the internal and external validity of their research. Among their criteria for assessing psychobehavioral technology, Miller (1973) and Schwitzgebel (1976) also emphasized reliability. A procedure that is behavior guiding will be reliable inasmuch as its users carry it out in the same way when employing it. When the procedures of human service are not behavior guiding, the quality of the resulting service is likely to be variable and difficult to account for.

A procedure that is not properly behavior building may be incomplete or insufficiently specific. However, it is important to note that a relatively complete and specific procedure may still not be properly behavior guiding, particularly if its instructions are overly complex, not well organized, confusing, or otherwise poorly communicated. The failure of an intervention procedure to be sufficiently behavior guiding is a limitation that generally can be remedied through modification of the procedure or through increasing the practitioner's skills in working with it.

Ethical Suitability

An intervention that is ethically suitable is one that protects the rights of participants on whom it is used. In research, there are at least three important factors to be considered in the protection of participant rights. These consist of making provisions for informed consent, determining that any risks involved for the participant are outweighed in general by the benefits, and that information provided by the participant will be kept confidential. Guidelines in these areas have been drawn up to protect human subjects engaged in federally funded research projects (see Federal Register, 1974). Because these guidelines are equally relevant to participants involved in human service, protections such as these should be adapted for and extended to clients in human service.

In addition to protections such as these, there are court rulings (e.g., Wyatt v. Stickney, 1972) and ethical guidelines proposed by professional organizations (for example, the guidelines of the Association for the Advancement of Behavior Therapy given in Cameo 7.3). There are also articles on ethical issues and client rights that suggest and define special protections for clients in human service (for example, see Begelman, 1975; Davison & Stuart, 1975; Stolz, 1978; Wexler, 1973). Among rights that need to be considered are the right to treatment, the right to decline treatment, and, if the client is confined or committed, the right to "the least restrictive alternative" of confinement (see Friedman, 1975). Conditions that make the application ethically suitable should be formulated and introduced for interventions lacking such protections. This failing, the interventions should be appropriately redesigned or disbanded.

Usability

Usability refers to the extent to which the characteristics of the intervention itself make it likely to be used by the interventionists for whom it is intended. An intervention may have objective capability, its procedures may be adequate and ethically suitable, but it may still fail to be implemented. Among the factors that relate to the usability of an intervention are whether it is relevant, codified, simple, flexible, modular, inexpensive, satisfactory to consumers, sustainable, and socially and technologically compatible. These characteristics are largely those of what some call contextually appropriate technology (Fawcett et al. 1980). Deriving from the field of community development, "appropriate" technology refers to technology that is compatible with the social context and the needs of potential users (Fawcett et al., 1980). Such technology is intended to be relatively easy to implement and is advanced as being more likely to be adopted.

Relevant

An intervention is relevant if it is appropriate for the problematic human condition to which it is to be applied. As Miller (1973) put it: "A technique is socially relevant if it can contribute to the solution or amelioration of personal or social problems that are of wide public concern" (p. 259). Winner (1977) suggested that technology should be "appropriate to the circumstances at hand" (p. 327). An anxiety management intervention would not be relevant for a problem of stuttering if it could not be shown that anxiety was a factor in the stuttering or that the anxiety management technique was otherwise applicable. Use of interpersonal helping methods with the poor as a method of rectifying the poverty would not be relevant. To be relevant, there needs to be some match between the capability of the intervention and the problems to which it is applied. Interventions that are not relevant should not be applied, or they should be redesigned and developed to be made more relevant.

Codified

Codification is the extent to which the innovation and its related activities have been represented in writing, in audio or visual form, or otherwise. Codification facilitates careful examination of an innovation and makes it easier for others to learn about the innovation and adopt it. Without codification, widespread diffusion and adoption are severely limited. Limitations of codification can be remedied readily by documenting the innovation and its procedures in a form that can be made readily accessible to potential users.

Simple

A simple intervention is, of course, one that is relatively easy to use. Simple interventions are more likely to be used than more complex ones, as Fawcett et al. (1980) indicated. A simple technique should also be intelligible. As Miller (1973) said, "A technique is intelligible to the extent that we understand how and why it works" (p. 259). In his more general analysis of technology and its control, Winner (1977) recommended "that as a general maxim, technologies be given a scale and structure of the sort that would be immediately intelligible to non-experts" (p. 326). And as Fawcett et al. (1980) further observed, "Obviously, the complexity of the procedure should be tailored to fit the capabilities of the potential users of the behavioral technology. When necessary, simplifying such technologies removes unnecessary obstacles to their use" (p. 510). More generally, if the intervention has not been made sufficiently simple in its initial design, it should be simplified by redesign or abandoned.

Flexible

A flexible intervention is one that allows for some modification in its use without altering its fundamental character. According to Winner (1977), "technologies [should] be built with a high degree of flexibility and mutability" (p. 326). Flexible interventions allow for creative involvement, a sense of "ownership" and "commitment," all of which may enhance adoption and continued use by consumers (Fawcett et al., 1980).

The procedures for many interventions do not encourage extensive modification but rather emphasize strict use of the procedure in accordance with its specification. Fawcett et al. (1980) stated:

> Behavioral technologies that are specified so as to limit arbitrarily the ways in which procedures can be used or that restrict the range of acceptable responses are inconsistent with this criterion [of flexibility]. For example, a counseling training program that specifies an unalterable sequence of counseling activities for the convenience of the trainers, though no evidence supports the functionality of sequencing, needlessly limits consumers' opportunities to apply this program creatively. (p. 509)

The criterion of flexibility clearly poses a dilemma. Most procedures of intervention are designed expressly to limit variable and inconsistent application because such nonstandardized application could interfere with the effectiveness and other desired outcomes. Yet rigorous standardization may conspire against adoption and use. One possible solution to this problem is to design robust interventions that will yield the same results given variations in procedure (Fawcett et al., 1980). For example, many food companies test their products for robustness to be sure that the recipes for the packaged foods (e.g., a cake mix) allow for more or less of the optimum for certain ingredients while still providing about the same level of product satisfaction. The possible bounds of flexibility need to be taken into consideration when designing and developing interventions so that some balance is struck between reliability of results and flexibility of application. To be effective, some interventions may have to be applied relatively strictly, whereas others may allow for considerably more procedural variation.

Modular

An innovation that is modular is one that is relatively self-contained and "small," and is capable of being employed with other intervention components. When combined with others, it forms a loose bundle of components, a collection that is not highly interdependent and interconnected (Rice & Rogers, 1980). Such modularity facilitates adoption and widespread use (Rice & Rogers, 1980) through what Rogers and Shoemaker (1971) called "trialability," which is the extent to which an innovation may be experimented with on a limited scale. As Fawcett et al. (1980) observed in this connection:

> Small-scale behavioral technology should be divisible into pieces that permit a trial use with limited risk and cost to the potential adopter. For example, a comprehensive employment preparation program that may be divided into instructional, counseling, and social reinforcement components for separate trial by a county employment service may be more likely to be adopted than one that must be taken in its entirety. (p. 509)

It is thus that modularity facilitates the accessibility and distributibility of innovations.

Inexpensive

An inexpensive intervention, of course, is one that is not costly to use. Again, adoption and widespread use are limited by high cost. Considering the variety and complexity of interventions, there would appear to be no simple rule of thumb concerning what constitutes "inexpensive." In community development, an innovation is considered inexpensive if it is essentially cheap enough so that it is accessible to virtually anyone (see Fawcett et al., 1980). It is more difficult to reckon what is inexpensive in human service intervention. One needs to take into consideration the time and money involved in acquiring the skills to use the intervention, as well as the cost entailed in its implementation. Interventions requiring complicated apparatus, costly training, and long periods of implementation are likely to be relatively expensive. Expensive innovations may be justified if their effects are redeeming or funds are sufficient. Otherwise, such innovations should be redesigned to be less costly or abandoned.

Consumer Satisfaction

Considering the practitioner-researchers as well as the clients as the consumers of an intervention, the degree of satisfaction is important in appraising whether the intervention will be used. No matter how effective the intervention, if consumers are dissatisfied and have free choice, there will be retarded adoption and eventually discontinued use. In the long run, we judge that an intervention must be at least minimally satisfactory to its users if it is to enjoy continued application. Although largely neglected until recent years as a relevant outcome, there has been increasing interest in including consumer satisfaction as one of several aspects of outcome in the evaluation of interventions (e.g., Warrfel, Maloney, & Blase, 1981). Again, innovations lacking in consumer satisfaction should be redesigned for greater satisfaction or abandoned.

Sustainable

An intervention that is sustainable will make limited use of scarce resources (e.g., Fawcett et al., 1980). The assumption here is that if the intervention may be introduced and sustained with existing resources, it has a better chance of surviving. The importance of using local resources is marked in the following observation by Fawcett et al. (1980):

> When behavioral technologies, such as complex motivational systems, require outside professionals or grant funding for their continued use, they can rarely be sustained with local resources. By contrast, those based on local resources are more likely to survive the departure of the program developers and the discontinuance of the grant funding that may have supported the initial development of the behavioral technology. (p. 510)

Social Compatibility

Fawcett et al. (1980) defined "compatibility" as the extent to which an innovation is consistent with the existing values, past experiences, and needs of the potential users (also see Rogers & Shoemaker, 1971). This type of compatibility is referred to here as "social compatibility" to distinguish it from technological compatibility, discussed below. Fawcett et al. (1980) further indicate that "procedures that are inharmonious with local customs and practices may not be adopted; and if tried, they may soon be discarded as foreign objects or rejected by biological systems" (p. 510). Although social incompatibility in the short run can cause serious problems for adoption in human service, when considered over a long time, some social incompatibilities are subject to alteration. For example, personnel can be changed, practitioners may be trained, and organizational arrangements may be made more congenial. However, social practices, customs, norms, and community patterns that are strongly embedded would typically be much more difficult to change, and hence would tend to be adapted to rather changed.

Technological Compatibility

Technological compatibility is the extent to which the innovation is compatible with the other aspects of social technology to which it is related. Although the term "technology" is alien for some in human service, it captures an important idea for which there are few good synonyms. Technology may be thought of as the systematic application of scientific and practical knowledge to the accomplishment of practical objectives. Guided by important values and humane commitments, human service does its practical work with a technology, just as does engineering, medicine, or any field that treats applied and practical matters. Social technology in human service consists of all of the technical means by which human service objectives are achieved.

Altogether, there are at least nine general types of social technology. The characteristics for each type and examples are presented in Table 8.1. This typology is proposed here as one specification of social technology relevant to human service. The framework is intended to embrace all of the components of the helping strategy, as presented in Part II.

In this view, values and ideology provide an essential directive for all types and aspects of social technology, including human service policy, and each part presents an important and distinctive contribution to the larger fabric of human service. Further, in this perspective, human service policy is not the Mt. Olympus of social technology but rather is a specialized and more embracing component that, like the others, can exercise influence over the other types. Actually, each type is thought of as being capable of exercising directive and constraining influences on all other types. This necessitates integration among constituent parts of any given type (horizontal integration) as well as congenial interdependence between types (vertical integration).

Although the focus here is on intervention innovations, these innovations are clearly part of a larger assembly of social technology and must be developed in light of the other social technological components to which they will relate. This means, for example, that if the proposed intervention innovation is incompatible with the service programs in which it would be lodged, the intervention should be designed initially to fit with the existing service program, the service program should be redesigned to accommodate the new intervention, or each should be designed to fit together compatibly. Ideally, each

TABLE 8.1
Principal Types of Social Technology[a]

Types	Characteristics	Examples
Physical Frameworks	Static physical structures that passively control space, light, sound, and/or temperature variables, with some structural elements that may be movable or changeable[b]	Room size and arrangements in agencies and residential facilities
Electro mechanical Devices	Electronic or mechanical devices	Timers, counters, audio and video recorders, chart recorders, transducers, computers
Information Systems	Methods of collecting, processing, storing, retrieving, and/or displaying information by human or electromechanical means	Problem Oriented Medical Recording, automated intake, computer-assisted agency record keeping
Assessment Methods	Principles and procedures for gathering and evaluating diagnostic information about clients, families, and other clientele	Interviewing guidelines, intake questionnaires, family observational procedures
Intervention Methods	Principles and procedures for carrying out intervention and evaluating progress of human service activity	Particular change methods of behavior modification, task-oriented casework, insight treatment, transactional analysis, group treatment methods
Service Programs	Service components with distinctive objectives and clientele, usually part of larger systems of service	Day care, rehabilitation service, foster-home care, school psychology service, mental health service
Organizational Structures	Structures of human service agencies that provide financial and social services	Arrangements of power, authority, responsibility, and distribution of work and labor in agencies
Service Systems	Organizational structures designed to coordinate and deliver aspects of one or more human service programs	State and local departments of social welfare, mental health, education

(Continued)

TABLE 8.1 Continued

Types	Characteristics	Examples
Human Service Policy	Prescriptions, directives, rules, or regulations oriented to guide action in regard to particular financial and human service objectives	Systematic positions on preferred approaches to income distribution, health and welfare benefits, equal rights, and social and welfare service

a. A modification and extension of Table 1 from Thomas (1978).
b. Schwitzgebel (1976).

component would be designed in light of its compatibility with others, which, in some cases, might require design of an entire system of social technology.

Other Criteria

In addition to the criteria indicated above, there are others that have more specialized application. For example, when appraising innovations implicating assessment and measurement, reliability and validity of measurement would be relevant. When assessing electromechanical and physiological devices, there are considerations of ease of operation, durability, safety, size, weight, validity, reliability, and aesthetics (see Schwitzgebel, 1976).

Writers have also proposed additional criteria that are mentioned here because they mark a special dimension. Indicating the importance of individualization, Miller (1973) proposed the following: "The technique that respects individuality cannot be applied to a person without consideration of his personal characteristics" (p. 260). An additional criterion increasingly being applied to industrial and scientific technology is ecological safety, a factor that eventually may have application to human service interventions as well.

Because of its primary focus on D&D, the discussion here has emphasized criteria for assessing characteristics of interventions as interventions, not the characteristics of the host organization in which the innovation is to be introduced or the manner and characteristics of implementation—topics relating more to utilization. Although some of the criteria discussed here also apply to the adoption and diffusion of innovations, there are still other criteria that pertain particularly to these stages that follow design and development. For discussions of these other criteria, the reader is referred elsewhere (see Davis & Salasin, 1975; Glaser, 1981; Stolz, 1981).

SUMMARY

1. Criteria for appraising human service interventions are relevant in planning and selecting interventions for use in practice and in the design and development of new human service interventions.

2. Objective capability refers to the ability of the intervention to accomplish what it was intended to achieve and includes the appraisal criteria of effectiveness and efficiency.

3. Adequacy refers to aspects of the intervention procedure considered as a practical guide to action. Specific criteria include the validity of the informational basis for the intervention, the completeness, specificity, and correctness of the procedure, and the extent to which it is behavior guiding for those who use it.

4. An intervention that is ethically suitable is one that protects the rights of participants on whom it is used. Among the factors relevant here are informed consent, determining that risks for participants are outweighed in general by the benefits, and keeping information confidential. Among specific rights that need to be considered are the right to treatment, the right to decline treatment, and the right to the least restrictive alternative, in the event of confinement or restricted freedom.

5. Usability refers to the extent to which the characteristics of the intervention itself make it likely to be used by the helping persons for whom it is intended. Among specific criteria of usability are whether the intervention is relevant, codified, simple, flexible, modular, inexpensive, satisfactory to consumers, sustainable, and socially and technologically compatible.

6. There are also criteria having more specialized application, such as those for innovations implicating assessment and measurement and for those involving electromechanical and physiological devices.

NOTE

1. Criteria for selecting knowledge from behavioral and social science for practical utilization have been formulated, but they have limited value in this context because they apply to the characteristics of knowledge, such as research findings, that facilitate application rather than to characteristics of interventions, which are already in application form.

Generation Processes in Innovation

What is innovation in D&D, and by what process does innovation come about? These questions are most intriguing, for we are only beginning to understand what transpires when a practitioner-researcher designs an intervention and, more generally, what the analytic, logical, and empirical components are of design and development. The innovation process is central to intervention design, and it is especially deserving of further work. The presentation to follow is an attempt to extend the analysis, explication, and conceptualization of this important area.

Attention is given first to the types of innovation, the sources of information for intervention innovation, the nature of the process by which each source of information is transformed into results that may be employed in design, and to the role of creativity and problem solving. Because of its generality, the material presented here applies to most aspects of intervention design and development.

TYPES OF INNOVATION

The word "innovation" is generally understood to mean the introduction of something new. To qualify as an innovation, however, the change need not be entirely new. It may also be an adoption or modification of something already in existence, as many writers on innovation have suggested (see Eveland, Rogers, & Klepper, 1977; Mintzberg, Raisinghani, & Theorêt, 1976; Pelz & Munson, 1982; Rice & Rogers, 1980).

It is useful at the outset to distinguish between the "thing" innovated and how it is used—that is, between the tool and its use, as Rice and

Rogers (1980) put it. The tool may be novel or modified, and what is used may be employed in a novel or customary way. This suggests four types of innovation. The first is *invention* and is the novel tool, such as an entirely new drug or assessment instrument for adults. The second is *adaptation*, which is a modification of an existing tool, such as an established drug with additional ingredients to reduce side effects or an adaptation of an adult assessment instrument for use with children. The third is a *novel application* of an existing tool (often called technological transfer), such as the new use of a drug developed for other purposes or the use of a clinical assessment instrument, say, for research purposes. The fourth is *adoption* and is the use by a different user group of an existing tool for purposes for which it was developed. D&D can yield an innovation predominantly in one type or a product consisting of an assembly of different types of innovation.

SOURCES OF INFORMATION FOR INNOVATION

Data and resources relevant to intervention design derive from nine potentially relevant sources, as described below. The information from these sources constitutes the basic raw material used in the formulation of intervention innovations.

(1) Basic Research: Research findings and methods, primarily from psychology and sociology and secondarily from anthropology, political science, and economics; and selected research findings from natural science. Example in design: use of findings on reinforcement from psychology to design a motivation system for clients.

(2) Applied Research: Research findings from such fields as psychotherapy, applied behavior analysis, behavior therapy, educational counseling, classroom management, rehabilitation, nursing research, and psychiatric research. Example in design: use of research findings from psychiatric research on depression to assist in designing intervention for the care of depressed patients.

The importance of basic and applied research is that there are often new findings that have not yet been applied to helping methods in human service. The utilization of research findings in intervention design provides an essential means for keeping intervention developments consistent with advances in basic knowledge of human behavior.

(3) Scientific Technology: Technology from fields of engineering and electronic and telecommunication technology. Example in design: use

of a small computer to assist in assessment and monitoring of change in intervention.

Paced by advances in basic science, scientific technology is growing at an increasingly rapid rate and is a particularly important resource in intervention design. Developments in computer technology, for instance, have applications in many areas, including those of human service. Scientific technology is also producing more and more electronic and mechanical devices, some of which, again, will have human service application. The promise of making human service more efficient, rapid, economical, reliable, and effective through adaptation of relevant scientific technology is difficult to resist.

(4) Allied Technology: Technology and technical knowledge relevant to human service from such fields as hospital administration, public administration, business administration, education, rehabilitation, public health, behavior therapy, architecture, clinical psychology, nursing, social work, and medicine. Example in design: adaptation of the Problem-Oriented-Medical-Record used in medical recording for purposes of recording in a nonmedical human service agency.

Allied technology is likewise an exceptionally rich source because of vigorous intervention development in allied fields. Exchange and cross-fertilization between similar fields of human service provide an easy and inexpensive method of accelerating intervention development in one's own field.

(5) Legal Policy: The national constitution, national and state laws, judicial decisions and governmental regulations and other legally sanctioned statements and documents. Example in design: development of guidelines for ethical practice in human service from court decisions and judicial rulings.

The importance of law is indicated in the following:

The law is best seen as the active embodiment of a society's values (Tribe, 1973). It furnishes the architecture for social edifices ranging from marriage to representative government to economics. The law can operate negatively by constraining interactions (e.g., criminal law); it can operate positively by facilitating human relations and aspirations, or by establishing institutions and providing authority to perform designated functions.

Technological development can be influenced by such legal actions in three basic modes (Tribe, 1973): '(1) *specific directives* [e.g., human subjects protections] (2) *modifications of market incentives* [e.g., legal liability related to practice], and (3) *changes in decision-making structures* [e.g., Human Rights Committee].' (Porter, Rossini, Carpenter, & Roper, Larson, & Tiller, 1980, p. 335; italics added)

(6) Indigenous Innovation: Self-help groups, popular psychology, and sometimes social and political movements. Example in design: designing a group treatment program by making use of practices typically associated with self-help groups.

Although often acting in response to precisely the same human problems as those dealt with by professional helping persons, indigenous innovation typically pursues a different direction in the solution of these problems, thus suggesting leads about how helping methods might be improved. Indeed, indigenous innovation often arises precisely because of limitations of existing helping methodology (e.g., Killilea, 1976).

(7) Practice: Current practice in the individual's own field and in related fields of human service. Example in design: designing an intervention on the basis of practice carried out earlier by a practitioner in the same field.

Contemporary practice is frequently overlooked as a legitimate source of information for design despite the large numbers of practitioners who daily face problems for which their methods are inadequate and who consequently experiment with novel approaches, often successfully.

(8) Personal Experience: Experience of the individual practitioner-researcher gained in his or her personal life as well as the reports of the experience of others. Example in design: designing a component of a divorce counseling protocol based on one's own experience in having gone through marital discord, separation, divorce, and postdivorce readjustment.

Also often frequently overlooked, personal experience can be a valid type of knowledge, as highlighted by Borkman (1976) in her analysis of experiential knowledge and self-help groups. She has observed the following:

> Experiential knowledge is truth learned from personal experience with a phenomenon rather than truth acquired by discursive reasoning, observation, or reflection on information provided by others. *Ruperto experto credite*, goes the Latin proverb ("Believe Rupert, who's been through it"). . . .

> The type of information [in experiential knowledge] is wisdom and know-how gained from personal participation in a phenomenon instead of isolated, unorganized bits of facts and feelings upon which a person has not yet reflected. This wisdom and know-how tend to be concrete, specific, and commonsensical, since they are based on the individual's actual experience, which is unique, limited, and more or less representative of the experience of others who have the same problem. . . .

> There are also major differences between professional and experiential knowledge. In contrast to professional information, experiential knowledge is (1) pragmatic rather than theoretical or scientific; (2) oriented to here-and-now action rather than to the long-term development and systematic accumulation of knowledge; and (3) holistic and total rather than segmented. (Borkman, 1976, pp. 446-449)

Personal experience that is relevant and accurately represented is likely to be most useful as a source of information and can add a unique and invaluable dimension to the design process.

(9) Professional Experience: Experience of the practitioner-researcher gained in professional activity. Example in design: evolving a child abuse program on the basis of extensive professional experience in remedial work with child abusers and their victims.

Professional experience based on a foundation of professional training and disciplined observation and practice tends to be less subjective and biased than personal experience and may be essential for most, if not all, design problems in human service.

One or more sources of information may be relevant to any design task (see Figure 9.1). For example, if one were to endeavor to develop a procedure to help clients with severe pain for whom conventional medical solutions had been exhausted, the practice of helping persons working in pain clinics would be an important source of information (practice), as would medicine (allied technology), research on operant factors in pain-expressive behavior (applied research), findings on the neurophysiology of pain (basic research), and personal and professional experience.

Although several sources having approximately equal importance could be relevant to a given design problem, there is often a primary source and possible secondary sources to provide supplementary information. In any case, it is important not to overlook any potentially relevant source of information because it is not always possible to predict in advance the source that would be useful.

PROCESSES OF GENERATION

It is one thing to locate information from a source and another to make appropriate use of it in innovation. The information comes in raw form and generally cannot be used without some transformation and specific application. The changes required to transform and apply basic information from one or more sources into results or products that may be used directly in the design and development of innovative interven-

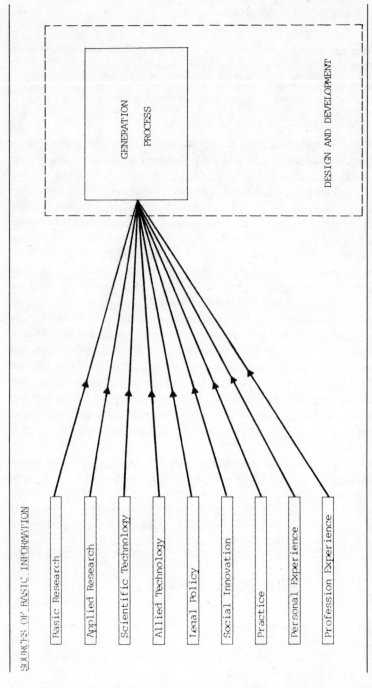

Figure 9.1: Sources of basic information for innovation and relation to design and development.

SOURCES OF BASIC INFORMATION

Basic Research

Applied Research

Scientific Technology

Allied Technology

Legal Policy

Social Innovation

Practice

Personal Experience

Profession Experience

GENERATION PROCESS

DESIGN AND DEVELOPMENT

116

tion are referred to here as the *generation processes* of intervention design. Each source of information has its distinctive generation process. Five such processes are presented below.

Knowledge Application

Beginning largely in the 1960s, inquiry was directed toward learning more about the utilization process itself. As recounted in Chapter 1, models of research utilization have been proposed (e.g., Bloom, 1975; Glaser, 1976; Havelock, 1973), the phases of the utilization process have been distinguished (e.g., Havelock, 1973), selection criteria for utilization of knowledge have been identified (e.g., Fischer, 1978; Tripodi et al., 1969; Thomas, 1964), and literature retrieval models to generate intervention guidelines have been developed (e.g., Mullen, 1978, 1981; Rothman, 1974, 1980). Although more work has been done in this area than in other areas discussed here, most of the prior work has pertained to the use of behavioral science knowledge in general rather than to interventional design.

Knowledge application is that process by which knowledge of human behavior from research is transformed into results directly applicable to the design of intervention methods. Rather than knowledge in general, it is important to emphasize that it is knowledge of human behavior that is the focus here, knowledge derived from the sources of basic research or applied research, generally in the form of research findings. There are two important components of the generation process in knowledge application. The first, called *transformation*, involves the process by which the research findings are transformed into relevant practice guidelines. The second, called *operationalization*, consists of making the practice guidelines operational in real-world terms.

Transformation

On the basis of prior work in the utilization of knowledge from behavioral and social science derived from literature review (see Rothman, 1974, 1981; Mullen, 1978, 1980), there would appear to be at least two important components in transformation. The first is the *formulation of empirical generalizations*, based on a review of the literature in the area of intervention. For example, if one were interested in the findings of social science that apply to social planning and community organization, as was Rothman (1974) in his attempt to formulate action principles from social science research, it would then be necessary to review the applicable social science studies. In their review, that researcher and his associates retrieved and processed 921 relevant studies. In his conceptualization of the research utilization process, Rothman indicated that the transition from raw, basic research to consensus generalizations depended on such constituent operations as retrieval, codification, and generalization of research findings. Illustrative activities here involved (a) location of the pertinent studies, assessing data for reliability, validity, and applicability; (b) codifying data into suitable categories; (c) constructing consensus findings from selected data; and (d) drawing appropriate generalizations and propositions from the consensus findings.

In his approach to literature retrieval applicable to the development of personal intervention models, Mullen (1981) followed a similar approach to deriving empirical generalizations (he called them "substantive empirical generalizations"). However, Mullen recommended that the practitioner-researcher also develop empirical generalizations concerning limiting conditions for the substantive generalizations as well as generalizations about the quality of evidence pertaining to the generalizations.

The empirical generalization that results from the literature review expresses as a minimum an associational relationship between two variables, X and Y. For example,

—depression (X) relates to anxiety (Y) for a given sample of patients;
—disordered thinking (X) relates to phobias (Y) for a given sample of phobic clientele;
—the "warmth" of the therapist (X) relates to the motivation of the client to change (Y).

These are descriptive relationships and most generally imply or assert that variable X is an independent variable that produces the effects for Y as a dependent variable. More specifically, the empirical generalization typically expresses an associational relationship that takes the following form:

Variable X relates to variable Y (generally expressly asserted), in certain ways and under given conditions, with a certain quality of evidence (preferably explicitly stated but often implicit or unspecified).

An example of a substantive empirical generalization is given below from the work of Mullen (1978), which, in turn, is based on a secondary review of Truax and Mitchell (1971) in which the correlates of accurate empathy were examined.

> An intervener's sensitivity to the moment-to-moment feelings of the client and the intervenor's verbal facility to communicate this understanding in a language attuned to the client's current feelings (as measured by the Accurate Empathy Scale) are positively associated with the client's depth of self-exploration (as measured by the Self-Exploration Scale), and are frequently associated with attitudinal, cognitive, and behavioral improvements in clients. . . . Empathy accounts for a relatively small amount of variance in intervention outcomes, yet this amount is often statistically significant. (Mullen, 1978, pp. 56-57)

An illustration of an empirical generalization concerning limiting conditions, as these apply to the substantive empirical generalization given above, is the following:

> Since most of the research has been based on interventions using intervenors trained in the client-centered approach, it is not known to what extent the substantive generalization would be valid for other types of interventions. Since most studies incorporated as techniques non-possessive warmth and genuineness, it is unknown to what extent the substantive hypothesis would be valid independently of warmth and genuineness. Limiting conditions concerning client characteristics and organizational contexts are of unknown relevance, based on the available information. (Mullen, 1978, p. 57)

Generalizations concerning the quality of evidence are illustrated in the quotation below:

> The substantive generalization is based on a relatively small number of uncontrolled field studies involving a relatively small number of investigators. The reliability and validity of the Accurate Empathy Scale is questionable, and the subject of much disagreement. It is unclear to what extent accurate empathy is independent of client qualities and the extent to which the qualities are reciprocal (interactive). (Mullen, 1978, p. 57)

The relationship expressed by an empirical generalization may be associational or causal. If it is merely associational, no causal association is asserted or necessarily implied, whereas if the relationship is causal, it is indicated that one variable may cause the other or that there are more complex causal relationships. For example, X may cause Y, Y may cause X, or X and Y may be mutually causal in their relationship. Further, X and Y may not be causally related but rather may covary together in time as a function of one or more additional variables. Any of the foregoing relationships, in addition, may be conditional on one or more additional variables that serve to moderate a given relationship. For example, X may cause Y, given condition Z or, still more complexly, conditions A, B, etc.

Associational relationships are much less informative than causal relationships because of the greater uncertainty concerning whether a change of variable X will have any predictable consequence for variable Y. Clearly, practical application based on empirical generalizations of an associational nature are more uncertain and risky than those based on a causal relationship. It is for this reason that empirical generalizations based on research that makes it possible to infer possible causal relationships are preferred.

The type and quality of the evidence on which the generalization is based provide important leads to the nature of the relationship. For example, when the research is nonexperimental and specialized analytic procedures are not employed, it is generally difficult to support inferences beyond an associational relationship. In contrast, when the research is experimental or quasi-experimental, it is often possible to infer that variable X, if experimentally manipulated, may express a causal relationship. It is important to recognize, however, that such an experimental study may still leave other questions unanswered, such as whether Y may cause X and the possible effects of other variables. The relationship of variables expressed in the empirical generalization should clearly be consistent with what has been established empirically and what is known theoretically.

The second component involved in the transformation of research findings involves *deduction of practice guidelines from the empirical generalizations.* The empirical generalizations are descriptive, whereas the desired practice guidelines are prescriptive—that is, they prescribe what the interventionist or others should do if certain desired objectives are to be achieved. The practice guideline generally takes the following form: "If you wish to alter condition Y, then bring about a change in condition X." Examples of intervention guidelines that might be deduced from empirical generalizations regarding accurate empathy are illustrated below, again drawing on the work of Mullen (1978).

> In practice situations where client self-exploration is desirable, intervener responses that reflect accurate empathy should be used to facilitate client self-exploration. Expression of low levels of accurate empathy should be avoided, especially with more fragile and vulnerable clients, to avoid harming clients. . . . Since accurate empathy at best appears to account for only a small portion of variance in intervention effects, other intervention qualities should be used to enhance effectiveness. (Mullen, 1978, p. 58)

In formulating practice guidelines, there would appear to be, first, the presumption of a causal relationship for the empirical generalization in question. Variable X is now presumed to affect variable Y. Thus, in this example of accurate empathy, it is presumed that accurate empathy on the part of the therapist is likely to bring about greater client self-exploration as well as greater client improvement. Second, the practice guideline generally prescribes either an increase or a decrease in condition X as a means of bringing about condition Y. Thus, as indicated above in the first intervention guideline, it is recommended that the practitioner increase accurate empathy to facilitate client self-exploration. Likewise, as indicated in the second intervention guideline, it is recommended that low levels of accurate empathy should be avoided to prevent harming clients. Third, the practice guideline can also include prescribed behaviors, events, or conditions presumed to produce the desired level of condition X. For example, in the case of accurate empathy, intervention guidelines could be proposed concerning recommended verbalizations of the practitioner (e.g., "I understand" or "You must be upset," when accurately used to reflect a feeling of the client), as well as prescriptions concerning appropriate attending behavior of the practitioner and ways to detect states of client feeling. Although not illustrated in the guidelines above for accurate empathy, such specific intervention guidelines have been formulated for the area of empathy (see Fischer, 1978, drawing in work of such writers as Truax and Carkhuff, 1967) as well as in other areas of intervention.

The examples above consist of empirical generalizations for the presumed effects of the intervener's behavior. This is appropriate, since an important portion of the research relevant to intervention design pertains to aspects of the intervener's behavior as it relates to client outcomes. However, there are other types of potentially relevant research findings. Important among these are the findings of studies that bear on the etiology and controlling conditions for the problematic conditions dealt with in human service intervention. The generation process described here is equally relevant in applying this research.

For instance, consider the proposition that disordered thinking about one's fears is evident in many persons with phobias. Despite the endorsement of this proposition among cognitive theorists and most practitioners, unfortunately there has been little empirical corroboration (e.g., see Rimm & Lefebvre, 1981). Treating this for illustrative purposes as if it were an empirical generalization from the literature, the formulation of practice guidelines would involve the same considerations as described above. First, although only associational, the relationship between disordered thinking and phobias would typically be presumed to be causal—that is, that the disordered thinking was a causal factor in the phobias. Second, by prescribing that disordered thinking should be a target of intervention in the alleviation of phobias, the descriptive relationship between the disordered thinking and the phobia has been converted into a prescriptive one. Third, particular behaviors, events, or conditions could be prescribed to reduce the disordered thinking. For example, practitioners could be enjoined to intervene to reduce such cognitive distortions of phobic clients as personalization, polarized thinking, arbitrary inference, and overgeneralization.

Operationalization

Following the transformation of research findings, the resulting *practice guidelines for intervention must be made operational in real-world terms.* For example, the practice guidelines must be made specific with a practice procedure, one that is carried out for specific change objectives, targets of intervention, target persons, and helping persons taking particular helping person and target person roles and doing so in given contexts of helping. Actually, before any concrete action can be taken, most or all components of the helping strategy need to be operationalized even though only selected and, in some cases, restricted aspects of the helping strategy are derived from the practice guidelines and the empirical generalizations on which they have been based. Thus, interventions based on knowledge application are likely to contain much more than those that derive directly from the empirical generalizations in question. Operationalization necessarily implicates other aspects of design, details of which are to be discussed more fully in subsequent chapters.

Modes of Knowledge Application

Application of knowledge from behavioral science to generate intervention innovation may be employed in one of two modes. In the *source-oriented mode*, focus in on what a certain domain of research findings may contribute to a range of possible areas of application. In this "supply-side" approach, the process begins with selection of an area of research findings for review, not necessarily or mainly with a specific human service problem, as would be the case with the other mode. The examples given above for accurate empathy and its correlates are illustrative of this source-oriented approach. The advantage of the source mode is that by surveying a given domain of research findings not yet considered for application, new, unanticipated, and sometimes ground-breaking applications may be disclosed. Approaches to knowledge utilization to date have been largely source-oriented (e.g.,

Mullen, 1978, 1981; Rothman, 1974, 1980), although the procedures of such retrieval approaches need not be restricted to this mode.

The second is the *need-oriented mode* in which a selected literature review is conducted in response to a specific requirement or design problem. Instead of asking what is known in behavioral science in a given area that might be relevant for application, the need-oriented question is as follows: "Given this particular action that I am considering taking, what is known in behavioral science that relates to it?" For example, consider the question of whether there is any support in research for the assumption, mentioned above, that disordered thinking will produce phobic behavior. Given this as the focus, the researcher-practitioner would then review the literature in this area to find out what was known and would make applications accordingly.

The advantage of the need-oriented approach is that it provides a relevant answer to a specific question; and no matter how the review turns out, there should be implications for action. This mode is thus efficient. The mode of literature review and knowledge application of this approach to intervention design is need oriented. It is recognized, however, that both the source- and need-oriented approaches to knowledge application have a place in intervention design, depending on one's purpose and the design framework employed.

Adoption

One important way by which innovations from scientific and allied technology, social innovation, and practice are made available in intervention design is by adoption. *Adoption*, as the term is used here, is the process by which an innovation is diffused from its field of origin to a different user group, to be used for the same purpose as that for which it was originally intended. An example is the ordinary pocket calculator, now used for financial and academic calculation, taken over by members of the human service fields for purposes of data processing in monitoring, assessment and evaluation. Another example would be if the *Diagnostic and Statistical Manual of Mental Disorders* (DSM-III) of the American Psychiatric Association were taken over for selective purposes of diagnosis and classification by members of human service professions other than psychiatry. Many of the interventions in the fields of human service began initially in one segment of that field and, through diffusion, were adopted by others (e.g., psychoanalytic thinking, behavior modification methods, family systems approaches). Adoption is clearly part of a larger diffusion process that implicates everyone in the intervention community.

Adoption presupposes the availability of an innovation that to some extent is already user-ready in its own field of origin. While adoption of someone else's innovation may not be viewed as particularly innovative, its selection calls for wise judgment; it may be novel in its new field; it may solve a design problem very well; and it may be part of an intervention assembly that in its entirety is innovative. Because the innovation to be adopted is already developed for another user group, adoption can be relatively easy and efficient. Adoption of intervention components is no doubt a major means by which innovations in intervention design are produced.

An innovation may be adopted in intervention design essentially without alteration, or it may need to be changed. In their analysis of the diffusion of innovations, Rice and Rogers (1980) indicated that the alteration of innovations in diffusion has been overlooked. They contend that alteration is actually common and they offer results from a case study of the diffusion of Dial-a-Ride to support their thesis. Consisting of 24 separate innovation components, Dial-a-Ride was studied in 10 case sites. It was found that there was alteration of 77 of these components when implemented in the different diffusion sites. These authors refer to such alteration as *reinvention*, which is defined as "the degree to which an innovation is changed by the adopter in the process of adoption and implementation after its original development" (p. 501). Reinvention is directly relevant to adoption of innovations in intervention design inasmuch as the adoption may involve alterations of the innovation as a *tool* and in its *use*.

An important factor affecting the degree of reinvention is the matching of the adopted innovation with the requirements of the intervention and the other components of the helping strategy. Adaptation of the innovation may be required in order that it match more appropriately. These researchers identified four types of reinvention, as follows:

1. *Planned*: the changes from the original innovation bundle are an expected part of the innovation process. . . .

1a. *Vicarious*: a planned reinvention which occurs as a preventive reaction to a problem experienced by some other adopting system. . . .

2. *Reactive*: reinvention required by unexpected and unsatisfactory consequences of the original innovation (for some component). . . .

2a. *Secondary*: a result of a previous reinvention's causing [sic] problems affecting some other aspect of the innovation bundle. (Rice & Rogers, 1980, pp. 508, 509)

Each of these types is relevant to interventional D&D but probably at different points. For example, the planned and vicarious approaches are probably most relevant in the initial stages, whereas the reactive and secondary would be more commonly involved in later stages, following some trial use.

Transfer

Transfer is the process by which an innovation from another field is taken over by a different user group for purposes that are different from those for which it was originally developed. Recall that although otherwise similar, adoption involves taking over an innovation from a different group to be used, at least initially, for the same purpose as that for which it was originally intended. In human service, the transfer entails transmission from areas outside the field as well as from those within the field to others in which that innovation has not yet been employed. A prerequisite for transfer is the availability of a sufficiently well-developed and potentially applicable innovation in another area. Like adoption, transfer of innovations is a major means by which interventions are generated that may likewise be relatively easy and economical, as compared with the alternatives.

The four sources of basic information from which innovations may be transferred provide rich sources. For example, among the contributions from scientific technology to human service are computer applications to assessment and change (e.g., Hansen, Johnson, & Williams, 1977), automated intake (Johnson & Williams, 1975; Vondracek, Urban, & Parsonage, 1974), information systems and data management (e.g., Young, 1974), and the use of videotaping in practice training (Katz, 1975). From fields of allied technology, for example, there are such human service applications as break-even analysis in budget planning (e.g., Lohmann, 1976), use of the Problem-Oriented Medical Record in nonmedical fields (e.g., Kane, 1974), and environmental design (e.g., Walz, Willenbring, & DeMoll, 1974). From indigenous innovation in the form of such self-help groups as Alcoholics Anonymous, Synanon, Alanon, Parents Anonymous, Neurotics Anonymous, and Overeaters Anonymous, there are implications for intervention design just as there are from indigenous innovation in the form of popular psychology and such Far Eastern practices as transcendental meditation, Yoga, and Zen Buddhism.

Further, any field of human service may be a source of innovation for others. For example, group methods, developed initially in recreation and social group work settings, have now been transferred to many other areas of direct service with individuals and families. Likewise, some of these skills of community action and planning have been applied by practitioners in direct service. Because of differences in clientele, setting, and objectives, the transfer of innovation from one domain of human service to another may entail as large a transition as borrowing from outside fields.

Types of Transfer

There are two types of transfer. The first is *transfer by direct importation* of innovation from an allied field in which the innovation is taken over directly from another field and is used with relatively few alterations. For example, single-case experimental methods have been taken over by some practitioners essentially without modification from applied behavior analysis and behavior therapy to be employed for purposes of service evaluation, not for research, which was their original use. Although innovations having potential for direct importation must be selected and evaluated carefully for their suitability for human service, they have the advantage, if directly taken over with success, of not requiring redesign.

The second is *transfer with alteration*, which involves at least some redesign of the innovation to make it suitable for use in its new domain. For example, rather than being over directly in exactly the form it was used for medical recording when applied to social work, the Problem-Oriented Medical Record has to be modified (e.g., Kane, 1974; Martins & Holmstrup, 1974). As is the case with reinvention of an innovation borrowed by adoption, the alteration of a transferred innovation also involves redesign.

Modes of Transfer and Adoption

Transfer and adoption may also be carried out in one of two modes, the source- and need-oriented modes, as discussed before. In the source-oriented mode, focus is on the general potential of given interventions for transfer and diffusion to other user groups and for other purposes. Considerable attention has been given in engineering and technology to the processes of technological diffusion and transfer (e.g., Brooks, 1968; Doctors, 1969; Gruber & Marquis, 1969; Schon, 1967; Spencer, 1970), and two transfer mechanisms are widely recognized, both of which are source oriented.

The first is the *passive method*, which consists largely of means by which scientific and technical information may be collected, screened, indexed, stored, and disseminated to meet requests of potential users.

The second is the *active method*, in which dissemination and processes by which innovations may be adapted for new users are pursued vigorously through diverse mechanisms. These include the publication of technical briefs, use of personal liaison between technology developers and potential users, employing the assistance of transfer agents and independent technology entrepreneurs, provision of specialized training programs, and fostering means whereby technical specialists with expertise in the innovation area may be systematically exposed to new user groups (Bastien, 1979). For example, the National Aeronautics and Space Agency has an applications engineering team whose function is to find outlets for aerospace technology in the public sector. If successfully pursued, the source-oriented approach can greatly increase the likelihood of diffusion and transfer of innovations to other user groups.

The need-oriented mode, in contrast, begins with a particular design problem or requirement and seeks innovations from other fields only as they may relate to these particular purposes. Thus, if one's task were to develop a method of computer-assisted assessment in a given field of human service, the researcher-practitioner would search for computer applications from scientific technology and allied areas having relevance to this task. If such innovations were located, they would be evaluated for adoption or transfer, and, if no applicable innovations were discovered, then the practitioner-researcher might want to design such an innovation, collaborating with computer specialists and others as necessary. The advantage of the need-oriented approach, again, is that it provides a relevant answer to a specific question. Although both modes of transfer and adoption are clearly applicable to intervention design, the need-oriented approach is the one emphasized here.

Legal Application

When dealing with legal policy in the form of a national constitution, laws of governmental units, judicial decisions, and governmental regulations, legal application is relevant. As the term is used here, *legal application* refers to the explication, specification, and operationalization required to make use of legal policy in human service. Although application of legal policy may affect any aspect of human service, in intervention design it generally entails at least the specification of guidelines involving client rights and practitioner, agency, program, or institutional responsibilities. More generally, when made operational for use in human service, legal policy may take the form of ethical guidelines, codes of ethics, grievance procedures, human rights, human subjects and peer review committees, mechanisms of client advocacy, and methods of monitoring and auditing for compliance.

Consider the court decision of Wyatt v. Stickney (see Martin, 1975). In this decision the court focused on the fundamental conditions for safe and adequate treatment. The court enumerated many rights that must be met, among them the right to the least restrictive conditions necessary for treatment, the right to be free from isolation, a right not to be subjected to unusual or hazardous treatment procedures without expressed and informed consent after consultation with counsel, and the right to keep and use personal possessions. In response to this court decision, articles then appeared dealing with some of the specific implications of the decision for the rights of the committed, thus setting the stage for altered intervention methods (Johnson, 1975; Martin, 1975; Prigmore & Davis, 1973).

Legal policy and its application is a broad and complex topic that goes well beyond the scope of the present work. However, given present objectives, several features are worthy of brief mention. Most content of legal policy is essentially prescriptive, indicating, for instance, that given behaviors or practices are obligatory, forbidden, or permitted. When the content is in this form, as is illustrated in the summary of Wyatt v. Stickney, there are relatively clear implications for service, at least as compared with some practices of the past. However, interpretations and specifications are required, and these must be consistent with the letter and intent of the legal policy in question. The methodology of legal research is clearly relevant here. Judgment of experts is generally a fundamental criterion of correctness of such applications. When legal policy is a significant source of information in the design of interventions, it would be important to supplement the skills of the practitioner-researcher with the contributions of members of the legal profession and to make use of a review committee whose members are competent to deal with the legal and ethical matters of human rights.

Like the other generation processes, legal application has two modes. In the source-oriented mode, emphasis is on the potential contributions to human service from one or more areas of legal policy. An example is Martin's (1975) *Legal Challenges to Behavior Modification: Trends in Schools, Corrections and Mental Health.* A work based on a comprehensive review of a large number of laws and court decisions rather than a narrow aspect of human service, this book has implications for virtually all of human service. The need-oriented mode, in contrast, looks to legal policy in response to a specific design or requirement, such as the rights of the clients in human service. An example would be the guidelines regarding the ethical treatment of clients proposed by the Association for the Advancement of Behavior Therapy (see Cameo 7.3). Again, both modes are relevant to intervention design. A need-oriented approach is the one adopted in this framework.

Experiential Application

Experiential application refers to that process by which the individual's personal or professional experience is transformed into results applicable to the design of intervention methods. Experiential application is complex, and the private experience involved in such application is not well understood.

Many would affirm the validity of personal and professional experience, at least under some conditions. More generally, an individual's experience, based on direct, firsthand knowledge, can yield valid information about (a) the problems that some clientele have or may have experienced, (b) potential solutions to such problems, (c) unlikely solutions, and (d) conditions under which a given intervention might or might not work for that problem area.

There are, of course, large differences in the depth, quality, and relevance of an individual's personal and professional experience. Likewise, there are large differences among individuals in their ability to benefit from experiencing events and to apply that experience to the solution of a design problem. There are at least the following requisites for the valid use of experiential information: (a) having had the relevant base of experience; (b) having recorded at least some parts of the experience accurately in memory; (c) possessing the ability to retrieve the information when needed; (d) possessing the ability to identify the innovative problem for which personal experience may be relevant; and (e) having the ability to apply the experience in question to the possible solution of the design problem. Given all of these, the practitioner-researcher is then in a position to make use of the personal experience in intervention design, using problem solving and other methods to be discussed subsequently.

Summary Overview

Up to this point, nine sources of basic information have been presented, each of which relates to at least one of the five generation processes. The generation processes are the processes by which the basic information is transformed into results or products that may be used directly in this design and development of intervention innovation. Figure 9.2 summarizes these relationships.

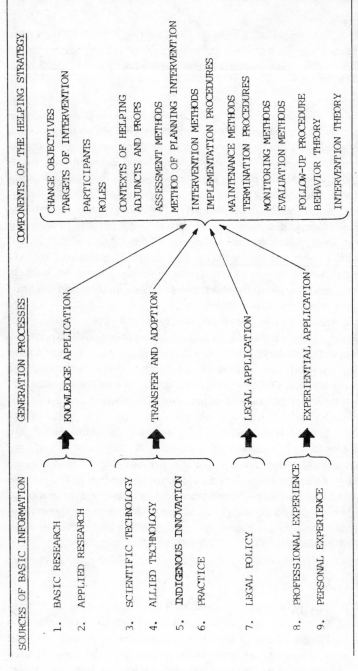

Figure 9.2: Relation between particular sources of information and generation processes, all as they relate to components of the helping strategy.

ON CREATIVITY AND PROBLEM SOLVING

Creativity

When asked about the nature of his creative experiences, Helmholtz, the distinguished psychologist, replied that after completing previous investigations of a problem "in all directions . . . happy ideas come unexpectedly without effort, like inspiration" (Moore, 1979, quoted in Bronson, 1979). Edison, the noted inventor, answered, "The key to successful methods comes right out of the air. A real, new thing, like an idea, a beautiful melody, is pulled out of space" (Moore, 1969, quoted in Bronson, 1979). No doubt some individuals possess extraordinary creativity and inventive ingenuity (e.g., Galton, 1869). In addition to exceptional intelligence, there may also be special abilities in creativity for divergent and "lateral" thinking and for bringing together remote associations, as well as distinctive personality characteristics (see Rothenberg & Hausman, 1976). Practitioner-researchers with creative talent can apply it to meeting the challenges of intervention design. However, to the extent that exceptional creativity is a gift few have and one that cannot easily be willed or prescribed, little can be gained by emphasizing it.

Indeed, much can be lost. Focus on creativity can foster the erroneous impression that extraordinary talent, if not genius, is required for innovation and that the result is somehow exceptionally novel. Such an approach to innovation obscures two important considerations. The first is the critical role of systematic procedures and problem solving, methods that all practitioners-researchers can use to facilitate the solution of design problems. The second is that although it is often seen as novel by the outsider, the solution response in design is generally plausible and not extraordinary when understood in the context of the information at hand and situation in which it was produced. Innovation is typically composed of a bundle of components, each of which may represent one or more solution responses to a design problem. Each solution response may or may not be novel in order for the entire innovation bundle to be distinctive and unusual.

Problem Solving

Problem solving has an important place in all of the intervention design. It should be used as a supplementary method in connection with the generation processes discussed above, as well as with the methods and techniques discussed in subsequent chapters. Indeed, much of the methodology outlined in subsequent chapters is a specification of concrete problems and solution methods that themselves are realizations of particular applications of problem solving to intervention design. More generally, problem solving should be viewed as a useful approach to any design problem in whatever context it emerges.

Although writers do not agree precisely on what the stages of problem solving should be, D'Zurilla and Goldfried (1971) identified five general stages that, in their view, come close to representing a consensus: (1) general orientation, such as "set" and attitude, (2) problem definition and formulation, (3) generation of alternatives, (4) evaluation and selection of an alternative, and (5) verification. These steps, plus an additional one, along with further details, are given below as they apply to intervention design.

General Orientation

Rather than to be seen as inviolate and unchangeable, contemporary helping methods are best viewed as state of the art, having both strengths and limitations. The strengths should not be overlooked but should be taken for what they are: components that at present meet at least some of the criteria of good intervention methodology but may be found wanting later in light of further developments. The limitations should not be feared or avoided, but rather should be seen as potential problems to be solved. While some problems cannot or should not be solved, each problem of design should be given an opportunity to be considered for possible solution within the methodology of D&D. It is thus that the practitioner-researcher should take an ambitious and activist approach to problem solving.

Problem Definition and Formulation

D'Zurilla and Goldfried (1971) recommended that in defining and formulating the problem, problem solving is likely to be improved if definitions of all aspects of the problem are given in specific, operational terms and a full and comprehensive description is provided of all the problem elements. In other words, problems of design should be partialized into concrete and manageable parts.

Gathering of Relevant Information

Facts as well as relevant opinions should be obtained as necessary through literature review and consultation with others who have special expertise. For example, the basic sources of information for innovation presented earlier should be drawn on for relevant data and resources.

Generation of Alternatives

To ensure that good ideas are not closed off by premature evaluation, alternatives should be generated in a brainstorming, free-wheeling fashion in which criticism and judgment are deferred until the point of evaluation. The goal is to obtain a rich, abundant, diverse set of alternatives so that a comparative context and perspective is created within which the relative merits of each can be evaluated. Some of the methods of "lateral thinking" may be helpful here (see Cameo 9.1).

Often the quality and quantity of alternatives generated may be improved by a period or incubation during which the individual or individuals involved engage in some diversion (e.g., exercise, relaxation, rest, sleep, recreation) while allowing covert mental processes to continue to solve the problem. Following such periods of incubation, the desired solution will sometimes suddenly present itself, sometimes called the "Aha phenomenon" or the "Eureka effect."[1]

Cameo 9.1
On Lateral Thinking

"Vertical thinking is concerned with proving or developing concept patterns. Lateral thinking is concerned with restructuring such patterns (e.g., insight) and provoking new ones (creativity). Lateral and vertical thinking are complementary. Skill in both is necessary" (deBono, 1977, p. 13).

Some techniques described by deBono to facilitate lateral thinking are the following:

(1) Deliberate generation of alternatives to any given way of looking at something.

(2) Challenging of assumptions.

(3) Suspension of judgment.

(4) Designing different ways of doing things.

(5) Fractionating to restructure a situation or problem.

(6) Use the reversal method to produce a different structuring of a problem.

(7) Brainstorming in which ideas are generated through cross stimulation in a formal group setting with judgment suspended.

(8) Use of analogies.

(9) Selection of different points of entry and foci of attention to restructure a problem or situation.

(10) Use of random stimulation (e.g., select inputs of unconnected pieces of information) to provoke restructuring.

(11) Application of new concepts or categories to a problem or situation.

Evaluation and Selection of Alternatives

Having been withheld up to this point, evaluation is now made of the alternatives generated earlier. Each alternative should be evaluated in terms of its ability to solve the design problem, given what is known about the intervention area, the feasibility of the solution, and its appropriateness otherwise.

At this point the ambitious and activist stance in problem solving must be tempered by a realistic approach to solutions. Rather than attempt to optimize by maximizing benefits and minimizing limitations, a solution that is essentially ideal given all the factors involved, it is better to "satisfice," to use the term of Newell and Simon (1972). The solution should be good enough to satisfy at least some of the criteria, given the realities of what is possible, practical, and relevant (see Newell & Simon, 1972; Janis & Mann, 1977).

To facilitate evaluation and selection, some of the guidelines proposed by Janis and Mann (1977) are relevant. Based on their analysis of a broad literature from many fields, these authors proposed seven criteria of good decision making (see Cameo 9.2). These criteria represent highly general and widely applicable guidelines relevant to this step as well as other steps of problem solving. Although not always attainable, the criteria can serve as an ideal in problem-solving design.

Taking Appropriate Action

It does little good to make a decision and not carry it out. Following the selection of an alternative, action steps accordingly need to be identified and carried out.

Verification

The adequacy of the solution can be examined by looking at its consequences, following its implementation. Many of the decisions made in intervention design have direct effects on subsequent activities in the developmental process; hence, it is generally possible to evaluate the adequacy of each solution, at least to a limited extent. Such feedback serves in the long run to improve the overall quality of the problem solving and, in the short run, may provide the practitioner-researcher with an opportunity to make appropriate changes before it is too late.

Cameo 9.2
Quality of Decision Making

Although systematic data are not yet available, it seems plausible to assume that decisions satisfying these seven "ideal" procedural criteria have a better chance than others of attaining the decision maker's objectives and of being adhered to in the long run.

The decision maker, to the best of his or her ability and within his or her information-processing capabilities,

(1) thoroughly canvasses a wide range of alternative courses of action;

(2) surveys the full range of objectives to be fulfilled and the values implicated by the choice;

(3) carefully weighs whatever he knows about the costs and risks of negative consequences, as well as the positive consequences, that could flow from each alternative;

(4) intensively searches for new information relevant to further evaluation of the alternatives;

(5) correctly assimilates and takes account of any new information or expert judgment to which he is exposed, even when the information or judgment does not support the course of action he initially prefers;

(6) reexamines the positive and negative consequences of all known alternatives, including those originally regarded as unacceptable, before making a final choice;

(7) makes detailed provisions for implementing or executing the chosen course of action, with special attention to contingency plans that might be required if various known risks were to materialize.

Our first working assumption is that failure to meet any of these seven criteria when a person is making a fundamental decision (one with major consequences for attaining or failing to attain important values) constitutes a defect in the decision-making process. The more defects, the more likely the decision maker will undergo unanticipated setbacks and experience postdecisional regret.

When a decision maker meets all seven criteria, his orientation in arriving at a choice is characterized as *vigilant information processing*.

From Janis and Mann (1977, pp. 11-12).

SUMMARY

1. Information and resources relevant to intervention design derive from nine potentially relevant sources, each of which yields basic data or material to be used in the formulation of intervention innovations. These sources of information are basic research, applied research,

scientific technology, allied technology, legal policy, indigenous innovation, practice, and personal and professional experience.

2. Generation processes are those processes required to transform and apply information from one or more sources into results or products that may be used directly in the design and development of intervention innovations. There are five generation processes, each of which is applicable to one or more source of information.

3. Knowledge application is the generation process by which knowledge of human behavior from research is transformed into results applicable to the design of intervention methods.

4. In this transformation, there is the formulation of empirical generalizations and the subsequent deduction from the generalizations of practice guidelines for intervention. Then the resulting practice guidelines must be made operational in real-world terms.

5. Knowledge may be applied in one of two modes, the source-oriented or the need-oriented mode.

6. Adoption is the generation process by which an innovation is diffused from its field of origin to a different user group, to be used for the same purposes as that for which it was originally intended.

7. Adopted innovations are frequently altered by their adopters, a result that is referred to as "reinvention."

8. Transfer is the generation process by which an innovation from another field is taken over by a different used group for purposes different from those for which it was originally developed.

9. Transfer may be accomplished by direct importation of an innovation from an allied field or by alteration, in which at least some redesign of the innovation is necessary to make it suitable for use in its new domain.

10. Transfer and adoption are generation processes that apply to the transformation of information and resources deriving from scientific and allied technology, indigenous innovation, and practice.

11. Transfer and adoption may be carried out in either the source-oriented or the need-oriented mode.

12. Legal policy, such as laws, judicial decisions, and governmental regulations, may be transformed by the generation process called legal application. This type of application refers to the explication, specification, and operationalization required to make use of legal policy in human service.

13. Experiential application refers to that process by which the individual's personal or professional experience is transformed into results applicable to the design of intervention methods.

14. Although creativity can greatly facilitate innovation, it is a talent that not everyone possesses in abundance or that can be reliably created and evoked. Emphasis here is placed instead on the vital role played by systematic procedures and problem solving, methods that can be used to facilitate the solution of D&D problems by all practitioner-researchers, given appropriate familiarity and training.

15. Problem solving is an important supplementary method that may be employed in connection with the generation processes as well as at other points in D&D.

16. Guidelines to aspects of problem solving were presented, including the following steps as applied to D&D: (a) general orientation; (b) problem definition and formulation; (c) gathering of relevant information; (d) generation of alternatives; (e) evaluation and selection of alternatives; (f) taking appropriate action; and (g) verification.

NOTE

1. This term, of course, comes from the story of Archimedes, who suddenly recognized the Principle of Specific Gravity while lowering himself into a bathtub and ran naked through the streets shouting "Eureka!" This word is Greek for "Good God, that water's hot" (Gardiner, 1970, quoted in Bronson, 1979).

Analysis

Beginning with this chapter, the first of the four phases of D&D is presented and discussed.

OVERVIEW OF THE DESIGN AND DEVELOPMENT SEQUENCE

Analysis is the first of four phases of D&D, the remaining being design, development, and evaluation. As may be seen Figure 10.1, each phase consists of one or more material conditions and activities. The material conditions are real phenomena that precede and essentially set the stage for subsequent activity. In later stages, the material conditions are also largely specific outcomes of D&D effort. The related activities, in turn, consist of methods appropriate to trying to solve problems presented at that point. Each of the activities may be thought of as a potential step if the entire sequence of phases and constituent activities is carried out in order. Each phase or component activity of a phase may itself be the main or sole focus of effort (segmented D&D), or most or all phases and their constituent activities may be carried out by one practitioner-researcher, project group, or organization (integrated D&D).

The activities have been selected and ordered such that if each activity is carried out successfully, the chances of solving the problems at the next step and of eventually producing a successful innovation should be increased. The overall strategy is to have the activities of D&D carried out in a systematic and orderly fashion by the same practitioner-researchers or by different ones, each of whom makes contributions to selected aspects of the developmental effort.

Figure 10.1: Developmental research and utilization (DR&U).

TWO PRINCIPLES

Two principles are relevant to this strategy. The first is the *principle of stepwise commitment,* as implied above. According to this principle, commitment is made to an activity only when preceding activities or steps have been carried out successfully by the practitioner-researchers involved or by others. This means that the activities of evaluation would not be carried out before those of development, that those of development would not be conducted until the activities of design have been performed, and that the tasks of design would not be completed until those of analysis had been finished. This principle also applies to the constituent steps within each phase.

It is recognized, however, that the recommended order may not always have been the sequence that practitioner-researchers followed in D&D that was successful, nor is this sequence necessarily always the most desirable. There may be times when activities have already been completed by others and next steps may therefore be readily pursued, or there may be occasions when several steps may be worked on at once or skipped entirely. However, if little or no developmental work has been done, it is best to start at the beginning and progress onward more or less in sequence. And if there has been prior work, effort should be focused on what needs to be done next.

The second is the *principle of least commitment.* According to this principle, "no irreversible decision should be made until it must be made" (Ostrofsky, 1977, p. 21). Serving to help avoid premature action, this principle enjoins the practitioner-researcher to hold off making irreversible decisions until all relevant data have been considered appropriately.

SOME CONSTITUENT ANALYSIS ACTIVITIES

Analysis embraces the relevant activities that necessarily precede design and development. The activities involved in the analysis phase relate to one or more of the material conditions. In this phase, there are three material conditions: a problematic human condition, state of existing interventions, and relevant information and resources. Each condition is critical to whether or not subsequent development may be engaged in and, if so, the direction it should take.

Some of the major activities of the analysis phase are described below. Each may be thought of as a step in the progression of D&D effort.

Problem Identification and Analysis

At the outset, before any developmental activity occurs, some *problematic human condition* is shown to exist. Examples are the abuse and neglect of children, physical abuse of husbands and wives, the emotional needs of the developmentally disabled, and individuals who are mentally and emotionally impaired. Problematic human conditions can embrace the gamut of personal, social, educational, and health difficulties of individuals and families. In this context, a problem is a recognized human service need for which existing approaches or methods are not satisfactory. In a word, something is not right, and what is being done about it is not satisfactory.

Identification of the Problem

Human problems are human made. They do not exist in the abstract or in absolute form; they are human conditions defined as problems by members of the professional community and the public at large. Underlying problem recognition are social, cultural, and economic influences that serve to bring the problematic human condition into existence and to make problem recognition possible.

There are at least two factors in the identification of a condition as a problem. The first consists of the standards (or norms) of the professional or nonprofessional community that are based on social values and that define given levels of behavior or well-being as appropriate. The second are discrepancies between the standards or norms and the existing behavior or states of well-being of given individuals or groups. When the discrepancy between the standard and what is judged is sufficiently large, the behavior or state of being is deemed to be a problem. For example, teenage alcoholism would be defined as problematic given values concerning desirable levels of physical and mental health, professional standards of alcohol abuse, and data indicating a high prevalence of teenage alcohol consumption.

Practitioners and researchers are often instrumental in the early identification of problems meriting intervention development. For example, child abuse has been common for a long time, but it is now recognized as a problem for which new procedures, programs, and policies should be worked out for prevention and intervention. Such abuse— particularly child battering—emerged as an important social issue through initial efforts of a small group of concerned physicians. Radiologists had reported multiple bone breaks in very young children in the 1940s and 1950s, but it was not until 1961, when investigators at the Denver Medical Center coined the emotionally charged diagnostic term "battered child syndrome," that professional and public interest in child abuse began to evolve (Antler, 1978).

Problem Analysis

Although critical in D&D, the identification of a problematic human condition is insufficient by itself. In addition, there needs to be at least some problem analysis. Such analysis consists of determination of one or more of the following: (a) the extent of the difficulty, such as its incidence of prevalence; (b) the component aspects of the problem; (c) the possible causal factors; (d) the effects of the problem including the behavioral, social, and economic accompaniments; and (e) intervention shortcomings in how the problematic condition is confronted.

Determination of the extent of the problem is important because it facilitates establishing a factual basis for the severity of the difficulty. For example, McShane (1979) indicated that:

> The pervasiveness of wife beating has not been fully documented. Experts believe that it is one of the least reported of all crimes relative to actual frequency of occurrence. Statistics from the Federal Bureau of Investigation suggest that wife beating is more prevalent than rape, one instance of which is reported every three minutes. Some professionals estimate that wife abuse occurs in 50 percent of all homes in this country. (p. 34)

The author establishes that the problem of wife abuse is far more severe and extensive than previously assumed.

Identification of component aspects of the problem is germane because it facilitates specification of problem elements. Such refinement is necessary to make it possible eventually to identify particular intervention objectives. For example, in Garbarino's (1980) findings on patterns of abuse among mistreated youths, he found that patterns of abuse could be divided into the following categories: "(1) mistreatment that begins with the onset of puberty; (2) mistreatment that represents a change in the quality or form of punishment (for example, from slapping to punishing), a change in parental affect (from tolerance to rejection), or a change in sexual conduct (from normal kissing to genital fondling); (3) mistreatment that is present only when the child is in the 'terrible twos,' and reoccurs when the youngster becomes an 'ornery adolescent,' and (4) mistreatment that merely continues a pattern of abuse begun in childhood" (p. 122). These patterns suggest special needs and different behaviors, each with its own directions for intervention development.

Possible causal factors are relevant because such conditions generally have important implications for treatment and, therefore, for intervention design. For example, if alcohol abuse is found to be a genetic or biochemical disorder, treatment could more justifiably be directed primarily toward medical and biochemical intervention; whereas if alcohol abuse is shown to be mainly learned behavior, intervention could more justifiably consist of modifying the drinking patterns and replacing them with alternative behavior.

The determination of effects also serves to emphasize the severity of the problem. In recent decades, for example, research on the effects of alcohol abuse has disclosed an impressive range of adverse consequences. Excessive drinking of alcohol may have serious consequences for the abuser's health, psychological functioning, work performance, family relationships, and the well-being of his or her children. In addition to establishing the importance of the problem, documentation of the effects of a problem helps define the scope and direction of desired intervention.

In the identification of intervention shortcomings, approaches to intervention may be found to be essentially nonexistent, as they often are in a new problem area, or somehow to be deficient. Substance abuse, for example, is acknowledged to be a prevalent and serious difficulty; yet despite recent improvements in treatment, existing intervention methods are less effective than desired.

Not all of the above aspects of problem analysis need to be carried out to justify the importance of the problem area for intervention development, but the more adequate and complete the analysis, the easier it is to judge the importance of the problem area and determine priorities for D&D. The practitioner-researcher often has the good fortune of finding that others have already carried out the research and scholarly work for analysis and all that remains is to review and evaluate the material. Indeed, in established areas generally enough work has been done in problem analysis so that nothing more is required to justify proceeding with development. However, if little or no analysis has been made of a problem, further work may need to be carried out before more developmental effort can be justified. The problems of analysis are themselves fully deserving of independent research, inquiry that may be conducted independently from or as an early and important part of D&D.

State-of-the-Art Review

Another material condition bearing directly on whether development can be embarked on is the *state of existing interventions.* The state of existing interventions is the base of information for conducting a state-of-the-art-review.

Successful identification and analysis of the problem serves mainly to establish the importance and dimensions of the problem area, but it does not rule out the possibility that relevant interventions are already available. The purpose of the state-of-the-art review is to determine whether relevant interventions already exist and, if so, whether further development is merited. A successful state-of-the-art review does not guarantee that someone else has not already come up with a satisfactory solution to the problem, but it does increase the likelihood of protecting the practitioner-researcher from making needless effort.

In his review of prior intervention efforts for child abuse, Antler (1978) discerned many limitations. Child abuse was being addressed as a crisis rather than as a complex set of problems requiring sustained intervention, and as a medical problem calling for protection rather than as a social problem with implications for social, economic, and other services. Antler noted that until recently the focus was on abuse at the expense of neglect, and there was greater emphasis on rehabilitation than on prevention. An alternative approach was proposed in which intervention and social services would be directed toward rectifying these shortcomings—an approach that could serve as the basis for further intervention development in this area.

State-of-the-art review is essential because it serves to identify the strengths and limitations of existing intervention methods. Without a careful review, directions for the development of new interventions cannot be knowledgeably charted or begun. Methods of information review and retrieval, including state-of-the-art review, are presented in Chapter 14.

Feasibility Study

The next step is to conduct a feasibility study. Study of feasibility provides some assurance (but does not guarantee) that the risks of further development would not entail wasted effort and resources. The material condition relevant to a feasibility study is the pool of *relevant information and resources.*

Engineers and researchers in industrial and scientific R&D have developed the feasibility study to a high art. No major engineering effort would be initiated without first conducting one. However, the feasibility study is a relatively new concept in the human services. Although questions of feasibility have no doubt been considered in the early stages of human service development, systematic analysis of feasibility has not typically been included as an early part of the developmental process. Study of feasibility in the human services will no doubt be less systematic, precise, and definitive as compared with its counterparts in engineering and science, but such study should be no less relevant or useful.

Feasibility will be employed here to refer to the practicality of the proposed development considering such factors as technical, organizational, economic, financial, political, and use feasibility. Each is discussed below.

Technical Feasibility

Technical feasibility refers to whether there has been sufficient prior technical accomplishment to provide a basis for developing the intended innovation. Clearly, if there is insufficient technical foundation for the desired innovation, the project will most likely fail. The data for technical feasibility consist mainly of information from one or another of the nine basic sources of information described in Chapter 9 and diagrammed in Figures 9.1 and 9.2.

Consider the following examples: At present computers cannot be employed reliably to analyze speech or to read handwriting, and thus it would not be technically feasible to try to develop a human service innovation that presupposed such computer capability. In contrast, however, now available are compact, relatively inexpensive and reliable microprocessors for potential adaptation in computer-assisted practice and administration in human service.

Organizational Feasibility

Organizational feasibility refers to the extent to which the individual and the organization of which he or she is a part have the ability to carry out the proposed development. Often, only individuals or a small group of practitioner-researchers would be involved, but sometimes there are many individuals or a team functioning within a larger organization.[1] There are at least three aspects of organizational feasibility.

The first is whether the personnel to be engaged in the development have the proper training, skill, and talent to carry out the proposed development. Among the capabilities that should be represented are knowledge and skill in the practice area involved, knowledge of D&D, and familiarity with conventional behavioral science research methods. In addition, the individuals should be flexible, imaginative, diligent, and capable of working with others. One or more individuals combining this profile of capabilities would be highly desirable indeed, but other combinations of capability are also advantageous. For example, a team can be composed of individuals who bring different and complementary talents. The more complex and ambitious the proposed development, the more likely it will be that single individuals will not possess everything desired. Limitations of personnel can sometimes be remedied by bringing in outside consultants, but if the core people lack basic competences, no amount of consultation can compensate.

The second aspect of organizational feasibility consists of top administrative support. If the director of the organization, for example, is opposed to the development and withholds support, the enterprise is likely to fail. All relevant personnel at the top of an organization should provide the necessary support and not impede the proposed effort.

Top administrative support by itself, however, will accomplish little without also having operational administrative assistance. This third aspect of organizational feasibility is particularly applicable to larger projects. Operational administrative support, for example, includes secretaries, research assistants, technical support services in a research or service organization (such as data processing and analysis facilities and the requisite personnel), and middle-level administrators.

The fourth aspect of organizational support consists of organizational resources, such as duplicating equipment, typewriters or word processors, telephones, and (increasingly) a computer with related supports.

Economic Feasibility

Economic feasibility refers to the extent to which the expected benefits exceed or equal the expected costs. Although the costs of D&D, like research costs, are often difficult to anticipate, they can be projected, allowing ample room for unanticipated factors and error. Anticipated benefits, in contrast, often entail qualitative human factors that currently are difficult (if not impossible) to translate into quantitative or monetary terms. However, often some component of the effort can be at least grossly quantified in monetary terms, such as the monetary value of restoring former alcohol abusers to regular employment. Because of the difficulty in quantifying anticipated benefits, Hussain (1973) suggested that one alternative is to compute the expected cost of the anticipated innovation and to obtain judgments from those actively involved in the proposed intervention area concerning anticipated benefits. One would then have to decide whether an innovation expected to cost, say, $20,000 would provide benefits equal to or in excess of this for given periods.

Financial Feasibility

Financial feasibility refers to the extent to which funds are available to meet the anticipated costs of the development. Even if a project is economically feasible, it may not be financially feasible. Likewise, a project may be financially feasible but not economically practical. There must be financial feasibility at the outset as well as the promise of economic feasibility over the long term.

Political Feasibility

Political feasibility refers to the extent to which a proposed development is acceptable to those who have the power to affect its initiation, reception, or continuation. Human service interventions in health, education, and welfare often entail charged political issues. For example, an alcohol or cigarette smoking prevention program that promised to be genuinely effective and that infringed on the business interests of the alcohol or tobacco industry would most certainly have political opposition. Clearly, lack of political feasibility can result in blocked development or other complications.

Use Feasibility

Use feasibility refers to the extent to which the proposed innovation promises to be adopted in the area of intervention for which it was developed. Will administrators and other members of the organization and the interventionists and their clientele find the intervention acceptable? Although initially important as an impediment to development, constraints on use in the long run are altogether less important than constraints for the other types of feasibility. A successful innovation that at first lacks use feasibility may eventually become feasible through education of the users and increasing acceptance of the innovation.

Methods of Study

Data relating to feasibility are often readily available and known to the practitioner-researchers. However, when not available, information relating to feasibility must be gathered and evaluated. Review of the literature, consultation, and gathering original data in exploratory inquiry are among the ways in which the researcher-practitioner may obtain the relevant information. Search methods should be resorted to only when it is not clear at the outset that there is obvious feasibility or the lack of it. However, when constraints to feasibility are not clearly evident at an early point, the researcher-practitioner faces an uncertainty that can be remedied only by gathering additional information. Although single individuals can often carry out the entire process, it is frequently useful to have the study conducted by a team of individuals, each of whom brings specialized contributions.

The feasibility study may disclose constraints that may be remedied with additional effort. For example, if an organization lacks the requisite capability for a project, it can often be acquired; if the personnel are less skilled than is desirable in a particular area, training can often be given or new personnel acquired; the absence of financial feasibility can sometimes be overcome by obtaining additional funds; lack of political feasibility can sometimes be surpassed with the mobilization of critical support; and limitations on future, anticipated use, as indicated before, may be removed following the development of a successful innovation. If a feasibility study does no more than identify constraints that need to be addressed, it has been justified (Hussain, 1973). When constraints cannot be remedied, however, the proposed development should be reconsidered or disbanded. Commitment to further action on the project should be made only if constraints can be removed or if there appears to be feasibility in all areas. The successful study of feasibility should culminate in a *statement of feasibility*, the last material condition for the analysis phase.

SUMMARY

1. As the first phase of D&D, analysis consists of those activities that necessarily precede design and development.

2. The constituent steps of the analysis phase, like those for the other phases of D&D, ideally are carried out in a systematic and orderly fashion.

3. Two principles apply to design and development—the principle of stepwise commitment and the principle of least commitment.

4. Before any developmental activity can occur, there must be a problematic human condition that may embrace any of a large variety

of personal, social, educational, and health difficulties of individuals and families.

5. The first step of the analysis phase consists of problem identification and analysis, activities that serve to define and explicate the importance and dimensions of the problem.

6. Identification and analysis of the problem have often been completed by others, particularly in well-established problem areas, but when this has not been done, additional inquiry is required in the area before development can continue.

7. The second step of D&D is to conduct a state-of-the-art review to determine whether relevant interventions already exist and, if so, whether further development is merited.

8. The base of information drawn on in a state-of-the-art review consists of the state of existing interventions.

9. Directions for the development of new interventions can be charted knowledgeably on the basis of information concerning the strengths and limitations of existing intervention methods.

10. The third step of analysis is to conduct a feasibility study to determine the practicality of the proposed development.

11. Drawing on relevant information and resources, the feasibility study given attention to such factors as technical, organizational, economic, financial, political, and use feasibility.

12. The feasibility study should culminate in a statement of feasibility that indicates that the proposed development is feasible or, if not, what constraints need to be remedied before development may be pursued further.

NOTE

1. Organizational feasibility is sometimes viewed as the capability of an organization to adapt and make use of innovation, something that will be discussed later in connection with use feasibility.

Design

The design phase consists of a series of related activities that result in generation of an innovation.

THE CONCEPT OF DESIGN

Although the concept of design is well established in science and engineering, it is new to human service. The following definition from Ostrofsky (1977) conveys an important aspect: "Design is purposeful planning as revealed in . . . adaptation of a means to an end or the relation of parts to a whole. . . . Design implies an iterative problem-solving process" (p. 6). Design has been defined variously with emphasis on such features as bringing something new and useful into being, conceiving something new and building an experimental model of it, translating existing knowledge into applications, the systematic creation and application of knowledge through organized effort, and as an imaginative leap (e.g., Rothman, 1980). All these features may be applicable here. As used in this context, design is the planful and systematic application of relevant scientific, technical, and practical information to the creation and assembly of innovations appropriate in human service intervention.

Drawing on his analysis of characteristics of design and development in engineering and industry, Rothman (1980) provided a useful characterization of the design process. First, it is utilitarian and goal oriented. For example, knowledge is used to solve problems rather than to build on prior knowledge to acquire refined or more valid knowledge. Second, design entails a synthesis inasmuch as knowledge of different types and from different fields is blended in ways that typically call for diverse skills, capabilities, and talents. Third, design is an art inasmuch as the discovery of the untried and new calls for imagination, inventiveness, and creativity. Fourth, design is tentative and exploratory, requiring further application, testing, and validation. To these we add that design is also systematic, disciplined activity that calls for the orderly analysis and solution of a series of design problems.

ROLE OF CONCEPTS

Concepts can play a critical role in the solution of design problems. As it applies to design, Ostrofsky (1977) said: "A concept is a basic approach to the solution of a design-planning problem. The basic approach relates to the depth defined by the needs and the problem identification" (p. 47). As a basic idea about how to solve a design problem, the concept serves to direct the designer to alternatives that may serve as solutions.

Concepts may vary in their inclusiveness, ranging from the general to the specific. Thus, one may have a concept that embraces an entire helping strategy—for example, to apply behavioral methods or systems theory to family intervention. The application of any developed mode of treatment to a new problem area or clientele would also be illustrative. More specific would be the concept that applied to only one aspect of a helping strategy component (e.g., to use intervention only in the home), leaving other aspects unstipulated. Still more specific would be the concept that applied only to a particular aspect of a helping strategy component, leaving out other options. For example, in regard to the assessment, the concept could be to use only clinical interviews, not other sources of assessment data. Still more specific would be the idea that a given intervention should be used with a given client under given conditions.

Because they express potential solutions, concepts should be encouraged throughout the design process. Essentially all ideas should be welcomed, even those that appear at first to be implausible or impractical. Concepts may be facilitated by brainstorming, periods of incubation following previously unsuccessful efforts to solve a problem, a permissive and nonjudgmental atmosphere when holding design sessions, and the rewarding of imaginative concepts, among other methods (see deBono, 1977; Janis & Mann, 1977).

SOME CONSTITUENT DESIGN ACTIVITIES

Although design is not yet well understood in human service, it is evident that it is complex and much enters into it. Many different activities are involved. Nine have been identified for presentation here (also diagrammed in Figure 10.1).

Determination of the Innovation Objective

General Objective

An early step is the determination of the innovation objective. This serves to provide necessary focus for design effort. Based on problem identification and analysis, the statement of the general innovation objective indicates such factors as the area of developmental effort and the persons and behaviors that are to be the focus of intervention. Examples of such statements are the following:

(1) develop a marital problem-solving program to assist parents of child abusers;

(2) develop a resource and counseling center to assist adult singles (i.e., unmarried and maritally estranged);

(3) evolve methods of maintenance to sustain gains achieved in an obesity control program;

(4) develop a family therapy for alcohol abuse applicable to intact families having at least one alcohol abuser;

(5) evolve a prevention program for teenage alcohol consumption; or

(6) devise an assessment procedure for assessing the capability of a cooperative marital partner to serve as a mediator in rehabilitative efforts to reach another family member who is a hard-to-reach substance abuser.

The innovation objective should be consistent with and justifiable in terms of prior work on problem identification and analysis carried out in the analysis phase.

Domain of Design

It is difficult to imagine an area of development in which all components of a helping strategy are left open for design. The realities of D&D call for fixing at least some aspects of the helping strategy, leaving a *domain of design* for concentrated effort. Stipulations for a proposed program in child management could be to restrict objectives to remediation for parents and children, target behaviors to child management, participants to parents of children up to age 17 who present child-management problems, helping persons to professionals in counseling and mental health, roles of helping person to clinician-behavior changer for the professional and mediator for the parents, role of target person to changee for the parents and children, the helping situation to the professional's office and the parent's home, and the service setting to a private family and child agency. In this example, all other components of the helping strategy could be left open for D&D.

In the domain of design, the number of fixed components may vary from a relatively small number, such as the eight illustrated in the top half of Figure 11.1, through all but one of the intervention components, as illustrated in the bottom half of that figure. Clearly, the larger the number of fixed parameters for components, the narrower the domain of design.

Because any component may be partially or fully stipulated, one can imagine many profiles of fixed parameters. It seems plausible, however, that there is a span of development that would be too broad and overly ambitious. Not everything should necessarily be open for design. Further, some components would appear to be a fixed "core," serving as context and framework for D&D in other areas. What this core should be is difficult to say, but one possibility would be those eight intervention components in the top half of Figure 11.1, in which stipulations have been indicated.

This illustration in the top of Figure 11.1 is of a broad domain of design, which leaves everything from adjuncts and props to intervention theory open for development—a very large domain indeed. The advantage of having a broad domain is that it allows for development in many components, thus increasing the likelihood of evolving complementary and integrated components. The disadvantage is that intervention effort may be spread too thinly, thus weakening the potential contributions of the effort. To reduce the likelihood of this disadvantage, the components in a large domain can be ordered in terms of priority, giving primary attention to the higher priorities.

A narrow domain of development, in contrast, may embrace only a few intervention components or even one specialized facet of a component. Thus, assessment and intervention methods could be the intervention components for development or, more narrowly, just the assessment methods alone. Even more refined would be focus on one aspect of a component, such as a specialized checklist for assessing the ability of family members to serve as mediators in helping efforts. The advantage of a narrow domain is that intervention effort can be focused sharply and intensely, thereby increasing the chances of successful

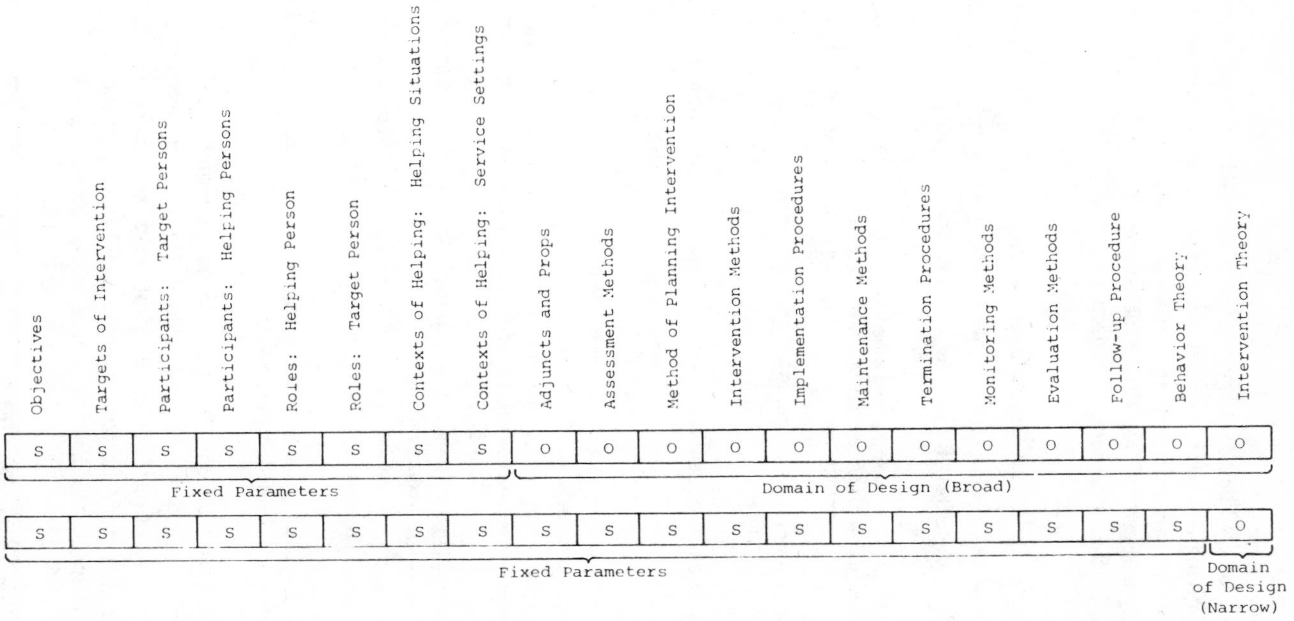

Component	Row 1	Row 2
Objectives	S	S
Targets of Intervention	S	S
Participants: Target Persons	S	S
Participants: Helping Persons	S	S
Roles: Helping Person	S	S
Roles: Target Person	S	S
Contexts of Helping: Helping Situations	S	S
Contexts of Helping: Service Settings	S	S
Adjuncts and Props	O	S
Assessment Methods	O	S
Method of Planning Intervention	O	S
Intervention Methods	O	S
Implementation Procedures	O	S
Maintenance Methods	O	S
Termination Procedures	O	S
Monitoring Methods	O	S
Evaluation Methods	O	S
Follow-up Procedure	O	S
Behavior Theory	O	S
Intervention Theory	O	O

Row 1 brackets: Domain of Design (Broad) covers the "O" cells; Fixed Parameters covers the "S" cells.
Row 2 brackets: Domain of Design (Narrow) covers the "O" cell (Intervention Theory); Fixed Parameters covers the "S" cells.

Figure 11.1: Illustrative fixed parameters and domains of design for components of a helping strategy. S = stipulated; O = open.

accomplishment. The disadvantage is that such a narrow focus precludes giving attention to other components that ideally should be included to be compatible with the focus of design.

An early and critical task is to establish the domain of design and to include it in the statement of objectives.

Identification of Innovation Requirements

Identification of innovation requirements provides further specification of what requisites the innovation must meet. Rosove (1967) said:

> A "requirement" . . . may be defined as a characteristic which a system or one of its elements should possess if the system is to accomplish a given objective. Requirements . . . tell us *what* the system is supposed to do in both qualitative and quantitative terms rather than *how* it is to do it. It is the function of system design, by contrast, to answer the question: how? (p. 225)

Examples of requirements are given below for each objective listed above:

(1) The program must not be seen or connected with the law enforcement system and must serve to reduce child abuse.
(2) The program must meet the social and emotional needs of participants in a time for most individuals of stress and disruption of past living patterns.
(3) The maintenance program must provide for sustaining gains following initial weight reduction for a period of 18 months or more.
(4) The program must be capable of handling possible domestic violence.
(5) The program must cover all types of beverage alcohol and reach children able to read.
(6) The procedure must provide for appropriate human rights protections for the spouse and substance abuser.

Actually, rather than one, there may be many requirements, some for each component of the helping strategy open for innovation. When specifying innovation requirements, it may be useful to make a systematic inventory of requirements such as that afforded by the Design Specification Chart presented in Appendix A.

Identification of Design Problems

As has been indicated, D&D is thought of as the systematic solution of a series of problems in the developmental sequence. In the context of intervention design, a design problem is a specific aspect of a helping strategy that is undeveloped, unspecified, or otherwise unresolved, the solution of which will facilitate the achievement of the innovation objective. Some examples follow:

(1) Whether to develop special selection procedures to screen spouses for their ability to serve as prospective mediators in family intervention and, if the decision is affirmative, what the criteria and method of selection should be.
(2) Whether to use the interview to assess the adequacy of family functioning and, if so, what areas of content the interview should cover.
(3) Whether to conduct intervention for anxiety alleviation in the office, the natural environment, or both settings.
(4) What intervention to use to enable a cooperative spouse to enhance marital decision making when his or her partner is unwilling to be involved in treatment (providing appropriate ethical protections are observed).

There are many potential design problems in a helping strategy, and these embrace essentially everything in the strategy not stipulated in advance. Recall that each component of the helping strategy (e.g., assessment methods, intervention methods) is composed of many options, and each option (e.g., whether to carryout assessment in the home) in actuality represents a potential design problem that may have to be solved at some point. The earlier chapters on the components of the helping process provide a guide to many (but not necessarily all) of the design alternatives that may need to be formulated as design problems for a given innovation objective.

The main function of identifying design problems is to provide a bridge between the innovation objectives and requirements and subsequent steps of D&D. When design problems have been formulated satisfactorily, a *statement of objectives and design problems* should be prepared.

Selection of Information Sources

Selection of the information sources is important because it is at this point that the design problems are connected with the basic information that can aid in the solution of the design problem. Each design problem has one or more source of information that is potentially relevant. Recall that when selecting sources of information, selection may be made from one or more of the following sources: basic and applied research, scientific and allied technology, legal policy, indigenous innovation, practice, and professional and personal experience. One or more primary source may be suitable as well as one or more secondary source. In selecting the appropriate source or sources of information, there are at least two selection criteria: *relevance to the design problem* and *adequacy of the source*. Each of these is discussed below.

Relevance to the Design Problem

There are no hard and fast rules for connecting design problems with relevant sources of information, but, obviously, the more one is conversant with the design problem and the sources of information, the easier it is to make connections. Familiarity with the design problem generally implies one or more relevant source. For example, if the design problem is how to measure depression, assessment methods to measure depression developed in fields of allied technology should be pertinent. Design problems that implicate electrical, mechanical, and physiological instrumentation clearly suggest contributions of scientific technology. Design problems involving particular intervention methods may be solved with already developed intervention methods from allied technology, indigenous innovation, or practice. Further, each source also implies a certain range of potential design problems for which the information of that source might be relevant. For example, legal policy is likely to be clearly relevant to design problems involving client and subject rights and protections.

Practice is often the only valuable source, particularly new programs in uncharted areas in which the practitioners are essentially the only ones who have attempted to come to grips with the problems. Personal and professional experience can be uniquely valuable in solving design problems, particularly when that experience is in an area directly related to the development task. Professional practice may also be used systematically to provide the professional experience for the refinement and design of intervention methods. For example, by seeing clients regularly in "developmental practice" having service as well as D&D purposes, the practice may provide for the ongoing design, development, and testing of innovations.

All relevant sources of information should be selected for each design problem.

Adequacy of the Source

After having selected one or more sources of information, the information should then be evaluated in terms of its adequacy.[1] For example, in regard to research, adequacy for purposes of using the information in design would consist of the amount of research, its soundness and the ability to apply it. In regard to innovations from such fields as scientific technology, allied technology, indigenous innovation, and practice, adequacy would consist of how well developed the innovations are, the extent to which their capabilities match the requirements of the innovation objectives, and the transferability of the innovation.

Adequacy of information in the context of legal policy is more difficult to appraise, since most legal policy already has some statutory or judicial legitimacy. Even so, legal policy that is clear, relatively uncontroversial, and consistent with human services values should be more adequate for design purposes than policy that lacks these characteristics.

Adequacy of information based on practice would consist of innovations in the area of intervention carried out by competent interventionists under conditions that allow for individual discretion, problem solving, and inventiveness. The quality, depth, and extensiveness of professional experience in the design area indicate pertinent aspects of adequacy for this source of information. Personal experience may be considered adequate to the extent that it relates to the area of intervention and is sufficiently extensive.

Gathering and Processing Information

After sources have been selected, information is then gathered from the relevant sources, recorded as appropriate, stored, and evaluated for subsequent processing. Methods of information retrieval and review should be employed at this point (see Chapter 14). The successful gathering of information should yield *relevant data.*

In the normal course of completing the above design activities, most likely the designer will not have arrived at solutions, although he or she may have gotten some good ideas along the way. To facilitate the generation of potential solutions, the relevant data must be transformed by means of generation processes such as those described in Chapter 9. The reader will recall that each source of information was indicated as having its distinctive generation process (i.e., knowledge application, relevant to utilizing the knowledge from basic and applied research; adoption and transfer, relevant to borrowing innovations from scientific technology, allied technology, indigenous innovation, or practice; legal application, relevant to legal policy; and, experiential application, pertinent to making use of professional and personal experience). For any given design problem and source of information, each generation process provides a basis by which that information may be transformed and applied to the solution of the design problem (see Chapter 9).

Generation and Selection of Solution Alternatives

The most appropriate time to generate alternatives is after relevant data have been gathered and processed. In addition to any good ideas that may have evolved earlier, the processing of relevant data should have produced several potential solutions. The advantage of having alternative generation as a separate activity, following the processing of relevant data, is that this provides an opportunity for evolving still other alternatives based on familiarity with the design problems gained up to this point.

When generating solutions, it is desirable to view the generation of alternatives as an aspect of problem solving in which alternatives are generated freely in a permissive, nonevaluative atmosphere. The objective is to evolve a set of alternatives that is large and fertile enough to provide one or more potential solutions. Design sessions can be held until an adequate set of alternatives has been generated. There are also other means of facilitating the generation of alternatives, as discussed in Chapter 9.

Many factors must be considered when selecting an alternative. Among these are the following:

(1) *Likelihood of problem solution.* Is the alternative likely to solve the design problem in light of the design requirements and innovation objectives?

(2) *Relative advantage.* Does the solution alternative have anticipated advantages compared with its competing alternative or the existing intervention or practice it is to displace?

(3) *Engineerability.* Do the practitioner-researchers have the technical ability to pursue D&D successfully with this alternative?

(4) *Cost.* Is the cost acceptable in terms of time and money?

(5) *Compatibility with other intervention components.* Does the alternative fit compatibly with the other components that are to comprise the innovation assembly?

(6) *Anticipated objective capability.* Is the alternative, when considered as an intervention, likely to be effective and efficient?

(7) *Anticipated useability.* Is the alternative, when considered as an intervention, likely to be used by the interventionists for whom it is intended? Aspects of usability include relevance, simplicity, flexibility, modularity,

expense, sustainability, compatibility, ethical suitability, and capability of satisfying consumers (see Chapter 8 for details).

Failure to meet one or more of the criteria may seriously jeopardize the success of the design effort.

Assembly

Design yields many things—new concepts, solutions to design problems, and different ways to put things together. Not everything to be assembled is new, although some or many of the elements are. The elements to be assembled range from minute details, such as a minor tactic, through such larger elements as new techniques of intervention,

---

Cameo 11.1
A Seemingly Simple Problem

Design Problem: How to have a spouse measure the alcohol consumed relatively precisely from an irregularly shaped 1.5 liter whiskey bottle without the alcoholic marital partner knowing about it? (Assume that proper ethical protections can be observed.)

Possible Solution Alternatives: Have the spouse

(1) Estimate the amount consumed every day.
(2) Purchase another bottle having exactly the same shape, mark it for measurement purposes, and use it as a basis of comparison.
(3) Pour the contents into a measuring container every morning, measure the amount consumed since the last measurement, return the remaining amount to the original bottle, and return.
(4) Remove contents from the bottle, etch in millimeter levels on the bottle, and return the whiskey to the bottle.
(5) Weigh the bottle, including contents, determine the weight of the amount consumed each day (subtracting the weight of the bottle), convert the weight to a liquid measure of the alcohol consumed, and return the contents to the bottle.
(6) Devise and attach a counting device for pouring.
(7) Use a special measuring tape, prepared by the practitioner-researcher, to be placed along the bottle vertically in a given place using a scale marked on the tape that progresses in 5 milliliter units from 0, when placed at the top of the bottle, to 1500 milliliters, at the bottom.
(8) Note when the bottle is empty, determine the number of hours since the previous bottle was emptied, and calculate the amount consumed per hour.

Acceptable Alternatives: 7 and 8.

groups of techniques on the approach, and details for each component of a helping strategy. Whatever the size, the elements must be composed sensibly and meaningfully in light of the innovation objective. At least three criteria bear on the adequacy of assembly:

(1) *Completeness* is the extent to which relevant components of the helping strategy have been specified. For example, if intervention methods were the primary focus, specification would be incomplete if only the techniques were specified but the details of program format were not. Or if the main focus of intervention were on assessment methods and only some of the content of assessment was specified in the design with other areas left open, this too would be incomplete. If the design has a broad domain and components are omitted or weakly specified, this too would indicate incompleteness.

(2) *Compatibility* is the extent to which the elements of a helping strategy are not conflicting or mutually interfering. Some examples of incompatibility follow: a definition of the helping person role as clinician-behavior changer and researcher-evaluator such that performance of one tends to interfere with the performance of the other; specification of a large amount of data to be obtained in assessment but allowing only a short time for gathering such data; including intervention techniques based on behavioral, cognitive, and psychodynamic assumptions when only one type of theoretical assumption would be appropriate for the behavior in question.

(3) *Relatedness* is the extent to which the components of the helping strategy are related and relevant to each other. For example, the focus specified for the methods of assessment should yield data relevant to the proposed intervention methods; the data to be gathered in monitoring, evaluation, and follow-up should relate to the target behaviors dealt with by the intervention methods; the objectives specified for the helping strategy should be matched by intervention methods appropriate to the achievement of such objectives; and the behavior theory employed should address the target persons and behaviors actually included in the intervention area.

Before the innovation is actually brought into being in the real world, it exists as a *symbolic representation of the intervention*. Analogous to a blueprint, this may consist of the ideas of the designers or, more commonly, of a written statement, such as a proposal describing the innovation. Other symbolic forms might be algorithms, such as flow charts and electrical schematics for electronic equipment, or audio- or videotaped records as models of the behavior desired in the innovation.

Real-World Representation

Symbols are important, but without bringing the innovation into being in real-world form, design would be incomplete. If the product is a device, realization would be a prototype apparatus; if it is a practice procedure, its realization would consist of carrying it out in practice; if it is an assessment instrument, its realization would consist of a typed or printed version of the instrument. When realized in real-world form, the resulting material condition is an *intervention innovation*.

Proceduralization

What It Is

As applied to intervention design, proceduralization is the process by which desired activities of the helping process are described, explicated, and made into procedures that helping persons and others involved in the helping process may follow. Proceduralization results in *innovation procedures*, an important aspect of intervention theory. Such procedures prescribe desired intervention activities in terms of who does what, where, when, how, for whom, and under what conditions. They often take the form of practice principles, practice guidelines, and ethical codes. Most typically in written form, procedures can be represented as ordinary prose, a list of recommended activities, instructions, or as a manual of operation. They may also be depicted symbolically, as in a flow chart or lattice.

The Importance of Proceduralization

Most procedures are actually a form of algorithm, which is an orderly sequence of instructions for solving a problem (Lewis, Horabin, & Gane, 1967). By reducing complexity, distilling essentials, and leaving out the unnecessary, procedures like algorithms in general make it easier for their users to make decisions, follow guidelines, and carry out the desired behaviors. Procedures have the additional advantages of being specific, public, repeatable, and capable of being scrutinized readily and made accountable.

Despite its importance, proceduralization has not progressed far in most fields of human service. Much of helping methodology is represented in the memory and habits of interventionists and is what has often been called "practice wisdom" (see Greenwood, 1955). Among the factors that conspire against proceduralization in human service are the diversity of cases, time and effort required, lack of a

---

Cameo 11.2
On Practice Wisdom

I believe that the issue of systematic formulation of practice wisdom is one of the unrecognized critical issues of the helping professions. Vast numbers of individual and agency innovations are effectively lost to others who might profit from this knowledge. There are a small number of outlets such as workshops and professional journals, but reports of case illustrations without the accompanying conceptual analysis—abstracting beyond a particular case to derive the intervention ideas applicable to other situations—have little value beyond their human interest descriptions. Is there no way to make use of this reservoir of experience?

From Bloom (1975, p. 66).

---

tradition to develop procedures, rapid change of some helping methods, lack of required analytic skills, and a sense on the part of some that there is something impersonal, inflexible, constraining, and mechanical about procedures. These can be real impediments. However, the long-term effect of failure to formulate helping methods into suitable procedures is that the field has less to show for its prior effort, there have been few cumulative advances, and the development of intervention theories and helping methodology has been retarded.

Types of Intervention Activities

Desired intervention activities consist largely of the behavior of the helping person and, to a lesser extent, of others in the helping process. When the intervention activities are analyzed further, it is possible to break them down into five types. These are recurrent activities that are (a) continuous, (b) nearly continuous or (c) intermittent and nonrecurrent activities that are (d) stepwise or (e) episodic. All are important, and a complete procedure would generally contain specifications for all types in the intervention area. Most often, however, the stepwise activity is most important because so much helping behavior is differential, sequential, and ordered. Examples of stepwise activities are those depicted in the 15 steps of the PAMBOS case-management procedure given in Cameo 7.2. An early task in proceduralization is to identify the desired intervention activities.

The Process

Early in proceduralization, desired intervention activities are generally vague and poorly conceived. As proceduralization progresses, more intervention activities are isolated and specified until eventually most, if not all, of the major areas of intervention activity have been noted, their components isolated, connections between and among component activities determined, and the conditions under which given activities are to be performed have been stipulated.

Procedures can be employed in D&D as an ongoing *product* and *tool*. By means of a series of successive approximations with revisions and extensions, proceduralization should entail a systematic interplay between the actual intervention, its description and explication, and the subsequent reformulation of procedures. The resulting procedure, in turn, is then used as a tool to guide intervention when next carried out. Every time an intervention is carried out in this way, it provides an occasion for description, explication, and procedural reformulation—a process that, when repeated, should result in cumulative refinement of the procedure. This process of successive procedural revision is part of trial use, described more fully in Chapter 12. Chapter 15 on empirical techniques and Chapter 16 on analytic techniques present tools useful in specifying and explicating procedures.

USER PARTICIPATION IN DESIGN

It is thought by many that design and the other phases of D&D can be enriched greatly by including potential users of the innovation in the process. These potential users include the interventionists who might adopt the innovation, their supervisors and administrators, as well as potential clients. Involvement of such potential users has many advantages over having only the researchers or practitioners and other outside experts complete the D&D largely by themselves (e.g., Benn, 1977; Hussain, 1973; King & Cleland, 1975; Poertner & Rapp, 1980). Among the possible advantages are the likelihood that through such participation the innovation will be more acceptable, more compatible with existing methods, simpler, sustainable, and, in general, more contextually appropriate.

However, there are also possible disadvantages, and these could outweigh the advantages. Among the possible limitations are the added time and effort required to engage users in the D&D process, restraints on designing and developing innovations at an appropriately high technical level, and, in general, needlessly compromising design and development on the basis of considerations relating to adoption, a process that should be addressed later on its own terms and as a separate phase of utilization.

Considerations such as these must be weighed when deciding how much user participation to include. Some participation would appear at this point to be highly desirable, particularly in some of the steps of design. How much to include beyond this is another matter. It is also important to recognize that diffusion and adoption are themselves phases of the larger process and call for special efforts beyond designing an innovation that is more or less user-ready.

SUMMARY

1. Design is the planful and systematic application of relevant scientific, technical, and practical information to the creation and assembly of innovations appropriate in human service intervention.

2. Concepts can play a critical role in design because they direct the designer to alternatives that may serve as solutions to design problems.

3. Design is a complex process that embraces a number of constituent activities, nine of which were identified and presented.

4. The first step of design is determination of the innovation objective that serves to provide necessary focus for the design effort.

5. In this determination, one must establish the domain of design. In a large domain, many aspects of the helping strategy are open for design, whereas in a narrow domain, most components of the helping strategy are fixed by prior stipulation and are not subject to D&D. The advantages and disadvantages of broad and narrow domains of design must be weighed when establishing the appropriate domain for D&D.

6. Identification of the innovation requirements, the second step of design, provides specification of what the innovation is supposed to accomplish.

7. Identification of design problems, the third step, serves to specify the problems that must be solved in order to achieve the innovation objectives. Typically many design problems must be addressed in the design phase.

8. To aid in the solution of design problems, the fourth step specifies that information must be selected from one of a variety of sources of basic information. Sources of information are selected on the basis of

relevance of the source to the design problem and adequacy of the source.

10. When gathering and processing information from relevant sources, the fifth step, the designer engages in one or more of the generation processes that facilitate transformation and application of the information to the solution of the design problem. Each source of basic information has its distinctive generation process, as described in Chapter 9.

11. The sixth step consists of building on information and ideas obtained earlier in the design process, and calls for the generation and selection of solution alternatives to provide a set of alternatives rich enough to yield one or more potential solutions. When selecting an alternative as a solution, the designer must consider such criteria as the likelihood of problem solution, relative advantage, engineerability and cost, compatibility with other intervention components, and anticipated objective capability and usability of the alternative.

12. Design yields many products, all of which must somehow be assembled sensibly and meaningfully. When assembling elements, which is the seventh step, the designer must give attention to the extent to which the resulting assembly is complete and the elements are compatible and related.

13. Design activities such as these should yield a symbolic representation of the intervention, something of a blueprint, which then serves as a basis for producing a real-world representation of the innovation, the eighth step.

14. Proceduralization is the process by which desired activities of the helping process are described, explicated, and made into procedures that helping persons and others involved in the helping process may follow. As the ninth and last step of design, proceduralization results in innovation procedures, an important aspect of intervention theory.

15. A procedure consists of an orderly sequence of instructions for solving a problem and makes it easier for its users to make decisions, follow guidelines, and carry out the desired intervention activities.

16. Formulation of helping methods into suitable procedures consolidates intervention accomplishment, provides a basis for cumulative advancement and development of intervention theories and helping methodology.

17. Procedures are also important because they can be employed in D&D as an ongoing product and tool in such a way as to achieve successive procedural revision and refinement of the procedure.

18. Inclusion of potential users of the innovation in the design process can be beneficial, particularly when such participation enhances the usability of the innovation without limiting the design process.

NOTE

1. Although related to the validity of the basis discussed in Chapter 8 as one criterion for evaluating the adequacy of an intervention procedure, the adequacy of the source of information is broader and applies to evaluation of the information for purposes of possible use in design.

Development

Development is the process by which an innovation is implemented and used on a trial basis, tested for its adequacy, and refined and redesigned as necessary. Some design activities continue in the development phase, depending on the revision required in development and possible new design problems that come up. As Ostrofsky (1977) observed, design is iterative, allowing for successive revision and reconsideration in light of new information. Development also involves some evaluation, particularly the adequacy of the innovation. Even so, however, development has its distinctive activities and is best viewed as a separate phase that is largely different from the phase of design that precedes it and the phase of evaluation that it follows (see Figure 10.1). The main activities of development are discussed below.

FORMULATION OF THE DEVELOPMENT PLAN

When planning the strategy of development, the researcher-practitioner faces major decisions that have important consequences for most aspects of subsequent developmental effort. Among the issues are the scope of anticipated development, the type and amount of concurrent evaluation, whether there is to be research concurrent with the development, and the setting in which trial use is discussed below.

The Scope of Development

How development is planned and conducted depends largely on its scope. Although the actual progress made in development is affected by many factors that are difficult to anticipate in advance, certain aspects of the scope of development are subject to control from the outset.

These are the domain of design and the general directions set for the depth and generality of development.

The *domain of design* is a function of the number of design problems and the number of components of the helping strategy open for design. As discussed in Chapter 11, the domain ranges from a narrow band in which many, if not most, aspects of the helping strategy are stipulated in advance and are not open for design to a broad domain in which most or virtually all components are available for design. The areas open for design in the domain of design are those potentially open for development. Obviously, the scope of development should not exceed the domain of design. The domain of design is generally set earlier in the design phase.

Depth is defined by the extent of trial use. This may range from initial through extended developmental testing to the replication of successfully tested innovations. Each innovation in each area may be pursued with more or less depth. The greater the depth of development, the greater the confidence the practitioner-researcher and others can have in the adequacy of the innovation. Trial use is discussed more fully later in this chapter.

Given unlimited time and resources, development should be pursued in considerable depth. However, practical limitations make this ideal difficult to achieve in any given developmental effort. The scope of development may be restricted by limiting the domain of design or depth of development, or both. One strategy is to pursue a broad domain with limited depth. An advantage of a broad domain is that by exploring many areas, the chances of successful innovation may be greatly increased. However, a disadvantage is that with a broad domain, effort may be thinly and superficially distributed and yield few innovations that would survive developmental testing if trial use had been extended.

A second strategy is to restrict development to one or a few innovation areas and to pursue development in depth. The advantage here is that each innovation is pursued in sufficient depth to yield a relatively reliable and useful product, which is what development is intended to accomplish. However, to the extent that developments in excluded areas could have a bearing on the eventual development in areas selected for intensive effort, such development in depth could be premature and misguided. Inasmuch as innovations developed in each area are likely to have implications for innovations in other areas, one approach would be to pursue a strategy in which initially the domain of design is relatively broad, developing innovations in depth only gradually as their relationship to the other intervention components becomes apparent.

The third aspect of the scope of development is *generality* over cases. By carrying out development over many varieties of cases, one would hope to evolve broadly applicable innovations. While at first it might appear that the best strategy to achieve generality would be to have a large variety of cases from the outset, this has important disadvantages. For one, developmental effort may easily be dispersed superficially. Generality over cases can be facilitated by starting with a selected sample (e.g., typical cases), leaving to subsequent development exposure to different cases that systematically expand the types of cases and potential design problems that need attention. There are also questions of sampling, discussed below, that must be considered in this connection.

In regard to generality over interventionists, a matter more relevant to field testing, actually only a few competent practitioner-researchers are generally required to evolve interventions, and these are likely to be atypical to start with. Later, after the innovations have been developmentally tested, they may be submitted to field tests to see how they work in the hands of typical interventionists working under common service conditions.

As the above discussion has endeavored to indicate, there are conditions under which varying domains of design and depth and generality of development might be justified. Because there are practical limits on the time and resources for D&D, the challenge is to set the scope of development to obtain the greatest developmental gain, given the innovation objectives, while still mounting a manageable and workable project.

Concurrent Evaluation

Another issue is the type and amount of evaluation that may be carried out concurrently with development. The problem is that innovations are frequently subject to redesign in the course of development, and changing innovations provide a moving and elusive target for evaluation. Development must allow the practitioner-researchers the opportunity to try new things as necessary, depending on what is encountered along the way. At the same time, however, a well-developed innovation is of little use if it is not effective. There should be enough evaluation to appraise the adequacy of the innovation (a topic discussed more fully later), yet at least some evaluation of outcomes that does not interfere with developmental freedom. Evaluation is discussed more fully in the next chapter.

Concurrent Research

A third issue concerns how much research is to be carried out concurrently with the development. Development in human service often presents valuable and tempting opportunities to collect research data relating to behavioral questions in the area of innovation. The advantage of gathering research data must be balanced against the added time and effort required and the possible adverse effects of the research on the development. There is generally more than enough to do in D&D; hence, any proposal to conduct research concurrently needs to be evaluated critically. In any case, the objectives of development should be kept foremost in intervention design, and any concurrent research should be restricted to what may be carried out readily and compatibly with D&D.

Setting

The fourth issue concerns the setting in which the trial use is conducted. The ideal setting for trial use includes one in which there is ready access to a sample of relevant clientele, supporting administrative arrangements, and few or no additional obligations beyond those directly related to the developmental task. The regular practice setting is one alternative and so is the setting established especially for the D&D. Each has its advantages and limitations and both can be made to work, if properly structured in light of the above considerations.

When these issues have been considered and resolved, a *development plan* should be prepared prior to moving on to the next developmental activity.

OPERATIONAL PREPARATION

Requirements to put developmental activities into operation are similar to those needed to set up a small human service or research organization. The reader can see what this covers by reviewing the considerations listed in Cameo 12.1. Although not comprehensive, this list includes much of what is required to get development going. Many of the considerations are self-evident. However, some involve special application in development. These are staffing and development skills, supervision and project management, and sampling. Each is discussed further below.

Staffing and Development Skills Required

Based on his experience using agency practitioners in a field test of selected social science application concepts, Rothman (1980) concluded that there were three basic qualifications of what he called "social engineers." These were conceptual thinking capability, as indicated by familiarity with and facility in regard to theoretical writings; practice competency, as indicated by familiarity with and skill in dealing with application situations; and dependability-reliability, as evidenced, for example, in reporting and task completion. These are also germane to intervention development.

Some additional qualifications important for practitioner-researchers who are to be actively involved in D&D follow: (a) familiarity with intervention design and development; (b) knowledge of conventional

---

Cameo 12.1
**Overview of Elements in Establishing a Field Operation
in Development**

The general plan or design:

Administrative responsibilities, arrangements, lines of authority
Staff composition, function, and size
Auxiliary staff needed
Staff supervision, training, support, relationships
Field settings
Field arrangements, expectations, and limitations
Instruments for measuring process, outcomes, antecedent variables,
    participant characteristics, social structural variables, etc.
Sampling requirements and methods
Data analysis procedures
Data-processing methods and costs
Materials handling
Space requirements
Finances, including salaries, equipment, operating expenses
Timing and duration of development
Communications
Relationships to the funding or sponsoring body
Procedural difficulties and design flaws

From Rothman (1980, p. 115).

behavioral science research methods, such as research design, measurement, data analysis, and interpretation; (c) observation skills, including accurate observation, memory, and recall; (d) ability to analyze and apply one's own experience; (e) ability to solve problems systematically; and (f) dedication to the developmental mission, including willingness to work hard on difficult tasks. Abundant creativity and imagination would be good, too. Realistically, however, these are elusive and rare qualities and, as valuable as they are, are not essential for one to be innovative in D&D.

Clearly, not every practitioner-researcher will possess the above skills and abilities in equal measure, or possess them at all. However, each participant in D&D should bring at least some of these characteristics to the task. The more, the better. What is important is that the profile of qualifications represented by those involved in the development reflects characteristics such as those given above, and involves no large gaps.

Supervision and Project Management

Most of what is learned in development is based on firsthand experience in the developmental process in which innovations are tried out, appraised, and modified as necessary. Decisions are usually made hour by hour and day by day, and everyone involved in development needs to stay close to what is going on. Ongoing supervision and project direction are critical. Organizational arrangements that entail complex hierarchies and place distance between the developmental activities and the managerial and supervisory personnel can be deadly. The challenge is to provide proper direction and coordination of the developmental task and achieve necessary compliance while at the same time allowing for discretion, innovation, and adequate practitioner autonomy.

Based on my experience in design and development, the following would appear to be important considerations in project organization and management:

(1) Data relevant to ongoing development should be gathered and processed with a minimum of delay, thus keeping everyone close to current progress.

(2) Monitoring of practice and innovation needs to be close and ongoing.

(3) Information needs to be recorded promptly and kept in accessible, orderly form.

(4) Supervisors and others engaged in project direction should be closely engaged in the developmental process.

(5) Easy access to supervisors, project director, and all others needs to be provided.

(6) Frequent and timely team sessions should be conducted in project-based development, or of consultation, supervision, or peer feedback, in individually oriented efforts.

(7) Early commitment should be made to new developmental directions when the results of prior effort have been processed and understood.

Different patterns of supervision are possible. Use of a team with colleagial supervision and consultation can be valuable in group efforts, even for talented and experienced practitioner-researchers, whereas in smaller projects, individual supervision and/or consultation is another alternative. One structure for providing relatively close supervisory involvement in the developmental process combined with allowing developmental discretion for the practitioner-researchers is illustrated in Figure 12.1. As may be seen, the practitioner-researcher may work on and implement innovations directly and independently at several points. However, the team (or superviser) is kept continuously informed of developments, and if the practitioner-researcher cannot work out a solution independently, a conference is held with the project team (or superviser) to try to resolve the issues. In order not to retard progress with practice and development, there should be frequent meetings with the project team (or superviser).

Sampling

When drawing a sample in development, criteria need to be established for the selection of cases (a term used here also to include practice situations). In conventional behavioral science research, criteria such as representativeness are important in drawing a sample. The criterion in development is different. Although cases are in fact typically the units sampled in development, the sample elements of actual interest are the design problems presented by the case. The case may be thought of as a set of potential design problems and events that present opportunities for innovation. Cases containing appropriate occasions for innovation and development are sought that meet the criterion of *developmental opportunity*.

Cases providing developmental opportunity are of at least two types. In the first, the cases present the occasion for developmental testing of innovations designed earlier. Such testing may necessitate redesign of existing innovations that are not adequate or replication of the innovations found to be adequate in testing. To afford the best opportunities for developmental testing, cases should be selected that

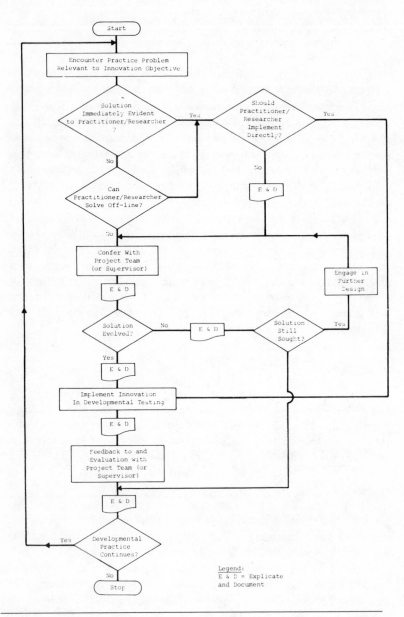

Figure 12.1: Example of practitioner-researcher team relationships in innovation process in development.

are likely to present design problems similar to those for which innovations have already been developed, thus providing occasion for applying the innovations again in the developmental testing. By continuing to sample similar cases, one increases the likelihood of furthering the depth of development, as discussed earlier.

In the second type of case, selection is made so that new design problems are presented relating to the design and innovation objectives. Such cases should be selected on the basis of their difference from those for which innovations have already been developed to increase the likelihood of encountering new and relevant design problems. By varying the types of cases from those dealt with initially, one increases the likelihood of expanding the domain of design and/or generality of development. Sampling of cases of both types clearly enlarges the scope of development and should be carried out consistently with the strategy of development adopted for the development phase.

There are important implications of developmental opportunity as a sampling criterion. It is clear that the design problems that define developmental opportunity will vary depending on the stage of development for that particular design problem. For example, in one instance it might be the occasion to test an innovation developmentally, in another to provide replicated use of the innovation following successful developmental testing and, in still another, an opportunity to evolve a new intervention. Thus, the design problems that provide developmental opportunity at one point would meet it differently or not at all at another point. To provide developmental opportunity, the types of cases selected will change throughout the course of development, as will the number required to meet the criterion. The cases are drawn purposively, not at random.

The number of cases should be large enough to allow sufficient trials of each innovation so that redesign may be carried out as necessary and to allow for the trial replication of innovations. *Trial replication* is the repeated use of the innovation to try to meet a design problem for which the innovation is appropriate. Trial replication allows for the opportunity to see whether the innovation is adequate and, if not, for its redesign. If the trial replication indicates no need for redesign, this successful repetition of the innovation is referred to as an *innovation replication*. If there is no trial replication of an innovation, there is no opportunity to find out if redesign is required; and, if there is no innovation replication, there is little assurance that the innovation will not have to be redesigned later. Both types of replication are required to increase the reliability of the innovations developed.

For purposes of initial development, the sample of cases need not be large, if the cases provide appropriate developmental opportunity. However, a fair number may be required to complete development. How large the sample of cases needs to be at any point in development depends on several factors. Among these are (a) the number of innovation replications needed across cases, X, (b) the total number of innovations dealt with in the development, Y, (a number that would have to be estimated if it is not known more definitely), and (c) the anticipated number of innovations involved for each case, Z. How these three factors interrelate in determining the number of cases is illustrated in the following formula:

$$\text{Minimum N} = \frac{X \times Y}{Z}$$

Consider the following example taken from the innovations dealt with on the unilateral family therapy project, in which the objective was to assist the cooperative spouses of uncooperative alcohol abusers to become a positive rehabilitative influence with the abusers. Let us set the desired number of innovation replications across cases (X) as 3. The total number of innovations involved in the development (Y) is at least 15, based on progress to date. (This is very much an underestimate.) These include such innovations as relationship enhancement mediated by the spouse, alcohol baselining and monitoring, assessment via the spouse, treatment planning with the spouse, programmed requests, programmed confrontation, spouse-mediated sobriety facilitation, spouse disengagement, spouse disenabling, spouse neutralization, and relapse prevention. About 9 of these innovations have turned up for each case (Z). Using the above formula,

$$\text{minimum N} = \frac{3 \times 15}{9} = 5$$

Actually, well over 20 cases have been worked with so far, and at least three innovation replications have been found for about 9 innovations, leaving at least 6 or more that have yet to be replicated that often. It turns out that about 7 of the 9 innovations are introduced essentially with every case (e.g., spouse-mediated relationship enhancement), and these consequently have ample chance to be tested and replicated developmentally. However, an average of about 2 of the remaining 8 innovations occur only occasionally in any given case, and a few rarely occur. Clearly, if all innovations are to be replicated, the actual N of cases required will have to be considerably larger than 20. Given more experience in the area, researchers will eventually be able to calculate the required N more precisely.

Several factors conspire to increase the N above a minimum level. The actual N of cases required will be high to the extent that the required number of replicated innovations needed across cases is high, the total number of innovations is high, a large number of innovations is involved per case, there is low likelihood of repeating an innovation with each case, and there is frequent need to redesign innovations, thus reducing the likelihood of successful replication of the innovation.

TRIAL USE AND DEVELOPMENTAL TESTING

Trial Use

Trial use presents the opportunity to implement innovations in practice with the clientele for whom the innovations were intended. By putting the development plan into operation, trial use results in *trial implementation*, as shown in Figure 10.1.

Trial use is similar to performance testing in industrial and scientific R&D inasmuch as the focus is on the reliability of the innovation, the conditions under which it works, and whether it functions as it was intended to. It is also similar to pilot testing in behavioral and social research, except that what is tested provisionally in such testing is research instrumentation, for example, not innovations. Trial use is a new concept in human service that has no real counterpart in this field. If systematically employed, trial use is a unique source of information concerning the adequacy of the innovations.

Outcomes of Trial Use

Trial use yields three principal types of outcomes, as Figure 12.2 indicates. Each of these—redesign, initial design, and replicated use— is critical in the developmental process. When the problem encountered in trial use can be handled appropriately with the innovation, opportunity is provided for replicated use. If the problem encountered is new for which D&D would be appropriate, then occasion is provided for initial design. If application of the innovation is unsatisfactory, opportunity is provided for redesign of the innovation. Clearly, the nature and variety of problems met in trial use will determine the extent to which each of these outcomes will be obtained.

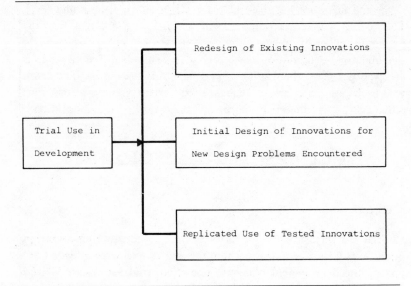

Figure 12.2: Principal outcomes of trial use in development.

Developmental Practice

These outcomes will not be forthcoming, however, unless trial use is conducted systematically in accordance with developmental objectives. Practice as carried out in regular service will not suffice. As Cameo 12.2 indicates, regular practice is ill-equipped to handle innovation development. Although innovations can and do occur in regular practice, such practice by itself is an uncertain and unreliable means of intervention development. To achieve the benefits of trial use, practice in trial use should be carried out with developmental objectives and methods, including developmental testing. Referred to here as *developmental practice*, this approach to practice increases the likelihood of obtaining the desired outcomes of innovative intervention methods as well as the benefits of service. Developmental practice may be carried out individually, without project or team affiliation, or with others functioning together in a coordinated effort.

Carrying Out Trial Use

To be useful in development, trial use should be conducted to provide opportunities to learn about the following: (a) What innovations need to be evolved to meet design problems encountered in

Cameo 12.2
Regular Versus Developmental Practice

Area of Difference	Regular Practice	Developmental Practice
Objective	Service	Intervention development and service
Practice methods	Regular intervention methods	Innovative intervention methods and others
How potential design problems are addressed	Ignoring, muddling through, trial and error	Intervention design and developmental research in general and trial use and developmental testing in particular
How results are monitored and appraised	Monitoring of possible changes in service outcomes	Monitoring of possible changes in service outcomes and of innovation-related outcomes through developmental testing
Outcomes	Possible service gains	Innovative intervention methods and possible service gains

implementation; (b) what revisions and alterations need to be made in redesign; (c) the operational feasibility of the innovation as indicated, for example, by whether the practitioner and client can carry out the innovation according to its requirements; (d) the appropriateness of the innovation for given practice situations and clients; (e) the adequacy of the innovation procedure as indicated, for example, by whether it guides the practitioner's behavior properly, whether it is descriptively complete and specific, and whether it is correct in terms of the practice

objectives that need to be met; and (f) what some of the outcomes
appear to be for the client (e.g., were the outcomes as anticipated for the
client, were there positive or negative effects otherwise, did the
innovation appear to be efficient or inefficient, and were the clients
satisfied with what happened?).

Some Guidelines

Although the process of trial use is not yet well understood, an
important aspect involves addressing practice problems systematically
and applying the appropriate intervention to the problems encountered.
Some of the decisions and activities involved in this process are outlined
in the flow chart of guidelines for conducting trial use given in Figure
12.3. In addition to the decisions involved in the process, the flow chart
also specifies many points at which explication and documentation are
required. The information thus obtained is particularly informative in
the developmental process.

The following are some of the important types of information that
may be obtained in trial use by following the procedure outlined in the
flow chart (the numbers below correspond to those associated with the
E&D points in the chart):

(1) What existing interventions or innovations are appropriate to use with
the practice problem encountered.
(2) What are the practice problems encountered for which it is not feasible
to design innovations and there were no actions taken relevant to design.
(3) What actions are taken that turn out to be relevant to the design after all
when it did not appear to be feasible to design innovation anew.
(4) What innovations are designed and why.
(5) What innovations are implemented in developmental testing.

Developmental Testing

Through its implementation in trial use, *developmental testing* is the
process by which an innovation is systematically tested, revised, and
redesigned as necessary. A major purpose of developmental testing is to
determine whether the innovation is adequate and, if not, to redesign
the innovation appropriately. The flow chart in Figure 12.4 contains
suggested guidelines concerning how developmental testing may be
carried out for each use opportunity.

There are many decision points in developmental testing, each of
which provides occasions to explicate and document what has been
learned. Among the types of information that may be obtained from

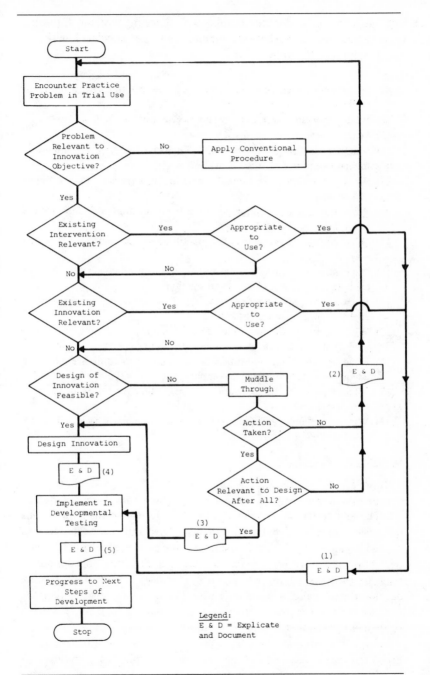

Figure 12.3: Some guidelines for conducting trial use.

following this procedure of developmental testing are the following (again, the numbers below correspond to those associated with the E&D points in the flow chart):

(1) What innovations are not appropriate or feasible to try with the client and why.
(2) What innovations are appropriate to use with a client and why.
(3) What interventions are feasible to try.
(4) Whether or not the innovation is appropriate after all, following implementation with the client, and why.
(5) What innovation procedures the practitioner-researcher cannot follow and why.
(6) When training is needed for aspects of the innovation procedure that the practitioner cannot follow.
(7) What innovation procedures the practitioner-researcher can follow and why.
(8) What innovations produce unsatisfactory client outcomes (e.g., insufficient client change, client dissatisfaction).
(9) What innovations produce satisfactory client outcomes (e.g., satisfactory client change, client satisfaction).
(10) What aspects of the innovation or innovation procedure are otherwise inadequate (e.g., lack of specificity or completeness).
(11) What aspects of the innovation or innovation procedure are otherwise adequate (e.g., are specific, complete).
(12) What aspects of the innovation or innovation procedure need to be redesigned and why.
(13) Whether enough replications of the innovation have been conducted.

Developmental Validity

Innovations introduced to the community of practitioners and consumers vary greatly in the extent to which they have been used, revised, and tested in practice. Unfortunately, too many innovations have been introduced but have not been tried out before, tested and revised as necessary. When innovations have been used adequately on a trial basis and have been tested developmentally, it is appropriate to refer to them as having *developmental validity*. Innovations lacking developmental validity have a greater likelihood of not meeting the practice needs for which they were introduced and of requiring subsequent revision to meet these needs.

Given the processes of trial use and developmental testing as presented here, the concept of validity as applied to development provides researchers and practitioners with a way to characterize

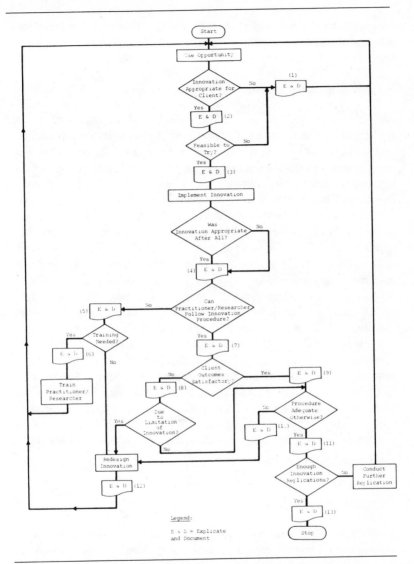

Figure 12.4: Process of developmental testing in trial use.

differences in the degree to which the development of an innovation has been adequate. Like the concepts of measurement and experimental validity, the concept of developmental validity implies particular criteria that should be met if an innovation is to be considered suitable developmentally.

Recording and Monitoring

The results of trial use and developmental testing need to be explicated and documented after important choice points and processes, such as those outlined in the flow charts in Figures 12.3 and 12.4. The main source of information consists of the careful observations of the practitioner-researcher combined with selected data gathered from clients and other participants. Much of the recording of qualitative material consists of written narrative, although special checklists and recording forms can often afford more comprehensive reporting. The monitoring and evaluation of client outcomes generally call for systematic recording—generally quantitative—and, in some cases, outcome measurement.

Although special instruments for recording, monitoring, and measuring may be needed, no elaborate research designs are necessarily required. Inferences concerning the effects of the intervention would be strengthened by use of single-subject or group designs. However, elaborate or rigorous designs to examine outcomes at this point in development would generally be premature and could interfere with the flexibility required in development. Recall that the objective at this point is the development of the innovations, not rigorous outcome testing.

Through recording and monitoring, trial use yields *trial use data*, as shown in Figure 10.1.

Directions for Analysis

When collated and evaluated for each case, the data gathered in developmental testing provide a basis for making many comparisons. Among the types of results that may be derived from the analyses are the following: (a) types of cases for which the innovation is appropriate; (b) practical impediments to implementation; (c) the sample of cases for which the innovation was implemented; (d) what went wrong with the innovation, if something did; (e) the extent to which the practitioner-researcher can follow the innovation procedure; (f) cases having satisfactory outcomes; and (g) cases for which the innovation procedure was adequate.

The Development Process

When conducting trial use in development, one or more practitioner-researcher is progressing from innovation to innovation and from case to case until development must stop. All developmental activity is carried out within a scope of development, consisting of a given domain of design with each innovation in the domain pursued to a given depth and generality of development. These three dimensions in effect represent an *innovation matrix.*

All trial use and developmental testing may be thought of as producing selected results capable of being entered into such a matrix. The depth of development for any particular innovation and type of case may vary from initial use to many replications of innovations that have been successfully tested developmentally. By monitoring effort on all dimensions, the depth of development may be charted across cases and innovations, thus facilitating periodic review of status. By noting the entries at a particular point in time and comparing progress in relation to developmental objectives, it is possible to determine what the next immediate step should be. When the time required to progress to a given degree of development is considered, rate of development can be estimated so that the amount of progress for any future date may be anticipated. By carefully monitoring and guiding the development process, fragmented and unsystematic development can be avoided.

How long should development be continued? Ideally, developmental testing needs to be carried out for each innovation until all innovations in the domain of design have been replicated successfully without need for major alteration or redesign. What the safe number of innovation replications should be depends on many factors, including how user ready the results should be. In general, however, it would be desirable to have at least several innovation replications before progressing to evaluation. Between two and three should provide at least some assurance that the innovation was designed appropriately. More would be better, of course. However, limitations of time and resources may make this impractical. In such situations, it may be sufficient to have tried all innovations at least once and to have redesigned several, leaving further development to another time.

In all development there is an inevitable "freeze point" beyond which further development cannot or does not occur. When this point is reached, there will most certainly be some unresolved issues and problems calling for redesign that cannot be addressed in the time remaining. All such unfinished business can be saved for "next generation" development when development is continued.

The result of the activities of trial use and developmental testing consists of *tested intervention innovations*, as depicted Figure 10.1.

SUMMARY

1. Development is the process by which innovation is implemented and used on a trial basis, tested for its adequacy, and refined and redesigned as necessary.

2. In the formulation of a development plan, the first step in the development phase, several major decisions must be addressed, among these being determination of the scope of development.

3. The scope of development shapes how development is planned and conducted. The three aspects that define the scope of development are the domain of design, established in the design phase, and the depth and generality of development.

4. The scope of development should be established to yield the greatest developmental gain consistent with the innovation objectives and the need to conduct a manageable and workable project.

5. Additional decisions that have important consequences for most aspects of subsequent development involve the type and amount of concurrent evaluation, whether there is to be research concurrent with the development, and the setting in which trial use is to be carried out.

6. The next step of development is operational preparation, a major component of which is to establish an organization for the field operation.

7. The organizational requirements for development are generally similar to those needed for a small human service organization, except for several areas of special application. One such area is the staffing and development skills required by the personnel. Although many special skills are needed, they tend to involve a blend of research, practice, and design and development.

8. Another area of special application is supervision and project management, where emphasis needs to be placed on means by which participants may be kept closely informed of relevant developments in a framework that allows for careful guidance of the developmental process and freedom of practitioners to innovate.

9. Another area of special application in development is sampling, in which cases are selected on the basis of the criterion of developmental opportunity.

10. One type of case that provides developmental opportunity is similar to those sampled earlier and presents the occasion for developmental testing of innovations designed earlier. By continuing to sample similar cases, the depth of development is furthered.

11. The other type of case that provides developmental opportunity is the one that differs from those initially dealt with and provides opportunities to address new design problems. By varying the types of cases from those dealt with initially, one increases the likelihood of expanding the domain of design and/or the generality of development.

12. The design problems that define developmental opportunity depend on the scope of development established at the outset as well as on the stage of development for that particular design problem. The types of cases selected will change throughout the course of development, as will the number required to meet the criterion of developmental opportunity.

13. To meet the criterion of developmental opportunity, a purposive rather than a random sample needs to be drawn.

14. The number of cases sampled should be large enough to allow sufficient trials of each innovation so that redesign may be carried out as necessary and successful innovations replicated. Trial replication and innovation replication are required to increase the reliability of the innovation.

15. The sample of cases need not be large for purposes of initial development if the cases provide appropriate developmental opportunity. However, a fair number may be required to complete development.

16. Although it is not yet possible to estimate precisely in advance the size of the sample required for any given development, it is clear that a number of factors affect the size of the sample, among them the number of innovation replications required across cases, the total number of innovations dealt with in the development, and the anticipated number of innovations involved for each case.

17. A formula for the minimum number of cases is presented, along with some of the conditions that should necessitate drawing a larger sample than the minimum.

18. The last step of development is trial use and developmental testing.

19. Trial use in development yields three principal types of outcome—redesign, initial design, and replicated use.

20. Developmental practice differs from routine practice and is identified as a method by which trial use may be conducted systematically in accordance with developmental objectives.

21. If systematically employed, trial use is a unique and valuable source of information in development.

22. In the first stage of trial use, the relevance of an existing intervention for the practice problem is examined and new innovations are designed, as necessary.

23. The second stage of trial use involves developmental testing, which is the process by which an innovation is systematically tested, revised, and redesigned as necessary. Guidelines are presented concerning how the researcher-practitioner may carry out activities in each stage of trial use.

24. The concept of developmental validity was introduced to designate the extent to which an innovation has evolved adequately through trial use and developmental testing.

25. Recording and monitoring during trial use and developmental testing yield information critical to both the process and the outcome of development.

26. The day-by-day activities of development may be charted and directed by recording progress in terms of the different dimensions of the innovation matrix.

27. Ideally development should continue until enough innovation replications have been completed to provide some assurance that a reliable and usable innovation has been obtained.

Evaluation

Evaluation in D&D is empirical inquiry directed toward determining the effects of the innovation. No matter how well designed an innovation is, it is of little value if its outcomes are not satisfactory. Indeed, if an innovation is designed or developed imperfectly but it has been found to produce satisfactory results, continued D&D with that innovation may be justified.

In some evaluative research, the evaluation turns out to be essentially an end in itself, often prematurely conducted before development has been completed or disembodied from earlier and subsequent development when completed. This is not the case in D&D and developmental research. Here the evaluation phase is viewed as an integral part of the innovation process, which begins with the earlier phases of analysis, design, and development. Evaluation provides the necessary feedback to determine whether the innovation should be retained and utilized more or less as it has been designed and developed or should be redesigned and developed further. To the extent that evaluation discloses that the innovation is less than satisfactory, it precedes subsequent design and development as well as follows them in a circular, interactive relationship. If the results of evaluation are satisfactory for any particular D&D effort, the phase of development proper may be regarded as completed and subsequent activities of utilization undertaken.

Unlike the methods and techniques relating to the other phases of D&D, those of evaluation are relatively mature. Evaluation methods in D&D include much of the already established research methodology of behavioral science and evaluation research. Because so much prior work has been done on the methodology of evaluation, details will not be repeated here. Readers not familiar with the basic methods of this subject are encouraged to refer to other sources (e.g., Bloom & Fischer, 1982; Campbell & Stanley, 1966; Cook & Campbell, 1979; Epstein &

Tripodi, 1977; Gottman & Markman, 1978; Grinnell, 1981; Hersen & Barlow, 1976; Jayaratne & Levy, 1979; Kazdin, 1980; Kendall & Butcher, 1982; Kiesler, 1971; Kratochwill, 1978; Mahoney, 1978; Miller, 1977; Tripodi et al., 1969). The focus here is on some of the major activities and decision issues that relate to evaluation in D&D.

FORMULATION OF THE EVALUATION PLAN

The first step of evaluation is to formulate an evaluation plan. There are at least six steps encompassed in making such a plan, each of which is discussed below.

Evaluation Objectives

When setting evaluation objectives, there are many options. Decisions need to be made, for example, about the areas of evaluation and the strategy of evaluation.

Areas of Evaluation

There are two areas of evaluation, outcome testing and field testing.

Outcome Testing. The principle focus of the evaluation phase is outcome testing and can include several different areas of outcome, as Cameo 13.1 indicates. All the areas are important, but effectiveness is critical because without it information relating to the other areas is of little consequence. At least four questions relate to effectiveness, ranging from outcome effects—the most general—through intervention effectiveness to comparative and component effectiveness. An ideal evaluation of effectiveness would include all four; but since each question is different and suggests a different methodology, any effort to evaluate all four at once would be unwieldy and impractical.

Actually, each aspect of effectiveness requires evaluation on its own terms and in its own time. For example, if there has been no evaluation of effectiveness, the first and most general question is whether or not *any* effects have occurred, irrespective of the various possible contributing factors. *Outcome effects* can generally be determined without using rigorous experimental methods and ordinarily do not entail constraints on service. Without knowledge that the outcome effects are mainly positive, there is generally little reason to consider other aspects of effectiveness.

Cameo 13.1
Some Areas of Evaluation

I. *Outcome testing* as determined by results such as the following:
  A. *Effectiveness*:
    1. *Outcome effects.* Has the innovation produced any change?
    2. *Intervention effectiveness.* For any change produced, was it the intervention that produced the change?
    3. *Comparative effectiveness.* Is the intervention more effective than some other intervention?
    4. *Component effectiveness.* What component of the intervention produced the effect?
  B. *Efficiency*: Does the innovation require time and costs that are not excessive?
  C. *Cost*:
    1. *Total cost.* What is the total amount required to implement this innovation, and is it excessive?
    2. *Cost effectiveness.* What is the relationship for this intervention between its cost and effectiveness, and how does it compare with the same information for alternatives?
    3. *Cost benefit.* What is the ratio of costs to benefits for this innovation?
  D. *Consumer satisfaction*: Are the clientele satisfied with the results produced by the innovation?
II. *Field testing* as determined by whether the results of the use of the innovation under normal operating conditions are satisfactory, using criteria such as those given above in A-D.

If the outcome effects are positive, then the next question is whether the given outcomes can be attributable to the intervention employed—a question of *intervention effectiveness*. In such evaluation, the intervention would be contrasted with appropriate control conditions. Because this aspect of effectiveness is essentially a matter of cause and effect, the strongest research design appropriate for the intervention situation should be employed.

More refined is the question of *comparative effectiveness*, which is evaluation directed toward determining whether the innovation is more or less effective than its intervention competitors. Examination of comparative effectiveness presupposes that there are effective competing interventions. Also, before submitting an innovation to comparison with alternative interventions, it is generally desirable to have shown the innovation to have been effective in its own right through examination of intervention effectiveness. Because it is necessary to compare two or more interventions when examining comparative effectiveness, the research design should allow for the systematic comparison of the effects of all interventions to be contrasted.

Still more specialized is the question of *component effectiveness*, which focuses on the contribution the constituent features of the intervention make to effectiveness. To examine component effectiveness, it is generally desirable to begin with an intervention that already has been shown to be effective. Experimental designs and research methods to examine component effectiveness should make possible the systematic comparison of the components of the intervention.

Although questions of effectiveness are central to outcome testing, *efficiency* and *cost* should also be examined in any comprehensive evaluation program. Inefficient or excessively costly innovations, however effective, may simply be impractical. Efficiency and most aspects of cost may be examined empirically with relatively well-established research methods. When effective interventions have been found to be more costly or less efficient than their competitors, appraisals of the tradeoffs between effectiveness, efficiency, and cost must be made, all of which involve social and economic priorities and judgments of value.

Consumer satisfaction is another area of outcome testing increasingly being included in evaluation programs. As was indicated in Chapter 8, consumer satisfaction is an important area of evaluation in its own right. The satisfaction of the consumers may or may not relate well with other evaluation areas, such as effectiveness. For example, an effective intervention may not be satisfying, and a relatively ineffective intervention may provide some satisfaction for consumers. Evaluation of consumer satisfaction can often be readily combined with evaluation of effectiveness.

Field Testing. Another aspect of evaluation is field testing to determine whether the innovation can be implemented appropriately under normal operating conditions. Among these conditions are service with typical clientele, usual human service practitioners, and customary work and administrative arrangements.

The areas of evaluation for field testing are generally the same as those for outcome testing (e.g., A-D in Cameo 13.1). However, field testing is distinguished here from outcome testing because each has its own questions and methodological requirements. In outcome testing of effectiveness, one attempts to obtain the best test of the innovation that is not confounded by the operation of extraneous factors. To accomplish this, it is often necessary to use especially trained practitioner-researchers to carry out the intervention with special subjects, or to employ an experimental design that requires some departures from the typical conditions of service. By submitting an intervention innovation in the early stages of evaluation to a field test before outcome testing has been completed, aspects of the normal operating conditions could obscure or confound the outcomes, indicating, for example, that the intervention was less effective than it would otherwise have been. More generally, if outcome and field testing are combined, unsuccessful results could be due to the confounding of effects of the field conditions, inherent ineffectiveness of the intervention, failure to implement the intervention appropriately in the field, or all three. Thus, while it might appear at first to be inefficient to separate outcome testing from field testing, such separation provides more accurate and interpretable results.

If outcome testing has been conducted first and the intervention has been shown to be satisfactory, failure to achieve satisfactory results in subsequent field testing is not necessarily a critical flaw inasmuch as the field conditions are themselves subject to change. In effect, the field conditions may themselves be redesigned as part of the D&D to make them more congenial to the proper use of the innovation. For example, among possible changes in field conditions are the provision of training to augment the skills of the interventionists, easing practitioner assignments to free time for using the new intervention, adjusting supervisory and administrative arrangements to facilitate implementation of the innovation, and monitoring of its use and provision of incentives for correct use to increase the likelihood that the innovation will be implemented as intended. However, if such modifications cannot be made, or if they are made and positive results obtained in outcome testing cannot be duplicated in the field, it is then necessary to redesign the intervention accordingly.

Clearly, at least some field conditions should be taken into consideration in the initial design, giving attention at the outset to such factors as contextual appropriateness (see Chapter 8). The more user ready the innovation is following initial design, the more likely it is that the results of outcome and field testing should agree. In any case, successful field testing ideally should yield a user-ready innovation capable of being diffused to relevant users and adopted widely.

Other Areas of Evaluation. In addition to outcome and field testing, evaluation can be focused on other areas as well. One of these is procedural adequacy, which includes such properties of the innovation procedure as its completeness, specificity, correctness, and how well it serves to guide the practice behavior of its users (see Chapter 8 for further details). An inadequate procedure is less likely than one that is adequate to be reliable, replicable, effective, and subject to interpretable evaluation. Defects of adequacy, however, cannot be determined directly by outcome testing, although such defects may have adverse effects on effectiveness or efficiency. Rather, distinctive methods are required that make it possible to evaluate the adequacy of the innovation procedure itself, such as the methods of developmental testing described in Chapter 12 and the empirical and analytic techniques discussed in Chapters 15 and 16. Although adequacy may be examined and improved at any point in development and evaluation, it is generally better addressed in development prior to conducting outcome or field testing.

Evaluation Strategy

The setting of evaluation objectives also requires consideration of an evaluation strategy involving which areas of evaluation are to be worked on and how the demands of service are to be met. Each is discussed briefly below.

Stepwise versus Nonstepwise Evaluation. A major decision is whether to conduct evaluation in a stepwise fashion progressing from developmental testing to outcome and field testing, to try to combine the evaluation areas by carrying out some or many of the evaluation activities concurrently, or to conduct a limited evaluation in only one area, eliminating the others. Stepwise progression has the advantage of being the most systematic, informative, and safest approach, but it can require considerably more time and effort than a combined approach. The combination of evaluation areas can also be difficult methodologically because each focus has its own purposes and methods. Elimination of evaluation steps can weaken the evaluation. Altogether, the stepwise approach is recommended for most developmental efforts, but, as is the case with all the steps of D&D, stepwise progression is not necessarily always required or the most advantageous approach. The choice of whether to conduct evaluation in ordered stages must be made on the basis of the conditions and opportunities afforded in any given developmental endeavor.

Role of Service in Evaluation. Another issue is how to combine service and evaluation so that the objectives of both can be achieved without detriment to either. This can be particularly challenging when attempting to carry out rigorous outcome or field testing that requires adherence to a given experimental design. In the case of single-case experimentation, for example, there are important differences between the requirements of the designs and those of service, as indicated in Chapter 6. The difference between the research methods of evaluation and the requirements of service may pose conflicts for the service, the evaluation, or both. Sometimes the potential for conflict is small, but more often it is large. There are at least five alternatives that may be employed to attempt to reduce conflict.

> *Alternative 1: Restrict service to the intervention innovation.* By restricting service to what is embraced by the intervention innovation, it is possible to meet most, if not all, of the requirements of the evaluation while still providing some service.
>
> *Alternative 2: Conduct evaluation as a component of service intervention.* Outcome evaluation is carried out as a separate segment in which the objectives of the evaluation are foremost and the requirements of service are not allowed to interfere with the evaluation. Likewise, in the service segment, service objectives are foremost and those of evaluation are secondary.
>
> *Alternative 3: Reduce measurement intrusiveness.* For example, baselines may be reconstructed from case records (Bloom & Block, 1977; Bloom, Butch, & Walker, 1979); archival data may be used for the baseline (Webb, Campbell, Schwartz, & Sechrest, 1972; Jayaratne & Levy, 1979) or use may be made of short baselines (Azrin, 1979) and single data points for pre- and postcomparisons (Jayaratne & Levy, 1979). The researcher may also employ less intrusive methods of gathering data.
>
> *Alternative 4: Reduce design intrusiveness.* For example, a multiple baseline design over behaviors or persons may be more suitable ethically or practically than a design calling for reversal of an intervention (Baer et al., 1968; Franks & Wilson, 1976; Hartmann & Atkinson, 1973; Hersen & Barlow, 1976; Kazdin, 1973, 1978a; Kazdin & Kopel, 1975).
>
> *Alternative 5: Conduct evaluation without experimentation.* Among the available methodologies for nonexperimental evaluation are time-series analyses (e.g., Jones, Vaught, & Weinrott, 1977) and methods oriented toward measuring goal attainment (e.g., see Kiresuk & Sherman, 1968). Design frameworks for evaluation include quasi-experimental designs, such as a time-series experiment and multiple time-series design (Campbell, 1969; Campbell & Stanley, 1966).

Innovations To Be Evaluated

At any point in development generally more than one innovation might be evaluated. With a broad scope of development, much or most of a helping strategy may be innovative and subject to evaluation. This entire strategy may be evaluated by comparing it, for example, with a control condition of no treatment. The outcomes of such comparisons reflect on the entire helping strategy evaluated and not necessarily on any particular component. Such global evaluation of a new approach should probably not be undertaken until it has progressed beyond the formative stage and some of the critical parts have been evaluated separately.

An alternative to such global evaluation is to evaluate a key segment, such as a component intervention technique. This segmented evaluation is characteristic of most contemporary evaluation of interventions. The key part is varied in the context and background of the other aspects of the helping strategy that are kept constant or relatively unvarying. For example, while using behavior therapy as the helping strategy, the constituent intervention technique of systematic desensitization could be the segment evaluated. As segments are evolved and reach sufficient maturity to merit outcome evaluation, they may be evaluated systematically, progressing from one to the next.

Indications of Success or Failure

When making operational definitions of the evaluation criteria, it is generally desirable to use multiple indicators rather than single operational specifications (Campbell & Fiske, 1959; Jayaratne et al., 1974; Kendall & Norton-Ford, 1982). For example, when specifying aspects of client change in measuring effectiveness, there are the indicators of self-report of change on the part of the client, observation of the client on the part of the practitioner-researcher, and observation of client change on the part of others who have had occasion to observe the client in the natural environment.

When selecting indicators of success or failure of behavior change, there are two important types. The first is *change of the target behavior* itself—the specific behavior to which the intervention innovation was applied. This is central inasmuch as the target behavior must change sufficiently in the desired direction for the intervention to be considered a success.

The second type is *change in relevant correlated behavior* not directly the target of intervention. For example, marital communication could be a correlated behavior when the target behavior involves aspects of sexual enhancement for marital partners. The marital communication may improve or deteriorate with improvements in the marital sex; or the marital sex may not change but the communication may improve or get worse following intervention for the sexual difficulty. Correlated behaviors may not change, may increase in a desired direction, or may decrease. Positive or negative changes in correlated behaviors may be as important as the changes in target behavior and provide valuable information for understanding the effects of the intervention. Thus, large positive changes in correlated behavior that occur reliably with modest changes in target behaviors can bode well for an intervention that otherwise could be judged as having weak effects; and negative changes in correlated behavior that reliably occur when the target behavior changes positively may offset or negate the targeted changes. Evaluation should include as potential correlates those behaviors that could plausibly change following application of the intervention for the target behavior.

Measurement Instruments

Instruments to measure relevant outcomes need to be assembled and, when possible, pilot tested before being incorporated into an evaluation. Many of the decisions relating to measurement instruments were considered in Chapter 3 and Chapter 6 and will not be repeated here. Again, measurement, like most of the methodology of evaluation, is a developed and established subject and the reader is referred for details to other sources that cover the basic content.

Research Design for Evaluation

One of the most important decisions in evaluation is selecting the research design. The research design provides the empirical and logical framework for inferring what the effects of the innovation are as well as the vehicle within which the evaluation is conducted.

Some Selection Criteria

There are at least four criteria in selecting a research design for the evaluation. The first is *experimental rigor*. The research design should protect the researcher-practitioner against the operation of extraneous causal variables that can weaken the validity of inferences drawn concerning the effects of the intervention—that is, the design should provide protection against as many as possible of the threats to internal validity. For this purpose, strong designs that afford powerful inferences concerning possible causal influences should be employed. This factor is particularly important in outcome and field testing.

The second criterion is *generalizability*. The design should facilitate ready generalization of the results to different subjects, settings and practitioner-researchers and, more generally, protect the researcher-practitioner from threats to external validity. For this purpose, designs should be selected, for example, that include a sample of subjects, settings, and practitioner-researchers appropriate for generalization. Although relevant in outcome testing, this consideration is particularly important in field testing.

The third criterion is *D&D flexibility*. The research design should allow the flexibility and discretion needed in practice to carry out necessary D&D. This condition is particularly important in developmental testing.

The fourth criterion is *intervention compatibility*. The research design should be compatible with the nature of the intervention, its requirements, and those of service. For example, if the intervention could not be reversed or removed once it was initiated, a design requiring reversal (e.g., an ABAB design as described in Table 13.1) would not be compatible. However, a multiple baseline design might be compatible inasmuch as no reversal of the interventions is required.

Each of these criteria will be discussed further below as they apply to the selection of a research design.

A research design may meet one criterion and not another. For example, a rigorous design calling for standardized intervention could disallow flexibility required by D&D. Actually, each design presents its own profile of qualifications for measuring up to these criteria. All things considered, there are few ideal designs, only designs better for some purposes than for others. It is generally necessary to weigh the ability of a design to meet one consideration against its ability to meet others. The presentation below is intended to highlight this differential applicability of designs, depending on one's purposes.

Single-Case Experimental Designs

There are two main types of research design: the single-case experiment and the more conventional between-groups design. Both types offer a large number of alternatives. Some of the main designs are covered briefly below. Again, this subject is well established and for basic details, the presentation of which is beyond the scope of this work, the reader is referred elsewhere (e.g., see Barlow et al., 1984; Hayes, 1981; Hersen & Barlow, 1976; Jayaratne & Levy, 1979; Kazdin, 1982; Kratochwill, 1978; Leitenberg, 1973).

Selected single-case experimental designs are summarized in Table 13.1. Among the advantages of single-case experimentation is its flexibility in application, allowing the practitioner-researcher to employ a design that is distinctly suited to the particular evaluation and practice problem presented. Such experimentation also allows for relatively inexpensive exploration and initial testing that can generally be undertaken without making any major commitments (Kazdin, 1982). Another advantage, as highlighted by several researchers (Hersen & Barlow, 1976; Leitenberg, 1973; Sidman, 1960), is that by applying the suitable design, individual sources of variability may be traced and isolated, thus facilitating the identification of effective intervention components that later may be combined with others into an intervention package. These advantages make single-case experiments as a whole relatively flexible in D&D and compatible with intervention and service requirements without sacrificing experimental rigor.

As indicated, however, each particular design may realize these advantages differently. For example, the AB design lacks rigor because it is subject to many possible threats to internal validity (e.g., history, maturation, statistical regression). However, this design can be relatively flexible in D&D and compatible with many intervention requirements. In contrast, the ABAB design is much more rigorous because it has a reversal and return to baseline following the initial baseline and intervention; but it may be incompatible with the requirements of intervention, service, and D&D because the reversal necessitates disbanding of the intervention.

The multiple baseline designs present still other profiles. For instance, the multiple baseline over persons does not necessitate removal of service through a reversal and, in this regard, has intervention compatibility, but this design does require delaying intervention while baselines are taken for all individuals in the design and until intervention has been applied for others who receive the intervention in earlier phases. The successive application of the same intervention with different cases greatly strengthens the rigor of the design and its generalizability; but, at the same time, the design requirement to apply the same intervention in the same way with each person may restrict the flexibility needed for D&D.

Some designs clearly meet a criterion better than others. It is not possible at this point, however, to appraise the designs too precisely or broadly. Even so, some generalizations may be put forward tentatively concerning the designs and the selection criteria.

Experimental Rigor. In regard to the criterion of experimental rigor, all the designs in Table 13.1 are subject to at least some threats to internal and external validity (e.g., see Kratochwill, 1978), but some are particularly weak. These include especially the B and AB designs and, although they are somewhat stronger, the BAB, ABA, ABAC, and

TABLE 13.1
Selected Single-Case Experimental Designs

Design Type and Examples	Design Procedures
Intervention only	
B	Intervention only
Baseline intervention	
AB	Baseline, intervention
Reversal	
BAB	Intervention, baseline, intervention
ABA	Baseline, intervention, return to baseline
ABAB	Baseline, intervention, return to baseline, reinstatement of intervention
ABAC	Baseline, intervention, return to baseline, a different intervention
ABACA	Baseline, intervention, return to baseline, a different intervention, return to baseline
Changing criterion	
$B_1.\ .\ .B_n$	Successive application of the same intervention, each with different criteria of behavioral performance
$AB_1.\ .\ .B_n$	Baseline followed by successive application of the same intervention, each with different criteria of behavioral performance
Multiple baseline across behaviors	
$A_1B\ B\ B$ $A_2A_2B\ B$ $A_3A_3A_3B$	Simultaneous baseline for three different behaviors in period 1 followed by introduction of intervention for the first while continuing the baseline for the other behaviors (A_2, A_3) in the second period, then introduction of the intervention for the second behavior while continuing the baseline for the remaining behavior (A_3) in the third period, with introduction of the intervention for the last behavior in the final period
Multiple baseline across situations	
$A_1B\ B\ B$ $A_2A_2B\ B$ $A_3A_3A_3B$	Same as described above for multiple baseline across behaviors except that instead of behaviors, the baseline are across situations or settings

TABLE 13.1 Continued

Design Type and Examples	Design Procedures
Multiple baseline across persons A_1B B B A_2A_2B B $A_3A_3A_3B$	Same as described above for multiple baseline across behaviors except that instead of behaviors, the baselines are across persons or groups
Alternating treatments (comparing A and B or B and C)	Rapid and random (or semirandom) alternation of two or more conditions (e.g., A and B or B and C) in which there is one potential alternation of condition per measurement opportunity. There is a single data point or set of data points obtained for each condition, which is preceded and followed by measurements associated with the other conditions
Construction ABACA(BC). . .B,C, or (BC)	For the intervention package (BC) systematic addition of each component alternated with baseline, ending with the component(s) that work most effectively
Strip (BC)ACABA. . .B,C, or (BC)	For the intervention package (BC) systematic subtraction of each component alternated with baseline, ending with the component(s) that work most effectively
Crossover B-C C-B	One individual (or family) is assigned at random to experience condition B while another is assigned simultaneously to experience condition C, following which each individual crosses over to experience the other condition, thus yielding a B-C sequence for one individual and a concurrent C-B sequence for the other
Multiple schedule	The same behavior is treated differentially under varying stimulus conditions. For example, two or more treatments may be offered by different therapists or be given in different settings in an alternating manner. The client may receive treatment C under one condition and

(Continued)

TABLE 13.1 Continued

Design Type and Examples	Design Procedures
	treatment B under another condition during the first phase of treatment, and these treatments would then be alternated between conditions in successive treatment phases

ABACA designs as well. The ABAB design is among the more rigorous single-case designs, and the multiple baseline designs can be relatively strong, particularly if there are many rather than few baseline-intervention segments included in the design. All the designs may be strengthened by taking measurements over many rather than few points in time during each phase of the design. Further details concerning the relative rigor of single-case experimental designs can be found elsewhere (e.g., Hersen & Barlow, 1976; Jayaratne & Levy, 1979; Kazdin, 1982; Kratochwill, 1978; Leitenberg, 1973).

Generalizability. In regard to the criterion of generalizability, questions are frequently raised about the representativeness of the findings from single-case experiments because these experiments typically involve one or a small number of subjects. A finding does not a generalization make. Or does it?

In his discussion of the basic principle of single-case experimentation, Chassan (1979) said the following: "Once a true process or effect has been established as having occurred in one person it can reasonably be inferred that there will be other persons as well in which the process or effect will occur" (p. 403). Dukes (1965) noted the special occasions when the sample of one would be likely to provide valid results. Among the conditions identified were the following: when between-individuals variability for the phenomena under investigation is known to be negligible, making results for a second subject redundant; when one case in depth exemplifies many; when negative results from one case are sufficient to demand revision or rejection of an asserted or assumed universal relationship; when the behavior studied is very unusual and there is limited opportunity to study it; or when the practitioner wants to focus on a problem by defining questions and variables that may lead to more refined approaches.

In his approach to studying the stability of behavior, Epstein (1980) indicated that intrinsically robust phenomena and potent, ego-involving events are among the conditions from which replicable results can be expected without aggregating results over stimulus situations and/or occasions. These are conditions that generally apply to the majority of single-case experiments. Also, as noted by Baer (1977) and Parsonson and Baer (1978), single-subject experiments typically have focused expressly on powerful variables having applied implications for which the effects may be discerned visually without the necessity of statistical analysis. In this context, Kazdin (1978a) further observed that interventions that produce dramatic changes in behavior are likely to generalize more broadly than interventions that meet the relatively weaker criterion of statistical significance based on group averages that characterize between-groups research.

Thus, any of the single-case designs may produce generalizable results, providing that conditions such as those outlined above are met. Even so, however, some single-case designs lend themselves more readily to yielding potentially generalizable results. These include the multiple baseline designs that allow for systematic examination of the extent to which the intervention is effective with different behaviors, persons, or settings.

When a sample of one or just a few is insufficient, researchers in the area of single-case experimentation typically turn to replication. Replication with single-case experiments has the advantage of being flexible, individualized, clinically relevant, and less costly than most conventional between-groups experimentation.

Sidman (1960) identified two types of replication relevant to single-case experimentation. The first is *direct replication* and involves repetition of the given experiment by the same investigator. Sidman further divides direct replication into two subtypes: repetition of the experiment on the same subject (within-subjects replication) and repetition on different subjects (between-subjects replication), the one having most relevance to generalization across subjects.

The second type is *systematic replication*, which involves replication to establish the generality of findings over a wide range of conditions. Following the successful completion of direct replication in at least several experiments, systematic replication is conducted by the successive replication of the experiment in which systematic variation of such conditions as clientele, therapists, or settings occurs.

The basis of generalization through replication of single-case experiments is an important concept. In this view, each successive positive replication increases plausibility multiplicatively, because a chance occurrence of such events becomes much more improbable with each additional replication. Even so, between-groups designs have particular advantages in extending the generalizability of findings, as will be highlighted below.

D&D Flexibility. Designs that most readily facilitate D&D flexibility are those that generally place fewest restraints on intervention. Restraints can take the form of the necessity to repeat an intervention or to administer a different one. Many designs in Table 13.1 place such constraints. However, the B, AB, and ABA designs do not require either repetition of the intervention or a different intervention; and the ABAC, ABACA and crossover designs, although not requiring repetition, do require a different intervention that may or may not be consistent with D&D requirements.

Intervention Compatibility: Design constraints can also interfere with ability to meet the criterion of intervention compa What is most important here is the match between what the design requires and what the service carried out with that intervention necessitates. For instance, the AB design would be better than an ABA design for interventions that can or should not be reversed. The BAB design is compatible with interventions that can be reversed and that should or can be introduced directly without taking a baseline. Actually, every design in Table 13.1 could be compatible with an intervention, under particular service conditions. However, the more the design requires, the more specialized and unusual the matching intervention requirements will need to be. Because they require so little, the B and AB designs are often readily compatible with intervention requirements.

Between-Groups Experimental Designs

Between-groups designs consist of groups of subjects, some of whom are exposed to experimental conditions and others to control or contrast conditions. Selected between-groups experimental designs are summarized in Table 13.2.

Although all of these are potentially relevant in evaluation, some are experimentally more rigorous than others. In general, they progress in order of presentation from the weaker to the more powerful. The first three are particularly weak and are not true experimental designs. The fourth and fifth are stronger quasi-experimental designs that have their uses and strengths although they are not as powerful as the last three, which are true experimental designs. The more powerful designs, of course, more readily meet the criterion of experimental rigor.

As in single-case experimentation, D&D flexibility is facilitated by designs that do not require repetition of the intervention or the necessity to apply a different one. By these standards, designs 1-7 have

TABLE 13.2
Selected Between-Groups Experimental Designs

Design Type	Design Procedure
1. One-time case study X O^a	Measurement (O) following introduction of the experimental condition
2. One-group pretest-posttest O_1 X O_2	Pretest measurement of a dependent variable (O_1) before introduction of the experimental condition followed by introduction of the experimental condition (X) and then posttest measurement of that dependent variable (O_2)

3. Static group comparison
    X O_1
    ———
    O_1
	Posttest measurement (O_1) of a dependent variable following introduction of an experimental condition for one group compared with posttest measurement for another group (O_1) that has not experienced the experimental condition and was not assigned at random

4. Nonequivalent comparison Group
    O_1 X O_2
    ———
    O_1 O_2
	Two different groups chosen without random assignment both receive measurement of the dependent variable at pretest (O_1) and posttest (O_2) but only one group receives exposure to the experimental condition

5. Interrupted time series O_1 O_2 O_3 O_4 X O_5 O_6 O_7 O_8 . . .	A series of repeated measures is taken at pretest (O_1, O_2, O_3, O_4) and at posttest (O_5, O_6, O_7, O_8) with introduction of the experimental condition intervening between

6. Posttest-only control group Design
    R X O_1
    R O_1
	Subjects are assigned at random to one of two groups, one of which receives exposure to the experimental condition and both of which receive posttest measurement (O_1) of the dependent variable

7. Pretest-posttest control group Design
    R O_1 X O_2
    R O_1 O_2
	Subjects are assigned at random to one of two groups, both of which receive pretest-posttest measurement of the dependent variable but only one of which receives exposure to the experimental condition

(Continued)

TABLE 13.2 Continued

Design Type	Design Procedure
8. Group cross-over $R \; O_1 \; X_1 \; O_2 \; X_2 \; O_3$ $R \; O_1 \; X_2 \; O_2 \; X_1 \; O_3$	Following pretest measurement (O), one group is assigned at random to one experimental condition (X_1) and the other group to the other condition (X_2), following which there is a posttest measurement for both groups (O_2); then each group crosses over to experience the other experimental condition, following which there is again a posttest measurement (O_3)

a. Meaning of the symbols is as follows: X = administration of the experimental condition, the independent variable, O = observation or measurement of the dependent variable, R = random assignment to a group, and — = no random assignment to a group.

some D&D flexibility. However, to the extent that the intervention must be standardized in a between-groups design—and this is highly desirable in outcome and field testing—D&D flexibility is reduced.

In regard to generalizability, between-groups designs allow for use of larger numbers of subjects, randomly selected samples, comparison of one or more interventions with separate control conditions, and systematic variation in the design of such variables as different interventions, therapists, and clients. These advantages can facilitate wider generalization than that typically afforded by single-case experimentation. In general, the more rigorous designs in Table 13.2 are also those that can be used to yield the most generalizable results, providing that the designs are structured to include relevant dimensions for generalization.

Intervention compatibility of between-groups designs in principle is the same as that which applies to single-case experiments, except that between-groups experiments have their own distinctive requirements. Depending on the design, these include random assignment of clients and control groups, such as a no-treatment condition. Both of these requirements can be incompatible with the needs of service as subserved by the intervention. By these standards designs 1-5 should generally be more compatible interventionally than the rest. However, to the extent that the interventions are standardized for all clients in a design, there may be some or many clients for whom the intervention would be individualized insufficiently. Standardization can be variable and, for any amount, it may be interventionally compatible to varying degrees. Thus, each intervention also has to be examined to judge the extent to which its evaluation with a given between-groups design is interventionally compatible.

As is the case with single-case experimental designs, every between-groups design has its own profile of advantages and disadvantages in terms of meeting the selection criteria discussed here.

Combining Single-Case and Between-Groups Experimentation

Single-case and between-groups experimentation may be combined. A series of single-case experiments, when aggregated over a number of experiments and cases, can add replication and other dimensions to the design. If enough single-case experiments of the same kind are aggregated, some of the benefits of both types of experimentation can be obtained. Jacobson (1977), for example, employed a series of ABAB single-case experiments with marital partners to examine the effectiveness of a marital problem-solving approach. The results were analyzed for each couple as well as for the aggregate of couples. Single-subject experiments may also be combined with conventional designs by employing a single-case experimental design for the subjects in the group experimental condition with a control condition in which all subjects receive no treatment (e.g., see Herman, de Montes, Domingues, Montes, & Hopkins, 1973).

Other Factors in Design Selection

Single-case experimentation is particularly appropriate when developmental flexibility is required and design and redesign are ongoing. At later stages of D&D and evaluation when interventions have been well established, between-groups designs may be employed for standardized, large-scale administration and appraisal, examination of the comparative effectiveness of approaches, and field testing.

The above presumes ready access to clients and adequate support to conduct the evaluation. However, practicalities may limit options. For example, if there are resources for only a few subjects or if only a few subjects are available, most between-groups designs are simply out of the question. Even if a sufficiently large number of subjects could be obtained but only with great delay and over long periods, options with group designs can be limited.

Still another factor in selecting the type of design is the nature of the evaluation problem. Azrin (1979) employed a variety of between-groups designs to evaluate the effectiveness of innovations he and his colleagues developed. In reflecting back on what entered into the selection, Azrin emphasized the importance of individualizing the research design in terms of the requirements for evaluation at that particular time. For example, if there was no established counterpart for the innovation, a no-treatment control was often employed. In contrast, if the new intervention had an already established competitor, the new intervention would be contrasted with an established treatment.

Sample Size

The size of the sample in single-case experiments depends on how many subjects are needed for the design and how many replications are sufficient to be persuasive. Herson and Bàrlow (1976) recommend at least three replications, but standards have not yet been established in this regard. If the designs are well chosen, the total number of subjects required for a series of single-case experiments need not be large.

Between-groups designs generally call for more subjects than single-subject designs, but what the number should be depends on many factors. If there is an ample supply of subjects and time and money, the size of the sample can be set according to relatively high standards, such as those employed by statisticians. In the practical world of evaluation, however, subjects are generally hard to come by and evaluation is costly. In recognition of such realities, Kraemer (1981) outlined "coping strategies" appropriate for clinical research in psychiatry and psychology. In this connection, she recommended 20 as a minimal sample size, with no fewer than 10 per group in a treatment-control trial. Kraemer based her judgment on what appeared to be acceptable in clinical research, as well as on statistical criteria. She also emphasized the critical importance of randomization.

All of the above is tempered by the focus and stage of evaluation. For example, in evaluation combined with developmental testing, only a few subjects in single-case designs might be needed, but if single-case or between-groups designs were employed for evaluation throughout development, a sizable number of subjects could be required. The number of subjects needed in outcome testing needs to be large enough to evaluate outcomes adequately in all areas involved. Field testing generally calls for relatively large numbers of subjects if between-groups designs embracing relevant varieties of subjects, settings, and practitioners are to be included.

Consideration of the above factors should result in preparation of an *evaluation plan* before conducting the evaluation. The evaluation plan should provide general guidance to the evaluation.

CARRYING OUT EVALUATION

It would be ideal if evaluation could be carried out entirely in accordance with the initial evaluation plan. It should be recognized, however, that the actual conduct of evaluation depends on conditions that cannot be anticipated fully. For example, if development is slow and not uniformly successful and calls for extended D&D, much more evaluation would be required than would otherwise be the case. If the evaluation is not done well, further evaluation would be called for. Thus, evaluation strategies may need to be altered and new plans formulated as the development and evaluation progress.

Gathering, Analyzing, and Appraising Data

It is highly desirable to analyze data early so that the results are known before next steps are charted. This means that analysis of any evaluation data will generally be carried out concurrently with the other activities of D&D. Analysis should focus not only on the effects of the intervention but also, when possible, on the variables that may affect the outcome (Gottman & Markman, 1978). This can help isolate some of the conditions under which the intervention is effective.

Taking Appropriate Action

The results of evaluation result in *evaluation data*. Clearly these may or may not favor the intervention. If the results are not favorable, further D&D is generally the next step. The D&D can often be a modification of the existing intervention to make it more effective, such as strengthening the intervention by intensifying it if it can be so intensified, lengthening it if it was not applied long enough, or augmenting it with strengthening components. Sometimes the clientele can be selected differently or the conditions improved for intervening. If the results are favorable, further evaluation involving replication or moving on to a new focus and stage of evaluation are generally appropriate. If the evaluation phase ends with favorable results, the intervention may then be considered for diffusion to other users and widespread adoption. In general, if the phase of evaluation is completed successfully, it should yield a user-ready innovation.

BEYOND EVALUATION

After the innovation has been evaluated and found to be worthy of use, additional phases of diffusion and adoption follow. Among the activities involved in diffusion are the preparation of dissemination and diffusion media, such as publications, in-service training programs, professional education, and field demonstrations—all of which result in *diffusion media* (see Figure 10.1). The final phase of adoption is entered after the phase of diffusion has been completed. If the implementation by users is widespread, this results in *broad use.*

An innovation may not be utilized if the activities of diffusion and adoption are not carried out. It is one thing to make a new mouse trap and another to have it adopted by potential users. This truth has long been recognized in the world of business and in industrial and scientific R&D. The important of utilization likewise is being emphasized increasingly in the human services (e.g., Rothman [1980] refers to the need for "social marketing"). Any developmental effort should embrace the full sequence of phases consisting of analysis, design, development, evaluation, diffusion, and adoption. These phases, along with their constituent steps and conditions, may be thought of as comprising developmental research and utilization (D,R,&U). The phases of utilization involving diffusion and adoption, although not the focus of attention here, have been included for brief comment because it is essential to view development as part of a larger process of innovation and its utilization. Unlike the methods and processes of D&D, more is known about the utilization of innovations. For further details concerning utilization, the reader is referred elsewhere (see Congdon, 1977; Havelock, 1973; Rogers & Shoemaker, 1971; Rothman, 1980).

SUMMARY

1. As empirical inquiry directed toward determining the effects of the innovation, evaluation in D&D consists of methods that include much of the already established research methodology of behavioral science and evaluation research. Focus here is on the major activities and decision issues relating to evaluation in D&D and on evaluation as an integral part of the entire D&D process.

2. The first step of evaluation is to formulate an evaluation plan that includes establishing evaluation objectives.

3. An important aspect of setting evaluation objectives is determining the areas of evaluation. Principal areas of evaluation are outcome testing (e.g., determination of effectiveness, efficiency, cost, and consumer satisfaction) and field testing, which is directed toward determining whether the innovation can be implemented appropriately under normal operating conditions. Other areas of evaluation include determination of procedural adequacy, an activity usually undertaken in developmental testing prior to embarking on outcome and field testing.

4. Other aspects of the evaluation plan include consideration of an evaluation strategy and determining the innovations to be evaluated, the indicators of success and failure, and what instruments will be employed to measure relevant outcomes.

5. A major aspect of formulating an evaluation plan is determining the research design for evaluation.

6. Among the criteria relevant to the selection of a research design are experimental rigor, generalizability, flexibility for D&D, and intervention compatibility. Each design has its own profile of qualifications for measuring up to standards such as these.

7. Single-case experimental designs have many advantages for evaluation, among them being their flexibility for purposes of D&D and their potential compatibility with intervention requirements without necessarily sacrificing experimental rigor. Such designs are particularly appropriate in the early stages of outcome testing.

8. Between-groups experimental designs have the advantage of facilitating wider generalization than that typically afforded by single-case experiments. Although such designs can be used at any point in the evaluation, they are particularly useful at later stages when the interventions have been established and can be evaluated comparatively and in field testing.

9. As with single-case experimental designs, some between-groups designs meet the selection criteria given above much better than do others. But here, too, each design has its particular profile of advantages and disadvantages for evaluation.

10. In some instances, it is possible to combine single-case with between-groups experimentation, thus capturing some of the benefits of both.

11. Other factors in design selection include the stage of D&D, availability of subjects and funds, and the nature of the evaluation problem.

12. Sample size, another aspect of the evaluation plan, depends on such factors as whether the evaluation is to consist of single-case or between-groups experimentation and the focus and stage of evaluation.

13. The last stage of evaluation consists of carrying out the evaluation.

14. Activities entailed in carrying out evaluation are the gathering, analyzing, and appraising of data and taking appropriate action based on the results of the evaluation, including further D&D.

15. After the innovation has been evaluated and found to be worthy of use, the additional phases of diffusion and adoption are important in determining the extent to which the innovation is utilized.

PART IV

Selected Tools and Techniques

In addition to the methodology of D&D presented in Part III, many tools and techniques have diverse and specialized application in D&D. There are four major types, each of which is represented by a chapter in this part. The first type is information retrieval and review, represented here by literature review and review of current practice as presented in Chapter 14. The second type is the empirical technique to assist in gathering data to address specific empirical questions that come up in the course of D&D. Empirical techniques presented in Chapter 15 are task analysis, the critical incident technique, and needs assessment. The third type is the analytical technique, mainly a logical and conceptual tool that may be used for the definition, explication, and analysis of problems and the synthesis of relevant information. Analytic techniques presented in Chapter 16 are flow charting, latticing, decision tables, and making recording forms. The fourth type consists of those practice techniques to assist practitioner-researchers in gathering and processing data for purposes of assessment and formulating intervention plans. Practice techniques presented in Chapter 17 are neutral interviewing, determining probable controlling conditions, the assessment experiment, and individualized, data-based intervention planning.

Information Retrieval and Review

D&D necessarily draws heavily on the work of others as reported in the literature and as found in current practice. It would be unthinkable to embark on intervention design without being familiar with at least some of the major contributions others have made to the area. Without proper prior review, intervention design can be misguided, inefficient, and repetitious of other work. Among the techniques covered in this chapter are literature review and the review of current practice.

LITERATURE REVIEW

Most readers are familiar with conventional literature review and have carried out such reviews at various points in their careers. The fundamentals of such reviews will not be repeated here. There are, of course, many similarities between a conventional literature review and a literature review conducted for purposes of intervention design. However, there are differences, most of which relate to the objectives, focus, and strategy of the review in D&D. Some of the steps of literature review in D&D are described briefly below.

Defining Search Objectives

Although literature review may be relevant to any of the developmental activities, it bears directly on those that rely most heavily on the contributions of others. There are at least five possible search objectives for literature review in D&D. These are literature review for problem analysis, state-of-the-art review, D&D feasibility, retrieval for design, and monitoring of current developments relating to the area of D&D.

Identifying Knowledge Areas
Relevant to the Objective

Although at first the identification of areas of knowledge relevant to the objective might appear to be easy and obvious, such identification requires some thought. It is helpful to recognize at the outset that the relevant areas of knowledge most likely will span different academic disciplines and/or professional fields and that more than one area of intervention is likely to be relevant.

Particular areas of knowledge are suggested by the search objective. For example, if the objective entails problem analysis, and if the problem area is wife abuse, studies bearing on the extent of wife abuse, the component aspects of the problem, possible causal factors, the effects of the problem, and intervention strengths and shortcomings would be relevant. Although the directions provided by search objectives provide important focus, there must be further specification. For example, knowledge relevant in a state-of-the-art review of interventions relating to the problem of attempting to reach and assist an uncooperative substance abuser through working with a cooperative family member could include substance abuse, behavior change with unmotivated participants, providing assistance and influence through mediators, and spouse and family treatment.

Identifying Data Sources

Ordinarily a large pool of data is potentially relevant to the search task, a reservoir of information stored in many different forms and accessible through numerous sources. There are the problems of the sheer quantity of information and of knowing where to look. Knowledge of relevant sources is thus invaluable in the search. In his work on literature retrieval, Rothman (1980) found it useful to break down the sources of information into four particular forms: computerized data banks, indexes to periodicals, review services, and synthesized works. The presentation that follows on data sources draws on aspects of Rothman's work, with extensions and applications to the task at hand.

Computerized Data Banks

With the advent of computer-assisted information systems, more and more computerized data banks are relevant to the social and behavioral sciences and the fields of human service.[1] These data banks have grown rapidly in recent years and have become a rapid source of information. Although the banks differ greatly in scope, form, and procedures of obtaining the information, they are generally readily accessible, given that the appropriate discriptors and procedures are used. In effect, the researcher-practitioner submits a request in the specified form to an information service for the information he or she desires and shortly thereafter receives computer output containing references, titles, abstracts, or summaries (e.g., Bloom, 1975).

The relative ease of obtaining such information can easily lead the user to believe that all that is required for a competent search is to submit a set of requests to the data bank and to examine the results when they are returned. It turns out that it is not that simple. The systems are often complex, cumbersome, and expensive to use; the information is often simply in reference form, with little more detail; and abstracts, when provided, sometimes give too little information about the findings and methods to be acceptable to the user (Rothman, 1980).

In my experience, the safest way to use such banks is as a source of references to enable the reviewer to decide whether a particular reference merits firsthand examination. Subsequent examination of the direct source, which should be the primary source in literature reviews, will determine the relevance of the contribution. There is no substitute for carefully reviewing the original source firsthand. Until data systems are available that are more user responsive, computerized data banks will probably continue to be more useful as sources of possible leads than as primary data for reviews.

Indexes to Periodicals

Indexes to periodicals generally provide bibliographic and abstracted information in a systematic way for a given field, discipline, or area of therapeutic or academic interest. Such indexes are generally well known and frequently used by students and others engaged in library research.[2] *Psychological Abstracts*, for example, is an invaluable source for reviewers interested in tracing down titles of articles or books in psychological research or therapy. The main value of such indexes, again, is to provide leads to publications that may then be examined firsthand. The indexes can be particularly informative when a careful search of all relevant indexes discloses essentially no entries in the area of interest, suggesting (but not necessarily confirming) that little or no work has been done in that area.

Many of these indexes also include books and monographs, in which case it would also be useful to consult such comprehensive listings as

National Union Catalog of the Library of Congress, which lists all of its own holdings plus those of other libraries.[3]

Review Services

Reviews and summaries of the literature relating to particular problems or fields of study are provided by selected organizations.[4] Most reviews covered by such services tend to be selective, and relevant information may not have been picked up in the review process. Thus, while citations in such reviews may offer useful leads that merit being followed up, the absence of information on a subject may not necessarily indicate that relevant work has not been done.

Synthesized Works

Scholarly works containing the synthesis and consolidation of contributions in specialized fields are often especially valuable sources. Such synthesized works make it possible for the reader to review and evaluate a large number of contributions, and if the work is comprehensive, it can provide a basis for determining whether certain interventions have been developed and, if so, with what success.[5]

Determining Appropriate
Descriptors for the Search

The reviewer needs appropriate descriptors to allow him or her to enter the literature appropriately. This is especially important because the literature is generally large, takes many forms, involves many sources, has considerable overlap, and is not necessarily ordered or catalogued in categories that are those of the potential user. The problem is further compounded by the fact that there is no shared language between and among practitioner-researchers.

Most descriptors used to enter an information pool are those provided by the source. For example, a large list of topics can be found in the Library of Congress Subject Headings that may be employed for purposes of locating relevant books and other publications in the card catalogue of the library. The *Social Sciences Citation Index* (SSCI) provides a Permuterm Subject Index useful for finding subjects that involve a combination of otherwise separate topics. Computerized data banks typically provide the user with a set of entry descriptors, and the indexes of abstracts, such as *Psychological Abstracts*, provide many index categories with subcategories, many of which involve cross classifications of two otherwise separate topic areas. In the face of categories that may be too broad or imprecise for the user's purposes, there is the temptation to search more broadly in order not to overlook relevant contributions. Experience with a given descriptor system and with what it yields is the best way to make accurate and efficient use of the descriptors in locating contributions.

Establishing Boundaries and Screening Criteria for the Search

The reviewer faces a large amount of information contained in many different sources and must strike a balance between the scope of review and feasibility. Although no precise guidelines can be formulated, establishing boundaries and screening criteria can help guide the reviewer in a situation that otherwise could be overwhelming and confusing. The reviewer needs to establish what sources to review, how much to review, and for what period.

The range of sources cannot easily be spelled out in general because the available sources and their appropriateness depend on such factors as the search objective and design problems.

However, in regard to how much information to review, it has been recommended in conventional literature retrieval that the number of sources, descriptors, and time frame for the review be specified in advance. This establishes a defined sample, which then represents the parameters of the retrieval search program (for example, see Rothman, 1980). Such a review directed toward covering a given sample of literature is here called the *sample-oriented review*. The objective is to draw conclusions from a given sample of sources and references embracing a given period. Reviews conducted to monitor current developments can be sample-oriented, as can retrieval for design, particularly projects that emphasize review of given behavioral science or practice literature for purposes of making applications of such knowledge to practice (e.g., see Mullen, 1981; Rothman, 1974).

Another type is the *decision-oriented review*, in which the focus is on obtaining information relevant to making a decision that leads to a given D&D action. For example, in a state-of-the-art review to determine whether a suitable intervention for a problematic condition has already been developed, the reviewer need only review that which is sufficient to decide whether a relevant intervention has been developed and, if so, if it is adequate. It may be that a suitable intervention is turned up right way, which leads to the decision not to pursue the proposed development further. From the point of view of the decision made, it does not matter that the review was incomplete or that other interventions were not suitable. In addition to the state-of-the-art review, search objectives involving problem analysis and developmental feasibility are likely to be decision oriented. Aspects of retrieval for design can be decision oriented also (e.g., adopting something from an allied field).

When selecting knowledge from behavioral and social science for use in practice, criteria for selection have been proposed by several writers (e.g., Fischer, 1978; Gouldner, 1967; Mullen, 1981; Rothman, 1974; Thomas, 1967; Tripodi et al., 1969; Zetterberg, 1965). Among these criteria, as the reader will recall, are those that relate to the extent to which the findings or theory would be practically useful. These criteria include content relevance, content inclusiveness, knowledge validity, knowledge power, and knowledge engineerability—all presented and discussed more fully in Chapter 7. When conducting literature retrieval for design, criteria such as these may be valuable in screening findings and theories in behavioral and social science for potential application.

Establishing Search Procedures

Search should progress systematically in terms of the search objectives and strategy. In most searches, it is best to progress from the most recent, comprehensive, and informative sources to the less recent and important. As applied to a sample-oriented review, this means that the most time-consuming and exacting work generally comes early and, as the review continues, it progresses more rapidly until the sample has been covered. In contrast, a decision-oriented review may disclose information sufficient to make a decision at any point.

Establishing Recording and Data Analysis Procedures

The reviewer needs to keep track of what has been covered and his or her progress through the search. When relevant results are found, they should be described fully, complete bibliographic citations should be obtained along with relevant information bearing on the search objectives and design problems. It is sometimes appropriate also to report on the adequacy of the study.

Data analysis procedures may range from qualitative review of recording made for each reference covered, often sufficient for most D&D purposes, to a meta-analysis that is a systematic, quantitative analysis of results. In the meta-analysis, the reviewed findings are treated as data and empirical conclusions are drawn about the reviewed findings—an approach particularly useful when one wishes to draw relatively precise descriptive conclusions about a given domain of inquiry (for further details, see Fiske, 1983; Glass & Kliegl, 1983; Mintz, 1983; Shapiro & Shapiro, 1983; Strube & Hartmann, 1983; Wilson & Rachman, 1983).

Implementing the Search

The reviewer should follow the search plan while simultaneously pursuing worthwhile leads, reference by reference. Relevant references should be flagged and followed up, progressing again in terms of the most recent and important. In reviews having fixed domains, the review should generally be completed as planned. Failure to complete a sample-oriented review can weaken or invalidate the conclusions.

In a decision-oriented review, as has been indicated, the review continues until enough information has been obtained to reach a decision. If this is early, so much the better. But this does not always happen. By proceeding from the most relevant to the least and from the most recent to the remote, the reviewer soon encounters increasing repetition and lack of new information until eventually it is concluded that what has been learned up to that point—for example, that there are no prior interventions suitable for the problem, and hence further development may proceed—is probably correct.

REVIEW OF CURRENT PRACTICE

The review of practice is typically a small inquiry with limited objectives designed to provide additional information bearing on one or another of the activities of D&D. Such a review can augment information derived from the literature and provide valuable information not otherwise available, particularly when problems are faced in practice that are not yet well understood and intervention efforts have been made to meet the problems that have not yet been reported.

There is a complementary relationship between literature review and the review of current practice that can be illustrated by how these types of review may be partnered in a state-of-the-art review. A state-of-the-art review of interventions in the current literature does not substitute for such a review of contemporary practice, particularly when new developments have emerged in practice that have yet to be reported in the literature. Further, each type of review should be conducted if the researcher-practitioner is not familiar with what is current in each area of review. The relationship between these two types of review is diagrammed in the flow chart given in Figure 14.1.

Defining Search Objectives and Illustrative Areas of Inquiry

The review of current practice may also be relevant to any of the developmental objectives, but, like the literature review, it bears directly on some more than on others. More specifically, the review of current practice may be focused on one of three major objectives:

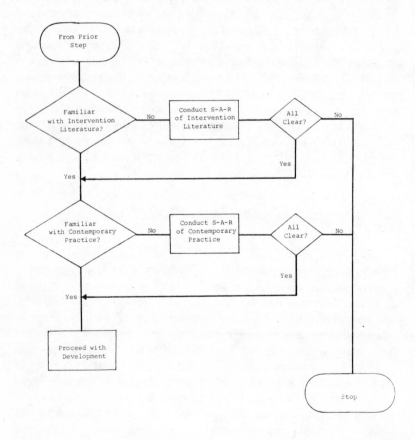

Figure 14.1: Relation between review of literature and of current practice in state-of-the-art review.

problem identification and analysis, state-of-the-art review, or retrieval for design.

Some Factors in Selecting the Sample

Generally exploratory and modest, the review of current practice is a limited empirical inquiry. For example, the practitioner-researcher could isolate the most relevant centers of practice, make contact with these centers, make a site visit to consult with key informants and observe their work, and then return home and draw the needed conclusions concerning the proposed development.

The sample of agencies, programs, or specialized practitioners ordinarily is biased intentionally in favor of what is most likely to be relevant to the search objective. However, the type and size of the sample depends to some extent on the review purpose. Thus, if the objective of the review is to further problem identification and analysis, a sample of practitioners or agency situations likely to indicate particular problems might be appropriate. (Here, a large sample could be sought in special instances.) In contrast, if the search objective were state-of-the-art review or retrieval for design, a sample of competently innovative practitioners in the area of development might be appropriate. Because the goal of the review is generally to obtain informative leads rather than to generalize about a particular sample, the size of the sample of practitioners and agencies ordinarily need not be large, providing that is is carefully selected.

Selection of the Data-Gathering Technique

Among the techniques for gathering data available to the practitioner-researcher are the observation of practice, interviewing key informants, and questionnaires administered to informants. Of these, direct observation has perhaps the most advantages inasmuch as it can provide the most accurate determination of what is going on. However, such observation is not always feasible. The interview is a good alternative, and, in any case, it is a flexible and versatile information-gathering technique. Questionnaires may also serve to generate the needed information. Whatever the type of techniques chosen to gather the data, there are no standardized instruments for the review of practice so the practitioner-researcher will have to construct a tailor-made instrument appropriate for the review.

Recording, Analysis, and
Drawing Conclusions: An Example

The results of the review should be recorded using a form appropriate for the purpose, the results analyzed, and conclusions drawn as they relate to the developmental task. These aspects of the review of practice are illustrated in the example below of a small, supplemental inquiry conducted in the early stages of the unilateral family therapy research to provide further information about the state of the art in this area and about possible intervention methods that might relate to the developmental objective.

The review was directed toward obtaining information concerning relevant approaches and interventions in the area of spouse treatment in situations involving an uncooperative alcohol abuser. The objective of the proposed development was to evolve methods to reach and assist an uncooperative alcohol abuser through working with a cooperative spouse who was not an alcohol abuser.

Ten open-ended interviews were conducted with knowledgeable and experienced alcohol counselors in selected outpatient alcohol abuse facilities located in the Ann Arbor area. A main focus in the interviews was on what was done with the spouse of an uncooperative alcohol abuser. The project was particularly interested in determining the extent to which alcohol counselors were placing emphasis on the rehabilitative role of the spouse as opposed to the more conventional role of assisting the spouse to distance herself from her partner and to realize her own aspirations.

The form used to record the interviews is illustrated in Figure 14.2, along with recorded entries for an interview. It may be seen that five areas of information were obtained and recorded: the philosophy and assumptions of treatment, the role of practitioner, intervention methods, target behaviors, and anticipated consequences—first as applied to the spouse and then for the abuser. Although these data could have been coded and quantified, a qualitative analysis seemed most appropriate.

The results indicated that in general there was little emphasis on the rehabilitative role of the spouse and, instead, focus was more on assisting the spouse to disengage himself or herself from the drinking situation and to encourage the spouse to pursue further self-actualizing activities. Even so, there was general recognition of the importance of family factors in drinking. The strongest aspect of the interventions reviewed appeared to be the alcohol education programs. This highlighted for us the importance of educating spouses and family members

Agency: Community Council on Alcoholism
Interviewer: C. Burnett
Person Interviewed: Harold Smith, Counselor
Date: 5-21-81

Area of Information	Spouse	Abuser
Philosophy and Assumptions	Alcoholism is a family problem with "sick behavior" (game-playing) occurring among family members. Spouse plays role of "enabler." There is no guarantee spouse can change alcoholism, so spouse must concentrate on taking care of self. Spouse has low self-esteem.	Alcoholism is a family problem, with family members playing roles that prolong the agony of the alcohol abuser facing his problem. The alcohol abuser must realize he has a problem and get into treatment to be helped. Alcohol is the primary problem. Stop drinking, attend AA, cooperate in therapy.
Role	Take care of self first. Then if decision is made to try to get abuser into treatment, spouse can follow Johnson method of confronting abuser.	Encouragement to be responsible for own behavior.
Intervention Methods	Refer to Alanon, individual counseling, and family group counseling (includes alcohol abuser). Encourage to get job skills and training, let alcohol abuser suffer consequences of drinking. Discuss roles family members play and give educational literature about alcoholism. Encourage to talk about feelings to break through denial.	Individual counseling. AA strongly encouraged, family group counseling. Exercises used in family group are assertiveness training, family conference exercises, negotiation exercises, instructions to use "I" messages instead of "you" messages.
Target Behaviors	Accepting responsibility for alcoholic in family, making excuses, putting alcoholic to bed, pampering alcoholic, making family decisions, playing martyr role eliciting sympathy from others. Stop blaming, avoid reacting to what alcoholic does. Assume a caring attitude but don't engage in enabling behaviors. Do something for oneself that will make one feel good.	Drinking, develop alternative behaviors to replace drinking that help person to feel good (social club, join athletic club, other activities of interest).
Anticipated Consequences	Improved self-concept, self-realization, distancing.	Ability to maintain sobriety, improved social functioning, and improved family relationships

FIGURE 14.2: Recording form for data gathered in interview on state of the art in current practice in the area of spouse treatment in alcohol abuse.

in the alcohol area. A particularly relevant aspect of contemporary practice was the use by a few practitioners of the Johnson (1973) approach. Although not used in any systematic way in the agencies with the cooperative spouse alone, this approach had sometimes been employed to have entire families and others confront the abuser to get him or her into treatment. Along with other methods, an adaptation of the Johnson approach involving carefully programmed confrontation of the abuser by the cooperative spouse was eventually designed and implemented on the project. Consistent with the results of the literature review conducted earlier and of consultation with various experts in the field, this review of current practice indicated that little had been done to preclude continued effort to develop a unilateral family therapy for alcohol abuse.

OTHER TECHNIQUES OF RETRIEVAL AND REVIEW

One of the fastest ways to become informed in a new area is to consult experts who have the relevant knowledge and experience. Equally valuable is attendance at professional conferences, conventions, and workshops where advances in the area are presented and where one may confer with key informants.

SUMMARY

1. Literature review and review of current practice are essential tools and techniques of D&D.

2. Objectives of a literature review in D&D include search of the literature for purposes of problem analysis, state-of-the-art review, determination of D&D feasibility, retrieval for design, and monitoring of current developments relating to the area of D&D.

3. Knowledge relevant to the search objectives is likely to span different academic disciplines and/or professional fields and to involve more than one area of intervention.

4. Sources of references for the literature review are computerized data banks, indexes to periodicals, review services, and synthesized works.

5. Among the additional activities involved in literature review are determining appropriate descriptors, boundaries, and screening criteria

and procedures for the search, recording, data analysis, and implementation.

6. As a small inquiry with limited objectives designed to provide additional information bearing on one or another of the activities of D&D, the review of current practice is another important source of information.

7. Among the search objectives in a review of current practice are problem identification and analysis, state-of-the-art review, and retrieval for design.

8. The sample in a review of practice need not need be large or representative, providing that key informants are chosen from appropriate agencies and programs in the area of concern.

9. Among the data-gathering techniques in a review of practice are observation of practice, interviewing significant informants, and questionaires administered to selected respondents.

10. As in any empirical inquiry, the findings of the review of practice should be recorded and analyzed and conclusions drawn from them.

11. An example was given of a recording from and the types of data gathered and some of the conclusions that may be drawn in a review of practice.

12. Other techniques of retrieval and review include consultation with experts and attendance at professional meetings.

NOTES

1. Many data banks are referenced in such sources as *Information Sources and How to Use Them*, Human Interactor Research Institute in collaboration with The National Institute of Mental Health, Rockville, Maryland, 1975.

2. Some relevant indexes are the following: *Reader's Guide to Periodical Literature, Social Sciences and Humanities Index, Social Sciences Citation Index, Science Citation Index, Psychological Abstracts, Sociological Abstracts, Bibliography of Medical Review, Cumulative Index to Nursing Literature, Excerpta Medica, Hospital Literature Index, Index Medicus, Child Development Abstracts and Bibliography, Coordinate Index Reference Guide to Community Mental Health, Mental Retardation Abstracts, Poverty and Human Resources Abstracts, Psychopharmacological Abstracts/Quarterly Journals of Studies on Alcohol, Rehabilitation Literature, and Social Work Research & Abstracts.*

3. Also relevant is Ulrich's *Guide to International Periodicals* (New York: R. R. Bowker, 1979).

4. For example, see *Alcohol and Health Notes* (National Institute on Alcohol Abuse and Alcoholism), *Crime and Delinquency Literature* (National Council on Crime and Delinquency), *Digest of Neurology and Psychiatry* (Institute of Living, Hartford),

Evaluation (National Institute of Mental Health), *Innovation Information and Analysis Project News* (George Washington University Policy Studies), *JSA Catalog of Selected Documents in Psychology* (Journal Supplement, Abstracts Service, American Psychological Association), *Project Share, Human Services Bibliography Series* (Washington; DC: U.S. Government Printing Office, 1976), *Schizophrenia Bulletin* (National Institute of Mental Health), *Smoking and Health Bulletin* (Center for Disease Control, HEW), *SSIE Science News Letter* (Smithsonian Science Information Exchange), and *Sources of Information in The Social Sciences* (White, 1973).

5. Examples are the *Handbook of Psychotherapy and Behavior Change: An Empirical Analysis* by Garfield and Bergin (1978); *Handbook of Behavior Modification and Behavior Therapy* by Leitenberg (1976); *Handbook of Clinical Social Work* edited by Rosenblatt and Waldfogel (1983); *Annual Review of Behavioral Theory and Therapy* by Franks and Wilson and published annually since 1973, the *Annual Review of Behavior Modification*; edited by Hersen, Miller, and Eisler and published annually since 1974; and selected sections of the *Annual Review of Sociology* and the *Annual Review of Psychology*.

Some Empirical Techniques

Three empirical techniques and their areas of application in D&D are presented here: task analysis, the critical incident technique, and needs assessment. These are in addition to the empirical methods described earlier, such as measurement and experimentation in evaluation.

TASK ANALYSIS

What It Is

Task analysis is a technique to analyze complex behavioral repertoires to isolate the constituent behavioral components required to accomplish given objectives. Consider the following example I and my associates faced when we began research in the area of marital decision making. It was not at all clear at first what components of decision making should be included in a training program to assist marital partners with difficulties in making decisions. Through trial and error over a period of many months, the research team finally evolved a five-step sequence: (a) agreeing to work on the problem; (b) choosing one part of the problem to work on; (c) listing possible solutions without evaluation, judgment, or commitment; (d) selecting a solution for implementation, a step in which evaluation of feasibility and of consequences was required; and (e) deciding on action (i.e., what is to be done, who will do it, when it will be done, and how). In the ensuing development using these as the decision-making steps, marital partners were trained to move through each step, one at a time, with the behaviors required for that step produced in the coaching process. The coaching with these decision-making steps made it possible in the training given to marital partners having disordered decision making to progress sequentially toward satisfactory, joint decisions (e.g., see Thomas, 1977a; Thomas, O'Flaherty, & Borkin, 1976).

As applied in D&D, there are several distinguishing characteristics of task analysis. First, the tasks to which the technique are applied are generally complex and/or difficult to perform, so that if they were not broken down into simpler, more elementary components, intervention would be difficult or impossible. Second, the elements taken together should comprise the entire task of which they are components. Third, the behavioral elements that are isolated, if they are client behaviors, should lend themselves to being targets of intervention or to facilitating greater understanding of the intervention process; and, if practitioner behaviors, they should be subject to training and change. Fourth, the behavioral components should be within the ability of the clients, or others who are to perform them. Fifth, when some components are prerequisite to others in a performance order, prerequisite relationships should be identified and preserved.

Uses of Task Analysis

Task analysis in D&D has many uses. For example, it can be employed to specify (a) the elements of competent and incompetent performance of clients, practitioners, or others; (b) the behavioral objectives of intervention; and (c) the tasks for which clients or practitioners may be trained. When appropriate elements of the task have been isolated, task analysis can facilitate pinpointed intervention, standardization of intervention, replication for purposes of practice and research, as well as documentation and codification of the behaviors involved. Through isolating the components of a task, task analysis can also facilitate study of the underlying psychological processes and organization of skills and knowledge.

Rational Task Analysis

It is useful to distinguish two types of task analysis. In *rational* analysis, no new data are systematically gathered, and the analysis is based on relevant experience of the analyst, logic, and a priori and hypothetical considerations. An example is provided by the research of Page, Iwata, and Neef (1976) in which basic pedestrian skills were taught to five retarded male students. Before carrying out training, the researchers identified five specific traffic skills in a rational task analysis. These were intersection recognition, pedestrian light skills, traffic light skills, and skills for two different stop sign conditions. A flow chart of the task analysis of the street-crossing skills is given in Figure 15.1. For each of the five traffic skills, correct and incorrect response definitions were evolved using a multiple baseline design over subjects and behaviors. It was found that after receiving training on each of the skills, each subject exhibited appropriate pedestrian skills under simulated as well as city traffic conditions.

Although not informed directly by empirical data, rational task analysis can be a valuable tool, particularly in isolating the components of tasks for which logic and judgment are important for the analysis. Indeed, even highly empirical task analyses involve rational considerations (Resnick & Ford, 1978).

Empirical Task Analysis

The second type of task analysis is *empirical*, in which data are gathered systematically to discern the behavioral components and/or the relationship between and among the constituent behavioral elements. An example is found in the research of Horner and Keilitz (1975), in which the investigators developed and evaluated a comprehensive tooth-brushing program to aid in the self-care of retarded individuals. In the task analysis, a sample of videotapes was obtained from three staff members considered "skilled performers" in brushing their teeth and from three retarded individuals selected because of differing tooth-brushing skills as assessed informally by their psychiatric aides. Through repeated observations of the sample videotapes, the behavioral components of tooth brushing were identified and described in detail. This analysis yielded 15 response classifications from "pick up and hold the toothbrush" to "discard the disposables." The specification of detail is illustrated in the following description for "apply the toothpaste to the toothbrush": "The student should pick up the toothbrush by the handle, hold the back part of the bristles against the opening of the toothpaste tube, squeeze the tube, move the tube toward the front bristles as toothpaste flows out on top of the bristles, and lay the toothbrush on the sink with the bristles up" (p. 303).

Using the response classifications from the task analysis in the ensuing training program, eight mentally retarded adolescents, in two groups, individually received acquisition training that included programmed opportunities for independent performances and, as necessary, verbal instruction, modeling, demonstration, or physical assistance. All eight subjects showed clearly improved tooth-brushing behaviors when compared to baseline.

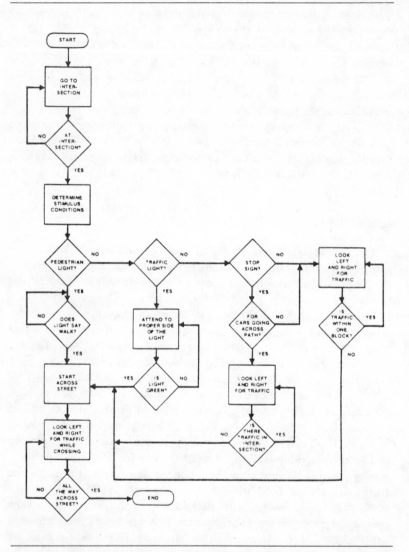

Figure 15.1: Task analysis of street-crossing skills. Diamonds represent decision points in the sequence; rectangles represent responses to be performed. From Page et al. (1976, Fig. 1, p. 436). Reprinted by permission.

Task Sequence

This study employed a fixed sequence of tasks in the training. Instead of displaying improvement following the introduction of training after baseline, it was found that three of the eight subjects performed worse in the early stages of training than they did before. The authors observed:

> This drop was largely due to the fact that during baseline, the subjects performed some steps correctly according to the response classification, but not in the order prescribed in the training program. Such responses were scored as correct during baseline sessions, before training was initiated, but were treated as incorrect responses during training. The drop in performance below baseline levels in the initial training sessions is thus attributable to the "undoing" of sequences of correct responses established during baseline. (p. 308)

Although there was a general advantage across subjects in the use of a predetermined sequence, as indicated, a linear sequence clearly may have some disadvantages for some individuals. For these individuals, alternative sequences, such as branching or nonlinear orders of responding, might be preferable.

Considered more generally, the sequence of behavioral components may be *linear* (a fixed, unvarying order), *branching*, or *nonordered*. The type of sequence chosen depends on the nature and type of prerequisite relationships between and among the constituent behavioral elements. Examples of how component orders may be determined are given in Resnick and Ford (1978). In any compete task analysis, there should be determination of the appropriate sequence for the participants involved.

Task Analysis of Competent Responding

A different approach to task analysis is illustrated in the study by Schwartz and Gottman (1976) in which the purpose was to explore what components are necessary to perform a competent assertive response. In a rational task analysis of the assertive response carried out prior to conducting the research, these authors speculated as follows concerning hypothetical relationships of the components: that knowledge of the content of a good assertive response (component one) would lead to ability to deliver an assertive response in indirect situations (component two) and that this, in turn, would affect physiological responses (component three), cognitive self-statements (component four), and perceived self-tension (component five)—each of the last three of which would affect the ability to deliver an assertive response in direct confrontation in life (component six). In the study, measurable responses were obtained for each of these component aspects of the assertive response for subjects who differed in assertiveness on the Conflict Resolution Inventory developed by McFall and Lillesand (1971). For a sample of 101 subjects, differences on measures of the assertive response between low, moderate, and high assertive subjects were analyzed to determine the nature of the response deficit in nonassertive subjects.

The results revealed a picture quite different from that hypothesized above. For example, there was no relationship between the measures of the knowledge of the content of a good assertive response (component one) or the physiological responses (component three) with degrees of assertive behavior. However, a greater number of negative and fewer positive self-statements (component four) were reported by low compared to moderate and high assertive subjects. The authors recommend this type of task analysis as a way to begin to specify the likely components of a competent response as a basis for testing the extent to which performance on the components discriminates between competent and incompetent populations. If the components discriminate appropriately, then they may become the foci of intervention in an intervention program (see Gottman & Markman, 1978).

THE CRITICAL INCIDENT TECHNIQUE

What It Is

Although the critical incident technique has been around for some time, it has been used primarily in such applied fields as personnel and engineering psychology. Flanagan (1954) defined the critical incident as

> any observable human activity that is sufficiently complete in itself to permit inferences and predictions to be made about the person performing the act. To be critical, an incident must occur in a situation where the purpose or the intent of the act seems fairly clear to the observer and where its consequences are sufficiently definite to leave little doubt concerning its effects. (p. 327)

Among the many areas of application of this technique are the measurement of typical performance, measurement of proficiency, training, selection and classification, job design and organization, operating procedures, equipment design, motivation and leadership, and counseling and psychotherapy (Flanagan, 1954). In connection with equipment design, for example, Fitts and Jones (1947, as cited in Flanagan, 1954) collected and analyzed 270 critical incidents relating to errors in reading and interpreting aircraft instruments. The results led to many specific suggestions regarding modifications in instrument displays. Another type of application is illustrated in the work of Hobbs (1948, as cited in Flanagan, 1954), in which more than 1,000 critical incidents of ethical problems of psychologists were contributed by the members of the American Psychological Association. Believed to represent one of the first attempts to use empirical methods to establish ethical standards, these incidents were analyzed by the Committee on Ethical Standards for Psychology of the American Psychological Association.

An Example

An example of an application of the critical incident technique is found in the methods used in an exploratory study of the adequacy of a case management procedure (Thomas, Bastien, Stuebe, Bronson, & Yaffe, 1982). The practice method examined was the Procedure for the Assessment and Modification of Behavior in Open Settings (PAMBOS), a 15-step, general case management framework to aid the practitioner in open service settings to organize practice activities in a sequential and systematic fashion. (The steps were summarized in another context in Cameo 7.2.) Although previous research employing PAMBOS had indicated that it was effective in guiding case management as well as in producing desired client changes with a variety of cases in an open community agency (Thomas & Carter, 1971; Thomas & Walter, 1973; Thomas, Abrams, & Johnson, 1971), it was not clear how complete and specific the guidelines were.

Data were gathered in the Family Service Agency over a 12-week period for all cases seen by two practitioner-researchers familiar with the procedure.[1] A critical incident was defined as any occasion when the practitioner's behavior during an interview session with a client was not guided by the PAMBOS procedural guidelines because the procedure was not complete or specific. After each interview, the practitioners recorded the incidents as procedural "issues" on specially prepared forms. Twenty-four clients were seen over the 12 weeks, resulting in a total of 104 client contacts.

Twenty-seven critical incidents were collected, yielding a rate of critical incidents per hour of practice of .25, or one every four treatment hours. The rate of critical incidents per case was 1.13 and likewise suggested a relatively low rate of procedural difficulty. In regard to

cases, it was predominantly those implicating child management that
yielded incidents; and in regard to the steps of PAMBOS, most of the
incidents pertained to steps of assessment in contrast to those for
modification, maintenance, or termination. Although in many areas the
procedure appeared to be adequate, the results of the study pointed to
several directions for procedural refinement for this approach to case
management.

Some Areas of Application in D&D

In general, the critical incident technique is particularly suitable for
gathering data that require simple qualitative judgments (Flanagan,
1954), a type of data needed at many points in D&D. One application in
the analysis phase is to isolate problems that may be candidates for
subsequent developmental effort. In the development phase the technique may be used, for example, to determine design problems
encountered in implementation; whether the practitioner and/or the
client can carry out the innovation according to its requirements; the
adequacy of the intervention; and the appropriateness of the innovation
for given practice situations or clients. These types of questions
frequently come up in trial use and developmental testing, a major area
for applying this technique. In evaluation, critical incidents of success
or failure of the innovation may be gathered in preparation for
developing more systematic methods of evaluation.

Procedural Steps

Because this technique is relatively obscure in the panoply of
behavioral science research methods, a few of the methodological
details are highlighted here. At least five procedural steps are involved
in the critical incident technique (Flanagan 1954).

(1) *Formulation of General Aims.* Critical incidents typically relate to
activities, and these, in turn, have what Flanagan referred to as a
general aim. It is necessary to formulate a general aim for the activity to
provide the context for specifying what is successful or effective in
regard to that activity. Most useful statements of aims, as Flanagan
further indicated, seem to center on some simple phrase or catchword
that has a slogan-like character. "Such words as 'appreciation,'
'efficiency,' 'development,' 'production,' and 'service' are likely to be
prominent in statements of general aims" (p. 337). For example, the
general aim of geriatric care in a residential facility might be
"enhancement of physical and mental well-being." When general aims

are not clearly evident, Flanagan recommended that the views of qualified informants be obtained to provide a basis for formulating a more widely acceptable statement of the general aim.

(2) *Formulation of Plans and Specifications.* To facilitate observation of critical incidents by observers, plans and specifications need to be prepared, such as the following: (a) the situations observed, including the place, persons, conditions, and activities involved; (b) the relevance to the general aim, with emphasis on particular activities that may have a significant effect on the general aim; and (c) the extent of effect on the general aim, including positive and negative contributions. "A definition that has been found useful is that an incident is critical if it makes a 'significant' contribution, either positively or negatively, to the general aim of the activity. The definition of 'significant' will depend upon the nature of the activity" (p. 338). Such incidents may often be defined as extreme behavior, either outstandingly effective or ineffective with respect to attaining the general aims of the activity. Another plan may specify (d) the persons to make the observations, including the selection and training of observers who are to make and report the judgments outlined in the step above.

(3) *Collection of the Data.* Data should be gathered, recorded, and processed while the facts are still fresh in the mind of the observer. Ideally, recording of the event should occur as soon after the actual occurrence of the events as possible, assuming that such recording does not interfere with the observation or the activities in question. As in all observation, attention needs to be given to the representativeness of the observations and their reliability and validity. The observations may be obtained through individual or group interviews conducted by trained personnel or through questionnaires or recording forms for respondents.

In regard to sample size, there does not appear to be a simple solution. If only a few negative incidents are required to make a decision, then the sample need not necessarily be large. Only one critical incident, after all, could occasion the redesign of an innovation. However, a different problem is posed if one needs a detailed description. For instance, Flanagan (1954) indicated that 2,000 to 4,000 critical incidents were required to establish a comprehensive statement of requirements for supervisory jobs. For objectives in D&D that call for extensive description, the size of the sample of critical incidents would also be relatively large, depending on how representative the sample needed to be and the extent to which representativeness could be achieved through drawing small, carefully chosen samples. Whatever the size, a useful rule of thumb for determining whether additional incidents are needed is to keep a running count of the number of new critical behaviors added to the classification system with each additional incident. One may conclude that adequate coverage has been achieved when the addition to the sample of a given number of critical incidents—say 10, 50, or 100—adds only a few or no more critical behaviors.

(4) *Analyzing the Data.* Data gathered by the critical incident technique typically yield a large variety of incidents for which some order and categorization are needed. In the formulation of categories, the incidents are reviewed in light of the analysis objective to form categories by induction that might be useful. The usual procedure is to sort incidents into a relatively small number of categories, using a small sample to start with as a basis for determining the categories. A more searching alternative is to employ a "free sorting" method, in which a reader reads one of the incidents (all incidents are first transferred to separate cards or slips of paper), writes a label for the type of incident, and places the incident under the label. Each label serves as a separate category. Then the next incident is read and, if similar in content to the previous incident, is placed under the same label; if dissimilar, a new label is created and the incident placed in that category. Labels are subject to change when a new critical incident adds another dimension to the concept that is being developed for a given category. This procedure is repeated until all of the critical incidents are read and placed into 10 categories (e.g., see Gottman & Clasen, 1972).

(5) *Interpreting and Reporting.* The results of the inquiry are interpreted and reported in light of the objectives of the inquiry and strengths and limitations of the study.

NEEDS ASSESSMENT

As conventionally employed, needs assessment is a methodology for determining empirically the needs for service. A needs assessment might be used, for example, to answer such questions as what the main needs of a community were, the types and degree of child abuse, the characteristics and number of elderly who have trouble caring for themselves, or the characteristics and number of mentally ill individuals residing in the community for whom service would be needed. Although developed for use in service planning and program management and development (e.g., see Neuber, Atkins, Jacobson, & Reuterman, 1980), needs assessment may be applied to aspects of problem identification and analysis in D&D. For example, it may be used to identify particular problematic human conditions for which development might be desirable; the extent of the difficulties, such as their prevalence and incidence; the component aspects of the problem; possible causative factors; the effects of the problem, including behavioral, social, and economic correlates; and how the problematic condition is handled, including intervention shortcomings.

As applied to the assessment of human service needs, there are at least three major approaches (Bell, Nguyen, Warheit, & Buhl, 1978), each of which may also have application in D&D. In the service utilization approach, the purpose of the needs assessment is to estimate accurately the needs of the community from a sample (or population) or persons who have received care or treatment. Data may be gathered from a sample of those who have already used the services and the records of human service agencies and other sources. The second is the social indicators approach, in which the needs assessment is based primarily on inferences drawn from descriptive, social, and demographic statistics found in public records and reports. In the third, the social survey approach, information is gathered directly from a sample of relevant informants in a community or other site. Each of these approaches has a relatively well-established methodology based in large part on applicable behavioral and social science research methods, such as demographic analysis and survey research.

Consider, for example, the methodology involved in conducting a social survey. Information is gathered by interview or questionnaire from a sample of relevant informants. Characteristically, there are the following five stages and activities in survey studies (e.g., see Bell et al., 1978): planning (e.g., identifying the potential utility and relevance of information that might be gathered); operational preparation (e.g., selecting data-gathering techniques and sampling procedures); data collection (e.g., contacting and interviewing respondents); data preparation and analysis (e.g., computing and generating new variables and indices and applying data analysis procedures to the data); and presentation of findings (e.g., formulating conclusions and recommendations and preparing a report for a wide audience). The literature on behavioral and social research contains many good texts on this and the other relevant methodologies and, hence, will not be detailed here.

SUMMARY

1. Task analysis, the critical incident technique, and needs assessment are three empirical techniques having specialized application in D&D.

2. Task analysis is a technique to analyze complex behavior repertoires to isolate the constituent behavior components required to accomplish given objectives.

3. Among the uses of task analysis of D&D are to isolate the elements of competent and incompetent performance, the behavioral objectives of intervention or the tasks for which clients or practitioners may be trained.

4. There are two types of task analysis: rational and empirical. The sequence of tasks in either type may be linear, branching, or nonordered.

5. The critical incident technique is a technique for isolating incidents that make a significant positive or negative contribution to the general aim of an activity.

6. Although critical incidents may be gathered at many points in D&D, a major area for applying the technique is in trial use and developmental testing in the development phase.

7. There is a distinctive set of procedural steps to facilitate gathering data with the critical incident technique.

8. Needs assessment is a methodology developed for empirically determining the needs for service, and it has application in several areas of D&D.

9. Approaches to needs assessment include examination of service utilization, social indicators, or data from a social survey—all of which involve well-established research methodology in social science.

NOTE

1. Family Service Agency of Genesee County, Flint, Michigan; Eugene Tulsma, Director, to whom I am indebted for his cooperation in the study.

Some Analytic Techniques

Among the analytic techniques that have diverse and specialized application in D&D are flow charting, latticing, making decision tables, and making recording forms, each of which is presented in this chapter.

FLOW CHARTING

Widely used in such fields as systems engineering and computer programming, flow charting is beginning to be applied in the fields of human service. For example, to assist helping persons in mental health to understand laws pertaining to children and mental health, the Local Government Training Board in the United Kingdom adopted flow charts to explain and communicate the requirements of the complex legislation (Local Government Training Board, 1969). Examples of flow charts given earlier in the book can be found in Figures 12.2, 12.3, 12.4, 14.1, and 15.1.

A flow chart can be defined as a diagrammatic representation of the sequence of activities (or operations) and the logic of the sequence. Flow charts make it possible to express graphically the logic of decision process and are particularly applicable to problems in which a series of alternatives and contingencies must be taken into consideration. The logic of some decision processes is often so complicated that people need a methodology to aid them in making sure that there are no errors and that all conditions are considered. Further, language is often an imprecise and awkward way to communicate. Using the graphics of diagrams, flow charts are an efficient way of expressing complex phenomena in terms of simpler components. Flow charts can be written to communicate at different levels, depending on the background of the audience.

Flow charts can also function as algorithms—that is, as orderly sequences of instructions for solving a problem (Lewis, Horabin, & Gane, 1967). For example, if we take as the problem the question of whether to make a flow chart, a flow chart can be made of some of the relevant decisions, as given in Figure 16.1. This flow chart can be used as a guide to whether or not a flow should be made.

Flow charting is useful in D&D for design problems and approaches to intervention innovation that require analysis, synthesis, and documentation. The procedures required in the use of an innovation generally involve many options, the actions of one or more persons, and conditions under which some alternatives are suitable and not others. Flow charting can be an important aid in establishing procedures for interventions.

Flow Charting Symbols

A flow chart is composed of symbols such as those given in Figure 16.2, representing the following functions:

(1) *Flow direction.* The flow of control or sequence of the procedure, activities, or phenomena being diagrammed is indicated by flow lines. Flow lines ordinarily progress from top to bottom and from left to right. When the direction of flow departs from these directions, arrows are necessary. Arrows are also useful for emphasis and clarity.

(2) *Process.* A rectangular process symbol denotes a process or activity.

(3) *Decision.* The diamond-shaped decision symbol is used to denote a decision that determines which of a number of alternative paths is followed. The question for decision should be posed in such a way that the answer involves two or only a few mutually exclusive alternatives. For example, the decision may be two-way (such as yes or no), three-way (such as low, medium, or high), or a multiple decision (such as the first, second, third, or fourth quartile of a distribution).

(4) *Start-stop.* The terminal symbol denotes the beginning, interruption, or end of a sequence.

(5) *Document.* The document symbol denotes recording or documentation of some result. In some cases, it may also be used to denote the need to refer to documents (see Foster, 1978).

(6) *Modification.* The modification symbol is used to indicate that at this point the options are unknown, complex, or changing (Foster, 1978). In modification, reconsideration, negotiation, or specification of options or further decision are required (Foster, 1978).

(7) *Connection.* The circle symbolizing connection stands for exit to or entry from another part of the chart. Connectors contain identifying numbers.

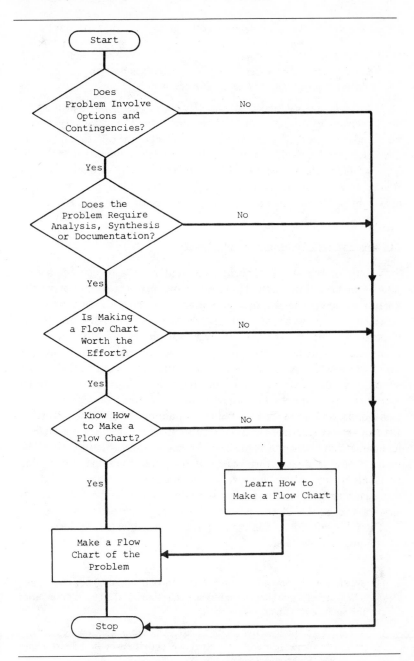

Figure 16.1: Flow chart of whether to make a flow chart.

The symbol for an off-page connector is used to symbolize entry to or exit from a page where it is given to the connector symbol containing the same number. For example, an off-page connector containing number 2 would direct the reader to the connector symbol (on the same or different page) with the same number in it.

The symbols presented in Figure 16.2 are those that appear to be most relevant to problems of D&D at this time. Unfortunately, as yet no standardization of symbols exists, although various organizations have published symbols that have been widely adopted by different groups.[1] Once the reader becomes familiar with the symbols given in Figure 16.2, he or she will be equipped to read and understand flow charts likely to be encountered in the fields of human service.

Suggestions for Making a Flow Chart

To my knowledge, no algorithm currently exists to instruct one in how to make a flow chart. However, if one exists it should assist the analyst in describing the problem prior to or early in the process of representing it diagrammatically. In general, the better the problem is understood, the easier it is to represent it graphically. A useful preliminary is to list everything that comes to mind that entails the problem for which a flow chart is to be made. For example, the analyst should write down such items as objectives, possible outcomes, essential activities, optional activities, and decisions, contingencies, documentation points, and areas of uncertainty and ambiguity. Producing such a list can often trigger a description of the problem, if one is not already evident. It can also serve as the basis for early drafts of parts of the flow chart. These drafts, in turn, can call to mind omissions and needed revisions. If everything goes well, each successive revision provides a more complete and accurate representation as well as further clarification of the nature of the problem being represented.

The following are among the questions to be addressed in the process of making a flow chart.

(1) When does the activity (or problem or set of operations) begin and end? The start and stop points need to be determined to define the boundaries for inclusion and exclusion.

(2) What are the main activities involved? For example, following a review of a list such as the one described above, activities should be sorted into processes, points of documentation, and modification.

(3) What are the main decisions that need to be made?

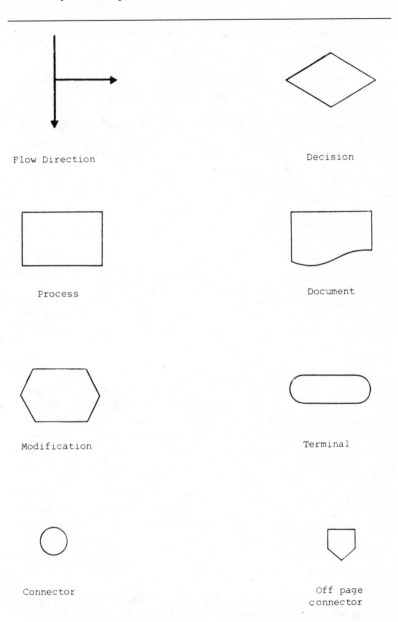

Flow Direction

Decision

Process

Document

Modification

Terminal

Connector

Off page connector

Figure 16.2: Flow-charting symbols.

(4) How does each decision relate to an activity, such as a process? Each decision involves two or more branches that lead to something else that must eventually be represented diagrammatically.

(5) What is the appropriate order for the main activities? All activities, such as processes and decisions, need to be placed in the appropriate temporal and/or logical order.

(6) What is the appropriate level of specificity? If the flow chart is intended to be general, then details may be omitted; but if the flow chart is intended to be detailed, all or almost all of the particulars need to be included. The level of specificity depends on the objectives pursued (e.g., to instruct the uninitiated precisely, to present a general visual reminder, to synthesize diverse components into a meaningful whole.) In Figure 16.1, for instance, details of how to make a flow chart are not included, since this would be inconsistent with the objective of representing the problem of whether to make a flow chart.

(7) Can a rough draft of a flow chart be made? If so, the draft should be prepared because even if it is incomplete and faulty, it can serve, as indicated before, to highlight omissions and areas requiring revision. To make it easier to draw the symbols, templates of the shapes of the symbols can be made or purchased (e.g., IBM sells a flow-charting template). Two or more drafts of a flow chart may have to be made before a satisfactory result is achieved.

(8) Has the "main line" been identified and represented properly? In moving down the sequence of decisions, the main line is generally that which is "desirable," with the desirable moving down the page and less desirable to the right. For example, given the objective of making a flow chart, the main line in Figure 16.1 consists of a series of "Yes" branches moving down the page toward the rectangle for making a flow chart, whereas the "No" branches are diagrammed to the right since they are less desirable, given the objective. It should be noted, however, that "No" answers may also be on the main line, depending on what is deemed to be desirable.

(9) Is there both an entry and an exit flow line for every symbol except the terminals? Ideally, all flow lines should be connected with a symbol or symbols that have flow lines leading to and from them. "Dangling" lines or symbols indicate omissions and leave the reader in limbo. For example, a "Yes" decision branch that is not connected to anything is inconclusive. Likewise, a process that does not have a line leading from it does not indicate to the reader what comes next.

(10) Has anything important been left out? Omitted factors need to be thought through in terms of what implications they have for the diagram, and then changes made accordingly.

(11) Is the problem represented adequately? Given the definition of the problem, is this the diagram that is desired? The diagram must match the definition of the problem, and the definition should be consistent with the analyst's objective.

Because of legitimate differences in the ways in which problems can be represented in flow charts, no one flow chart is necessarily the only way to represent a problem. No two analysts making flow charts would necessarily come up with the same diagrams. Beyond legitimate variations, however, there are correct and incorrect flow charts and differences in representational usefulness. In general, there are two sets of criteria for evaluating flow charts. The first is *technical*, in which emphasis is placed on such questions as whether the lines and symbols are diagrammed consistently with the conventions of flow charting. Some of the technical criteria have been outlined up to this point. Each decision, the reader will recall, must be represented in terms of mutually exclusive alternatives, thus disallowing questions such as "Why should one make flow charts?"

The second is *substantive*, with focus on whether the diagrammatic representation depicts the problem in terms of the objectives of the analysis. Some flow charts are intended to represent real-world events, such as behavioral sequences of intervention activities that are actually carried out. In such instances, an appropriate evaluation criterion would be the accuracy of representation. In almost all instances, the flow chart is also intended to represent the logical structure of alternatives and decisions, in which case the criterion of logical consistency would be critical. If the objective is also to educate the reader, educational value would be relevant. If the objective is to produce a prescribed outcome, such as specific practitioner behavior, the extent to which the behavioral outcomes conform to those prescribed would be important. If the chart is to function as an algorithm to assist the user in solving a problem, an appraisal criterion would be success in problem solution. It should be clear that more than one criterion would generally be applicable in evaluating a flow chart. Although technical criteria are important and cannot be ignored, the substantive adequacy of the flow chart is most important.

Advantages and Disadvantages of Flow Charting

Among the advantages of flow charting over a prose narrative is that reasoning is simplified, complexity and vagueness are reduced to a systematic order of simple questions and simply described processes, there are no redundancies, and the effort required on the part of the reader of the diagram to reach a correct decision is reduced to a minimum (Lewis et al., 1967). Additional advantages are that flow charts provide a shorthand analysis in which the logic of relationships can be expressed quickly and graphically and may be analyzed easily;

solutions may be synthesized by combining detailed elements into a whole; past efforts may be documented; and the diagrams may be used for purposes of communication, instruction, and visual and graphic reinforcement of narrative (Hussain, 1973).

Among the disadvantages of flow charting is that the diagram can become very elaborate, a "bushy mess" if the problem is complex. And flow charts are sometimes difficult to change. There are also occasional difficulties in interpretation when it is not clear that the sequential relationships are essential, desirable, or likely. Flow charts can also be difficult to make, particularly if the problem is intricate and the analyst is inexperienced in making flow charts. Most critical, however, is that flow charting requires that one describe the problem and diagram it at the same time (Katzan, 1979). This is fine if the analyst can do both, and, as has been emphasized, flow charting can be useful as a tool to assist in finding out how best to describe and represent a problem. Even so, however, it is not always easy to diagram what one does not yet understand. Flow charting can often be simplified by adopting techniques to describe the problem, such as decision tables, that may be employed independently from the diagrammatic representation (Katzan, 1979).

LATTICING

Latticing has been defined as "a technique of analyzing a complex abstraction such as a goal, objective, a problem or a procedure . . . into its more specific components. Not only does it result in specific components, but it also shows relationships between these components and the original, more general objectives" (Foster, 1978, p. 6). At various points in D&D, abstractions need to be analyzed to isolate specific components and the interrelationships of the components. For example, the objectives of intervention innovation could implicate such abstract goals as the following: enhancement of marital relationships, improvement of family functioning, betterment of residential care for the retarded, acquisition of social skills, or amelioration of interpersonal anxiety. Considering each of these as an objective, latticing can facilitate analysis of the subobjectives, their interrelationships, as well as the overt processes that relate to each subobjective.

Like the other analytic techniques presented in this chapter, latticing has its own symbols, rules, and format. These make it possible for the practitioner-researcher to analyze objectives into a graphic format so that misunderstanding is reduced and communication enhanced. In the presentation below, the terms of reference and conventions proposed by Foster (1978) are followed.

Nomenclature and Structure

That which is analyzed in latticing is called the *objective*. The aim is to analyze the objective into its less abstract specific components. The objective is divided into *subobjectives* that are component aspects of the objective that subserve achievement of the objective. The subobjectives, in turn, are broken down further into *processes*, which are specific, overt components. There are two characteristics of processes. One is that they should be directly observable and subject to measurement. The other is that they are events as distinct from activities. Whereas activities are things that are done and involve the expenditure of time, money, and other resources, events do not require the expenditure of resources but occur at a given point in time. Writing an article is an activity inasmuch as it involves the expenditure of time and other resources, but "article published" is an event that occurs on a given day.

Figure 16.3 depicts a lattice with one objective (given at the coordinates of E13), four subobjectives (given at B2, C5, D7 and, E13), and thirteen processes (A1 to A13). Processes 1 and 2 relate to and specify subobjective 1, subobjective 2 is specified by processes 3-5, subobjective 3 is specified by processes 6 and 7, and subobjective 4 is specified by processes 8-13. Achievement of all subobjectives, in this particular lattice, indicates that the objective has been achieved.

By way of format, note that one subobjective is placed directly under the objective, the next (subobjective 2) is placed one level lower, and the last (subobjective 1) is placed another level lower. The diagonal arrangement of subobjectives is called the *ridge line*. The thirteen processes are all on a horizontal line, an arrangement called the *baseline*. Notice that one process is placed directly beneath the subobjective to which it relates and that the subobjective farthest to the right, in turn, is placed directly beneath the objective. The solid lines with arrowheads that connect all of the elements in the lattice are *build lines*. Processes directly beneath subobjectives are connected by straight lines going up to the subobjectives, whereas the other processes are related to subobjectives by bent lines going from the process to the subobjective to which it relates. The subobjectives, in turn, may be connected by lines as well.

To make it easier to locate different parts of the lattice, the elements are numbered along the baseline from left to right and are lettered from

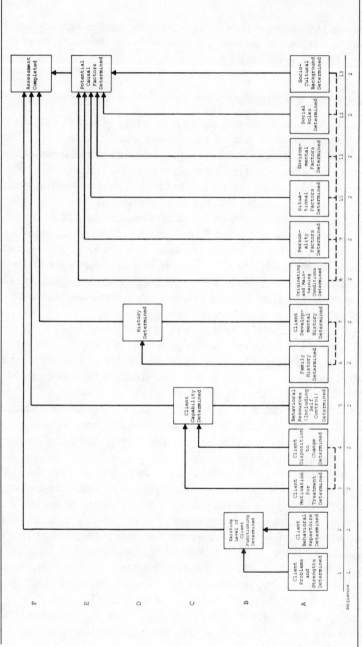

Figure 16.3: Lattice of selected aspects of assessment.

bottom to top on the lefthand side. When used in combination, the numbers and letters are *coordinates* that make it possible to identify the location of every element. These coordinates were used above to indicate the precise location in the lattice of objectives, subobjectives, and processes. This system is very helpful, particularly when the lattice becomes large, say 18 rows and 90 columns.

Relationship lines are dotted lines indicating that there is a strong but indirect relationship between the elements connected. Relationship lines are given in Figure 16.3 between elements A3 and A4, A6 and A7, and A8 through A13.

The reader will notice that there are two sets of numbers below the baseline in the figure. The set above the line is in numerical order and is used to locate coordinates, whereas the set below consists of sequence numbers employed to designate the order in which the elements should occur.

One more characteristic remains to be discussed: the type of build. The build line in Figure 16.3 goes from the subobjectives directly to the objective, bypassing other subobjectives above it on the ridge line. This is a *nonsequential build*. In a *sequential build*, the build line goes from subobjective 1 to subobjective 2 and from each other subobjective to the next.

Two Types of Lattice

Although all lattices have the same structural components and format, a distinction may be made between two types. In the *content lattice*, an abstraction is broken down into its content components, whereas in the *implementation lattice*, an abstraction is specified in terms of the procedures by which the objective may be implemented. Although it is not necessary to make both types, it is often helpful to do both. As Foster (1978) indicated, "first the content lattice shows you what you are really trying to do and then the implementation lattice delineates the procedure by which it can be done" (p. 14).

Figure 16.3 is a content lattice that depicts substantive areas in which information may be obtained in assessment. An implementation lattice, in contrast, would place emphasis on how such information might be obtained. For example, if one were to make an implementation lattice for selected ways to carry out assessment for the content areas given in Figure 16.3, the first four processes for the first subobjective of "assessment data gathered" might be "client interviewed," "nonclients interviewed," "other data obtained from clients," and "other data obtained from nonclients."

The reader will note that the lattice entries have been given in the past tense in such a way that a subject and a verb are included. Examples are "history determined," "potential causal factors determined," "assessment data gathered," and "client interviewed." Foster (1978) suggested that as an aid to developing a content lattice, one analyzes the subject word or phrase (the object of analysis) into its components. In the case of the content lattice, one would then ask, "What do I mean by the words for the subject?" In contrast, for an implementation lattice, one analyzes the verb into its components. Here one asks, for example, "What do I mean by ____ (the verb)?"

Some Suggestions for Preparing a Lattice

At the outset it should be recognized that any two people working on the same problem may come up with different lattices, both of which are useful and neither of which is right or wrong. Assuming that the lattice is technically correct in its assembly and format, there can only be lattices that differ in usefulness. No doubt there are also many different ways to go about making a satisfactory lattice. What might be a useful suggestion for one individual may be confusing for another. The suggestions given below are offered most tentatively. They entail three major steps: outlining potential elements, preparing a rough lattice, and preparing a finished lattice.

In outlining the potential elements, one begins with the objective, stating this, again, as a word or two for the subject (which is the object of analysis) and a verb (which is given in the past tense). One then generates as many subobjectives relating to this objective as easily come to mind. Subobjectives, in turn, may be divided further into additional subobjectives or processes, as appropriate. All of this should be done with the goal of making a content or an implementation lattice. Realizing that revisions may have to be made and some of the work reorganized, this process is continued until it has yielded enough so that provisional relationships between and among the elements can be noted. It is less important to get the proper format at this point than it is to allow one's mind free rein to come up with ideas about the subobjectives and processes.

The purpose in preparing the rough lattice is to explicate the objective further into its components and to begin to order the subobjectives and processes, doing so provisionally so that subsequent revisions may easily be made. The first thing in preparing a rough lattice is to take the objective and place it in the box in the upper righthand corner of the sheet of paper. Next, the subobjectives are placed along the diagonal ridge line. The first subobjective is placed farthest to the left, if sequence is important. Each subobjective is then divided into more specific elements, proceeding to divide components further as best one can until the elements are overt events, the processes. It is thus that the rough lattice is basically a work sheet. The baseline need not be straight, thereby allowing further elements to be added, and no coordinates exist.

The last step is to prepare the finished lattice by putting the rough lattice in a form consistent with the structure and format discussed earlier. In preparing the finished lattice, one begins with the processes instead of the objective. The processes are counted and then placed along the baseline. The higher-ordered elements are then located, beginning on the left with the subobjective to be placed first and moving from left to right, bottom to top, until the lattice is finished. Each additional subobjective should be higher on the ridge line than those to the left, with the final subobjective being located one row directly beneath the objective. Finally, the coordinates should be placed on the margins along with sequence numbers, if desired.

DECISION TABLES

Decision tables are an alternative to flow charting that is applicable to most problems for which flow charting would also be suitable. However, decision tables are more general because they can be used more widely to represent the logical structure of problems. A decision table represents the logic of a problem in a tabular display that specifies the resultant actions for a given set of possible alternatives. The table is composed of a set of mutually exclusive and collectively exhaustive rules. Each rule specifies a set of conditions and the actions to be taken if those conditions arise.

An Example

Assume for purposes of illustration that the focus of development has been to evolve intervention procedures to improve the bathing behavior of residents of a facility for the mentally impaired. Assume further that three types of intervention have been designed and developed successfully. The first is a bathing behavior training program, the second is a contingency program (such as providing reinforcement) for proper bathing, and the third is a program of suitable cues concerning when and how the bathing should be carried out. Among the questions still to be resolved is the issue of under what conditions the staff should employ each intervention alternative. For example, should all residents be trained in bathing behavior or only some and, if so, under what conditions?

One solution to this problem is presented in the decision table given in Table 16.1. It may be seen that five rules were evolved, three of which relate to the action alternatives described above (one for training, another for contingencies, and the third for cues) plus the additional alternatives of reassessment or not to intervene. Four conditions were found to be relevant, as the table indicates.

Structure of Decision Tables

The logical representation in decision tables follows a basic format and is completed according to specific conventions (see Hussain, 1973). The components and form of rules in a decision table are given in Figure 16.4. In the condition stub in the top half of the figure, condition statements are given in the top rows, whereas in the action stub in the lower half, action statements are given in the bottom rows. The condition and action stubs are separated by double horizontal lines. Further, all statements on the left of the double vertical line are called *stubs*, whereas those on the other side of that line concerning those statements are called *entries*.

TABLE 16.1
Decision Table for Selected Intervention Alternatives

	Rule 1	Rule 2	Rule 3	Rule 4	Else Rule
Desired behavior being emitted?	N	N	N	N	
Desired behavior in repertoire?	N	Y	Y	Y	
Appropriate contingencies applied?	—	N	—	Y	
Appropriate cues presented?	—	Y	N	Y	
Provide training for desired behavior	X	—	—	—	—
Provide for appropriate contingencies	—	X	—	—	—
Provide for application of appropriate cues	—	—	X	—	—
Reassess	—	—	-	X	—
Do not intervene	—	—	—	—	X

In making entries for conditions, entries of "Yes" and "No" are replaced by symbols "Y" and "N." The action entry "Yes" is replaced by "X." An irrelevant condition (that is, one that can be either Y or N) is denoted by a hyphen. A hyphen placed as an action entry indicates that the action in question is not to be executed.

When represented in terms of the particular entries just described, the table is a limited entry table to distinguish it from a table that involves extended entries to represent values of variables that are "extended" into the table. For example, instead of "rain forecast" in a condition stub, it might read "probability of rain" with the given probability values—for example, "<.5" or ">.05"—being entered into the table instead of a Y, N, or –. Aside from differences in entry, however, the logic and format for extended tables and mixed extended and limited entry tables is the same as for limited entry tables.

The rules of a decision table are presented in the columns, each column representing a set of conditions associated with the specific action or set of actions. Thus, Rule 1 in Table 16.1 indicates that if the desired behavior is not being emitted and that behavior is not in the repertoire, training should be provided for the desired behavior. It is thus that rules state an if-then relationship between particular conditions and action alternatives. There could be any number of rules, providing that they are mutually exclusive and collectively exhaustive.

Table 16.1 also may be used to illustrate the "Else Rule." The Else Rule serves to complete a table by ensuring that the remaining possible sets of combinations are included, providing that all of them result in the same action entry. By combining the remaining conditions that involve all other possibilities, the Else Rule simplifies the table and decision making. For example, in Table 16.1, in addition to Rules 1-4, four sets of conditions have been combined into the Else Rule. The four rules combined in the Else Rule are as follows: Y, –, –, –, for the column entries, beginning with the first row of the conditions and reading down the condition rows for that column; and Y, Y, –, –; Y, Y, Y, –; Y, Y, Y, Y, for the remaining columns. These four rules all involve the same action entry of "Do not intervene."

When making a decision table, the format presented in Figure 16.4 should be followed as well as the conventions described here. Although the format and conventions are to be adhered to carefully, the decision table is a relatively flexible instrument inasmuch as existing conditions and actions can be revised and expanded readily by changing the respective entry cells. Expansion of rules can be made by adding columns to the table and expansion of conditions and/or actions can be made by adding rows to the table. If the table gets to be too large, it can be segmented and the segmented tables linked together.

The conditions and actions of decision tables can have many different specifications in D&D. However, as is illustrated in Table 16.1, the conditions of the decision table can be used readily to represent conditions relating to the application of an intervention and the actions of the table can be employed readily to depict the desired actions to be taken. More generally, decision tables may be useful at any point in D&D to help understand and communicate the logical structure of problems, particularly those associated with intervention innovations and procedures for such innovations.

MAKING RECORDING FORMS

At various points in D&D the practitioner-researcher will encounter problems for which recording in some form is desirable. For example, forms are often needed in connection with client assessment, monitoring, determining the effects of the intervention, and evaluation. Forms may also be used to record ongoing problems of design and development for later attention. Because the situations encountered are typically new and unusual, it is rarely the case that an existing

		Rule 1	Rule 2	. . . .	Rule K	Rule:
Condition Stub	Condition 1? ⋮ Condition n?					IF all of these conditions apply
Action Stub	Action 1 ⋮ Action n					THEN all these actions must apply

Figure 16.4: Components and form of rules in a decision table. Adapted from Hussain (1978).

recording form is suitable. Being able to make a recording form when necessary is a very handy skill.

The first step in designing a form is listing the information needed and who should be the recorder of the information (e.g., the client, practitioner-researcher, or outside observer). The information needed is then converted to recording entries that are placed in some format for recording. An example of a tailor-made recording form for monitoring suggestions made to engage in nondrinking activities and their outcomes is presented in Figure 16.5. Space for entries is available at the left for the date, time, and place that the activity was suggested as well as who suggested it, what happened, and the time and place of the occurrence. The recording for this form was intended to be completed by a cooperative spouse being worked with in connection with unilateral family therapy for alcohol abuse. All of the entries are open-ended, thus allowing for possibilities that cannot or need not be specified in advance, as they typically need to be in closed-ended form. If it is not clear otherwise, it is generally good to have entires for the person who produced the recording, the date the recording was made, and the date and time to which the recorded entry applies.

Once the form has been drafted, it is then desirable first to have it evaluated by colleagues and then to have it pilot tested. The form should then be revised as necessary and used again on a trail basis to be sure that revision was sufficient. The final form should then be introduced for the routine collection of data.

OTHER TOOLS OF ANALYSIS

Among other tools of analysis are those that facilitate planning, scheduling, and managing project activities. Two techniques make it possible to synthesize a large number of components into a complex, sequential arrangement. One is network analysis (also called critical path diagrams) and the other is PERT (Program Evaluation and Review Technique). Techniques such as these are particularly appropriate in the management of large and complex developmental efforts.

There are other tools of systems analysis and engineering (e.g., input-output grids, morphological analysis, relevance trees, and operations research) that superficially might also appear to be useful in D&D. At this point, however, these other techniques appear to have limited utility. Among the reasons is that in most fields of engineering, variables and parameters are quantified more readily, inputs and

Area Name: Non Drinking Activities

Monitoring Form #3

Date	Time	Place	What Activity Suggested	Who Suggested	What Happened	Time	Place
11/27	6:00 P.M.	Home	Go to movie with David	I did	Went to movie. We enjoyed it.	7:30 P.M.	Bijou
11/29	5:30 P.M.	Home	Play cards with Taylors (they don't drink and don't like drinking)	I did	Played cards with Taylors; David had fun.	8:30 P.M.	Taylor's house
11/30	4:00 P.M.	Home	Go to church Sunday	I did	Didn't go. David said he'd rather watch T.V.	10:30 A.M.	Home

Figure 16.5: Illustrative tailor-made recording form for spouse recording of nondrinking activities suggested by her and her alcohol-abusing husband.

outputs defined more precisely, and costs calculated more easily than in human service. However, as more experience is gained in intervention design, special uses may also be found for such techniques. Readers interested in other techniques are referred to such sources as Foster (1978), Hussain (1973), and Porter et al. (1980), as well as to basic texts in engineering methods.

SUMMARY

1. Flow charting, latticing, making decision tables, and making recording forms are analytic techniques that have diverse and specialized application in D&D.

2. A flow chart is defined as a diagrammatic representation of the sequence of activities (or operations) and the logic of the sequence.

3. Flow charts can facilitate the logical explication of a problem, communication to diverse audiences, and serve as an orderly sequence of instruction—that is, as a algorithm—for solving a problem.

4. Flow charting is useful in D&D for design problems and approaches to intervention innovation that require analysis, synthesis, and documentation—all of which can aid in the proceduralization of interventions.

5. There are special symbols and rules for making flow charts and steps to aid in constructing the chart.

6. Two sets of criteria are applicable to evaluating flow charts: the technical and the substantive.

7. Latticing is defined as a technique of analyzing a complex abstraction, such as an objective or problem, or a procedure, into its more specific components, and of showing the relationships between these components.

8. Among the areas of application of latticing in D&D is analysis of the objectives of intervention innovation.

9. There are two types of lattice: the content and the implementation lattice.

10. There are also special symbols, rules, and format for preparing a lattice and steps to follow that may help in constructing the lattice.

11. A decision table is a tabular display that specifies the resultant actions for a given set of possible alternatives.

12. Useful in D&D for helping to understand and communicate the logical structure of intervention innovations and their application,

decision tables should be particularly applicable in the phase of design and development and in proceduralizing innovations.

13. There are also specific rules, symbols, and formats that must be followed in making decision tables.

14. Making recording forms is a handy skill for the practitioner-researcher because for many problems encountered in D&D recording on special forms is desirable.

15. Steps that may help in preparing tailor-made recording forms are offered, along with an example.

16. Other tools of analysis (such as those from systems analysis and engineering) in principle should be useful in D&D, and these may be found to have application to selected problems of human service when D&D is more mature.

NOTE

1. For example, see the symbols in the International Organization (ISO) International Standard 1028 — "Information Processing — Flowchart Symbols," and American National Standard, Flowchart Symbols and Their Usage in Information Processing, ANSI X 3.5-1970.

Some Practice Techniques

Although the primary purpose of practice is to give service, interventions evolved in practice for a particular problem may have broader application. Thus, the intervention devised to assist Mr. Jones with his seemingly unusual concern may later be found to be applicable with other individuals who have the same or a similar problem. Ideally, every practitioner-researcher should be equipped to evolve interventions for practice purposes that may have more general relevance. The purpose of developmental practice, described earlier, is precisely to evolve new interventions while also providing client service. Although many practice techniques could be helpful in D&D, four are emphasized here as having particular relevance. These techniques are neutral interviewing, the determination of probable controlling conditions, the assessment experiment, and individualized, data-based intervention. Each of these has in common emphasis on obtaining accurate, individualized information and of avoiding intervention that does not take into consideration the distinctive needs and conditions of clients.

NEUTRAL INTERVIEWING

To obtain accurate and useful information for purposes of planning and intervention, one must first gather and assess information. The interview, of course, is typically a major source of such information. However, if the interviewing is biased for whatever reason, the information thereby obtained may likewise be biased. Although they have been virtually ignored in most fields of practice, there are well-developed methods of asking relatively unbiased questions for purposes of obtaining information that may be used for scientific purposes. Guided in part by the research interview, the technique of neutral interviewing is intended to provide accurate information in those instances where other styles would not be appropriate.[1]

Interviewing Bias

The behavior of the interviewer is clearly a complex influence on the interviewee. Through eyes, face, vocal expression, body position, and words, the interviewer elicits emotional states, cues behavior, and provides feedback that may increase or decrease portions of the informant's verbal and nonverbal response. He or she can introduce unwanted biases and ad hoc and premature interventions all too easily. The interviewer provides a continuous stream of potentially active stimuli for the interviewee, so that the question is not how to make assessment completely neutral but how to reduce unwanted bias and intervention and still guide the interview toward objectives of assessment and intervention.

Examples of questions illustrating unwanted bias and influence are presented in Cameo 17.1, along with ways of asking questions in a less biasing manner. Several types of bias and influence are shown, and each can have adverse consequences. As I observed elsewhere (Thomas, 1973):

> Information may be distorted through influences brought to bear upon the display of the patient's responses. Thus, the negative or problematic aspects of behaviors can be emphasized at the expense of obtaining information about the pro-social features; the flow of information may be interrupted; the patient may be hurried by the interviewer's pace or questions; there may be excessive dwelling on a given topic; there may be questioning of the validity and accuracy of the patient's information; and there may be selective attention to some and not other aspects of what the patient says.

> Labeling of client behavior, whether done subtly or blatantly, may create problems where there were none before, exacerbate existing problems or contribute to the fulfillment of labeling prophecies. A false attribution of cause, in addition simply to being incorrect, may alter greatly the way the patient behaves toward himself. Any false representation of . . . therapy may lead to an incorrect commitment of the client to pursue therapy when a more accurate representation might not have encouraged him to continue. False hopes may clearly produce later disappointment and resentment. The providing of *ad hoc* or premature advice and modification is unwarranted if an assessment has not been completed. In cases not involving crises, assessment ordinarily yields several important classes of information needed in order to formulate rationally a modification plan and to select the appropriate technique of modification. (p. 109)

Reducing Interviewing Bias

Neutral interviewing is one way to reduce bias and unwanted influence. While such interviewing does not guarantee the reduction of unwanted influence, the interviewer's words can be expunged of most if not all distortion. When asked in a neutral way without biasing

---

Cameo 17.1
Examples and Types of Unwanted Bias and Influence

Example 1

Patient: "I enjoy going to parties."

Therapist: "Is that right?"

Commentary: Even if the therapist had not expressed amazement or surprise, his words were literally a question and could, of course, be construed as expressing reservation or objection.

Alternative: "Could you tell me more about what you enjoy about going to parties?"

Example 2

P: "Oral-genital sex makes me very anxious."

T: "What's wrong with oral-genital sex?"

Commentary: This question directly challenges the patient and is very nearly the equivalent of saying that there is nothing wrong with oral-genital sex. To express judgment is totally unnecessary and may inhibit the patient from describing openly what it is about oral-genital sex that makes him anxious. If one objective of assessment is to learn about what makes the patient anxious, then the therapist should seek more information about the cause of the anxiety and should do nothing to inhibit the patient from reporting this information.

Alternative: What is it about oral-genital sex that makes you anxious?

Example 3

Pt: "I had a nervous breakdown two months ago and I was in the hospital for . . . " (therapist interrupts)

Commentary: The interviewer's interruption may suppress the patients' subsequent response.

Example 4

T: "Let me ask you something about your nervousness. What do you think it does for you?"

Commentary: The therapist's question, of course, presumes that the nervousness actually has consequences of a given sort, which need not be the case. It is a loaded question.

Alternative: "Could you tell me more about what you have described as your nervousness?"

Example 5

Pt: "I don't enjoy the company of my children."

T: "You mean to say that you don't get anything at all out of your children?"

Commentary: The therapist's question, which needlessly expresses disbelief in what the patient said, is an inappropriate way to obtain additional information on this subject.

Alternative: "Could you tell me more about that?"

Example 6

T: "In other words, by drinking excessively you get back at your wife. Is that what you're saying?"

Commentary: Assuming that this was not precisely what the patient said, the therapist was making a presumption; it is a very biased question that could lead to a distortion of patient responses.

Alternative: "What do you think are some of the effects of your excessive drinking?"

Example 7

T: "When you hurt yourself, do you have sexual feelings?"

Commentary: Unless the patient had already indicated that sexual feelings might be involved, the question should be asked in a more open-ended way to find out the possible range of reactions concerning what happens when the patient hurts himself.

Alternative: "What happens after you hurt yourself?"

Example 8

T: "Why do you discipline your children so harshly?"

Commentary: This is a variation of the proverbial question, "Do you still beat your wife?"

Alternative: "Under what conditions do you find it necessary to discipline your children firmly?"

Example 9

T: "When was the last time you had to discipline your son? How often do you discipline him? What did he do?"

Commentary: Because the answers to each of these questions would probably be different, it would have been preferable to ask one question at a time, thus increasing the chances of obtaining the desired information.

Adapted from Thomas (1973).

inflection, questions can greatly increase the likelihood of producing undistorted information. The interviewer should not interrupt, hurry, or pace the interviewee too rapidly, and should let the interviewee finish what he or she is saying before going on to the next question. Although questions necessarily direct the respondent toward a group of potential responses, they should not be slanted toward a given response or type of reply, and queries should not be used to express opinions, judgments, and values.

Informants should understand that during assessment, when information is collected and appraised, the practitioner will delay in making recommendations and giving advice until the assessment has been completed. It should further be indicated that at this time, accuracy, specificity, and frankness are what is required. Advice should generally be avoided until assessment has been completed and intervention undertaken.

At the same time, however, it is important to recognize that there are areas in which the interviewer intentionally engages in influence to facilitate treatment objectives, and is thus nonneutral. For example, rather than to leave the interview entirely unstructured, it is generally necessary to guide interview topics in keeping with some plan or procedure of assessment and intervention. In the interviewer's demeanor to clients, he or she should be friendly, civil, and courteous. He or she would generally be biased positively toward the client's disclosure of information, particularly if it is accurate and honestly given. The interviewer also necessarily departs from strict neutrality when establishing a relationship, contracting for a working alliance, reinforcing appropriate client behavior (such as that involved in the production of good data), and handling crises.

Neutral interviewing can be conducted without losing a lively give and take or a pleasant and friendly relationship. As a tool that can add to the accuracy of the information obtained, it can be employed in practice without sacrificing other practice objectives or the ability to respond flexibly to diverse and shifting practice requirements.

DETERMINING PROBABLE
CONTROLLING CONDITIONS

Controlling conditions are those contemporary, environmental, or personal factors that serve to maintain problem behavior or conditions at their existing level. It is important to identify the controlling conditions for problem behavior since this knowledge very much determines the approach taken to intervention. Intervention not guided by such knowledge may miss the mark or leave untouched underlying conditions that continue to operate and that may eventually counteract the effects of the intervention. If interventions are based on careful determination of the controlling conditions, an empirical basis is provided for developing interventions that have application to other cases of that type.

Types of Controlling Conditions

There are at least four types of controlling conditions, as given below:

(1) *Repertoire deficit* occurs when the behavior in question was never acquired and consequently is not part of the repertoire. For example, a mother may never have learned appropriate child management, with the result that she cannot handle the children. When repertoire deficits are found, the focus of intervention should be on removing the deficit through providing training for the deficit behaviors.

(2) *Setting events* occur when states of the organism or environment affect how the individual reacts to stimuli that relate to the problem behavior or other behavior or interest. For instance, anger may be a setting event disposing marital partners to engage in verbal abuse in response to partner communication. Setting events dispose the organism to respond differently to a stimulus than it would otherwise (e.g., see Bijou, & Baer, 1966; Steinman, 1977). In addition to anger, common setting events are fatigue, hunger, anxiety, sickness, sexual deprivation, depression, and effects of medication and drugs. When setting events are discovered that increase the likelihood of problem behavior (or decrease its acceptable counterpart), intervention may then be focused on altering the setting events.

(3) *Stimulus antecedents* by their presence, serve to sustain undesirable responding or, by their absence, prohibit desirable responding. For instance, the erotic responses of the sexual deviant may be elicited by feet-related stimuli. When undesirable responding is found to be occasioned by stimulus antecedents, a focus of intervention would be to alter these antecedents. Likewise, when desirable responding does not occur because proper stimulus antecedents are not present, a focus would be to institute the appropriate antecedent conditions.

(4) *Stimulus consequences* serve to accelerate undesirable responding or to diminish desirable behavior. When functioning as controlling conditions, such consequences may serve to reinforce undesirable responding or not to reinforce or to punish desirable responding. For instance, the child may fail to keep his room tidy because the parents offer no reinforcement for doing so. When stimulus consequences are found to be operating as controlling conditions, a direction for intervention is to alter the consequences so as to reduce undesirable responding, increase desirable responding, or both.

It is not unusual to find that controlling conditions are largely one or another of the above types, thus simplifying the focus in intervention. However, more than one type may be in effect simultaneously, making it necessary to focus the intervention accordingly.

Furthermore, the practitioner-researcher should anticipate that there may be intricate interdependencies between and among individuals in marriages and families as well as in other interpersonal relationships. Each individual in the family, for instance, may be an important part of the behavior-guiding environment of others. It would thus be inappropriate to focus on the controlling conditions for one member's behavior without also identifying how that person's behavior and other conditions may have an effect on others with whom that individual interacts. When determining controlling conditions for more than one person, attention should be given to those conditions indicated in the types above, for each person, one at a time in relationship to all the others in the system. By this means, one may take into account aspects of the complex interdependencies and interrelationships present in interacting systems.

Obtaining Data on Controlling Conditions

In determining probable controlling conditions, it is essential to adopt an empirical approach. Problem or other behaviors may be identical in form but have different controlling conditions; likewise, those that are different in form may have similar or identical controlling conditions. Empirical data are generally essential to isolate the controlling conditions. The relevance of an individualized, empirically based assessment of possible controlling conditions is illustrated by the research on sexual deviation of Abel, Blanchard, Barlow, and Mavissakalian (1978).

Audiotaped descriptions of sexual experiences and measures of penile erection were employed in this research to specify precisely the erotic cues operating for sexual deviates. In the first step, subjects described the erotic experiences they had or would like to have while measurements were simultaneously taken of the degree of erection using a direct measuring device (a circumferential penile transducer). The researchers then listened to the subject's verbal description and observed the resulting changes in penile responses displayed on a polygraph record, thereby disclosing aspects of the subject's description that caused increasing or decreasing erections. Then the researchers questioned the subject about the content that was associated with increasing erection responses. In the second and subsequent trials, a researcher described the verbal cues that previously produced an erection while omitting content that failed to do so, again monitoring erections with the measuring device. Through repeating this process, the researchers were able to add or withdraw descriptive features that had or had not produced recorded erections, eventually obtaining an identification of the particular cues that were erection producing for a particular subject.

One of the subjects studied, for example, was a 22-year-old male who reported a two-year history of sexual arousal to women's open-toed sandals. He had reported that it was the sandals that "turned him on," and that feet without sandals were not erotic. It was not clear from the history whether the subject's sexual arousal was to sandals or to the girl's feet. Specific audiotaped descriptions subsequently were developed to determine whether sandals, feet, or the responsiveness of the girl were responsible for the subject's sexual arousal. In contrast to what patient had said initially, sandals did not appear to produce arousal; rather, it was the female's foot and her responsiveness to his attentions to her feet that were sexually arousing. By means of these data-based procedures, the investigators demonstrated that highly individualized erotic cues could be identified for particular sexual deviations, thereby providing the basis for precise, tailor-made interventions.

Two types of empirical methods may be employed in determining controlling conditions. The first is nonexperimental, the approach employed almost exclusively in most contemporary approaches to assessment. By means of such techniques as the interview, client records, or practitioner observation, information is gathered concerning conditions that appear to be associated naturally with the target behaviors of interest. For example, if the practitioner-researcher were interested in possible controlling conditions for excessive alcohol consumption, he might inquire concerning what factors seemed to increase and decrease drinking. The inquiry might reveal a profile of factors that increased and decreased the drinking with conditions such as hunger, for example, being an increaser and work a decreaser. The other type of method is experimental, discussed more fully below in connection with the assessment experiment.

The Functional Hypothesis

No matter what method is used, the basic form of information in determining possible controlling conditions is associational—that is, possible controlling conditions are found to be associated in time with variations in the problem or other behavior of interest. On the basis of such associations, inferences are drawn concerning possible causal relations. For instance, if marital arguments are found to correlate regularly with the couple's fatigue, one might infer reasonably that the fatigue served as a setting event for the arguments. It is on the basis of such relationships that *functional hypotheses* concerning probable controlling conditions are formulated.

In the functional hypothesis, a possible causal relationship between a controlling condition and a problem or other behavior is proposed. More than one functional hypothesis may be relevant, of course, in the determination of controlling conditions. Once formulated, it is desirable to obtain additional empirical data to help rule out alternative explanations and provide further corroboration or noncorroboration for the functional hypothesis. If the functional hypothesis is based largely on interview data, further information may be obtained, for example, by having the clients keep special records. The data gathered then provide a basis for hypothesis acceptance or rejection. The functional hypothesis, along with the other assessment data, provide the basis for formulating an intervention plan.

Hypothesis formulation in practice is an art that also involves gathering and interpreting data to confirm or disconfirm the hypothesis. Unfortunately, little is known about how to formulate hypotheses systematically in practice. However, one recent study provides some suggestive leads (Elstein, Shulman, & Sprafka, 1978). The purpose of the study was to learn more about clinical reasoning in medical problem solving. Data gathered from physicians who were given selected information about cases with known diagnoses provided the basis for the study's findings. Among the results having implications for hypothesis formulation were that correct hypotheses were often generated early, the hypotheses were limited in number, overinterpretation was the most common interpretive error, competence in diagnosis was case related, and having adequate information and experience were basic to diagnostic competence.

THE ASSESSMENT EXPERIMENT

Most assessment methodology is nonexperimental. That is, there is no intentional manipulation of some variables or conditions to determine their possible effects on others. The problem, however, is that there are limits to what nonexperimental assessment can reveal. Some conditions or variables of interest do not occur naturally or occur so infrequently that their effects cannot readily be assessed on the basis of what has happened before. If the conditions or variables of interest do occur, the relationships found as assessed by nonexperimental methods might be uncertain and make causal inference difficult. Some clients and other informants cannot identify relevant conditions bearing on the problem behavior or do so imprecisely. Difficulties such as these can often be overcome through the use of the assessment experiment, in which selected variables or conditions are manipulated systematically prior to beginning intervention to obtain assessment information that would not otherwise be readily available.

An Example

Aspects of the assessment experiment are illustrated with information drawn from a small experiment conducted with a 19-year-old male patient referred to me because of recurring, obsessive thoughts that his hair was falling out. These thoughts frightened the patient and he felt powerless to control them. He had a full head of hair and a dermatologist had affirmed that, in fact, the patient's hair was not falling out. Other than their evident delusional quality and the alleged high frequency of occurrence, however, little else was known about the recurring thoughts. Although the patient was cooperative and appeared to give valid self-reports, it was clear that an assessment experiment would produce information that would augment what could be obtained by patient self-report alone. Specifically, more information was needed about the descriptive aspects of the behavior, the extent to which the thoughts could interfere with other, ongoing behavior, and the extent to which the thoughts themselves were subject to voluntary control.

In the experiment, the rate and duration of thoughts were obtained under two conditions of reading, as an ongoing behavior with which the thoughts could interfere, and under two conditions of voluntary control.

As a first step, the patient's cooperation in conducting a small experiment was solicited. It was indicated that this was not yet treatment, that the experiment was being conducted to learn more about his thoughts, and that additional details concerning the purpose would be explained afterward. The patient was asked to raise his right index finger every time he had a thought and to lower it when the thought went away. This was practiced until he became accustomed to the procedure. It was then indicated that what the patient was to do in each part of the experiment would be explained at that point and that, once the signal to start had been given, he was to use the finger signal when he had the thoughts and to continue with the activity requested until he was asked to stop. The therapist sat quietly to one side out of the patient's vision, where he timed and observed the events.

In the first condition, the patient was given copies of the *National Geographic* and was asked to select and read silently any article he wanted to; in the second, he was given similar instructions and copies of *Sexual Behavior*, a semipopular magazine. In the conditions relating to voluntary control, he was asked first to try to have the thoughts and, in the next, to try not to have them. These four conditions lasted 12.7, 10.0, 7.0, and 6.0 minutes, respectively. Following the last, inquiry was made about selected aspects of the patient's experience during the experiment. The experiment took about 40 minutes.

Consider first the nonquantitative results. In response to questions asked immediately following the experiment, the patient indicated that he had trouble understanding what he read, that he read slowly, that there was nothing in what he read that seemed to occasion the thoughts, and that all of the thoughts pertained to the image he had of himself looking into a mirror and seeing his hair fall out. The therapist observed during the probe that every time the patient raised his finger he simultaneously looked up into space with a distracted stare. Further inquiry disclosed that he read only a few paragraphs in each condition, read slowly as he typically did, and had thoughts while reading about as often as he did ordinarily.

Analysis of the quantitative results indicated that when reading the *National Geographic*, the rate of thoughts was about one every two minutes and they lasted an average of 54 seconds. Altogether, thoughts occupied approximately 45% of the total time for this condition. The results for the condition involving the reading of *Sexual Behavior* were similar and also indicated that reading this potentially more engaging subject was evidently no less interfered with than was reading the *National Geographic*.

In the condition in which the patient was to try to have the thoughts, he had them for 92% of the time as compared with 6% of the time in the condition in which he tried not to have them. In the latter condition, the patient had a higher rate of very brief thoughts (2.1 per minute), whereas in the former, he had fewer thoughts (1.1 per minute), although, as indicated, they were very long.

It was concluded that the thoughts were incompatible with reading and that the thoughts occurred frequently enough and lasted long enough so that they could probably interfere with most ongoing behavior requiring concentration. The relatively high degree of voluntary control of the thoughts suggested that whatever else might have been operating to occasion the apparently delusional mental activity, the patient had some control over the thoughts. The thoughts thus might be subject to modification through self-control procedures and/ or alteration of consequences designed to reduce the thoughts. By means of this brief and simple experiment, important information was gained that could not be obtained easily through more conventional assessment.

Some Distinguishing Characteristics

Although generally less extensive than other types of experiments, the assessment experiment nonetheless has objectives, a design, a procedure, the collection and analysis of data, and conclusions. Each of these is briefly discussed below.

Objectives

Assessment experiments, as has been indicated, have assessment objectives, and these should be clear and justifiable at the outset. An assessment experiment should never be undertaken casually, but only when important information is needed that cannot be obtained by other means. There are at least four types of objectives. The first is to learn about possible controlling conditions for the target behavior, as was illustrated in the above example.

The second objective is to obtain information about possible behavioral resources that may be employed in intervention. Such resources ordinarily involve alternatives that may be employed in intervention when assessment has been completed. For example, in an assessment experiment carried out to determine the effects of self-monitoring on the rate of a barklike vocal tic in a young male with Gilles de la Tourette's Syndrome, self-monitoring was compared with working alone, the presence of the therapist, and the presence of a stranger. The presence of a stranger produced rates of about six per minute, incidentally confirming a hypothesis formulated earlier that strangers were tic producing for this patient. The self-monitoring, in contrast, produced the lowest rate—less than one per minute. On the basis of these results and other assessment data, self-monitoring was introduced as the intervention with the result that the rate of the tic dropped immediately and dramatically during intervention (Thomas, Abrams, & Johnson, 1971).

Assessment experimentation may also be undertaken to provide more adequate specification of target responses and to determine response levels for alleged response deficits, again when such information cannot be produced readily by nonexperimental methods.

Experimental Design

The experimental design should be suitable for purposes of exploring the questions for which the experiment is undertaken. Although in principle virtually any experimental design might be appropriate, single-case experimental designs are generally more suitable than between-groups designs because of their flexibility and ease of application. The full range of single-case designs should be potentially applicable (e.g., see Table 13.1).

Procedure

The procedure in an assessment experiment should follow the model of experimental method in regard to making procedural activities explicit, replicable, and objective. Further, participants must understand that the purpose is not treatment but to obtain additional information prior to embarking on intervention. The activity can be explained as a small experiment in which the practitioner would like the client to try to undertake what has been requested. However, it must be clear that no matter what happens, if the client tries to comply and accurate data are obtained, the results will be useful. If the participant tries to undertake what has been requested, he or she should not be made to feel that he or she has failed if the requested behavior cannot be produced for some reason.

Analysis

Analysis is similar to its counterpart in experimental research, except that the amount of data and complexity of the analysis may be less in the assessment experiment. The data generally need to be processed and analyzed quickly, sometimes immediately after obtaining them and before moving on.

Conclusions

As compared with conclusions that may be drawn from other experiments, those obtained from an assessment experiment are often modest inasmuch as the experiment was itself modest; in any case, the conclusions cannot be generalized safely beyond the particular individual or individuals involved. In all cases, the findings need to be evaluated in the context of the other assessment data.

When designed appropriately and carefully, an assessment experiment can yield valuable information no matter how it turns out.

INDIVIDUALIZED, DATA-BASED
INTERVENTION PLANNING

Data-based intervention planning presupposes an empirically based assessment in which careful attention is given to operational specification of the behaviors or conditions in question, to baselining (where appropriate), and to the empirical determination of probable controlling conditions and behavioral and environmental resources. An individualized data base serves to increase the likelihood of achieving a good fit between the capabilities and condition of the client (or clients) and the intervention. Such individualized intervention can increase the chances of success and is invaluable when working in new or difficult problem areas.

Among the questions the practitioner-researcher needs to address in this type of intervention planning are the following:

(1) Is the intervention to be applied to the relevant target behavior?
(2) Is the intervention to be applied to the relevant target person (or persons)?
(3) Does the client have the response capability to engage in the behaviors required in the intervention?
(4) Are the behavioral assumptions made for the client or others involved in intervention supported by data pertaining to the client situation?
(5) Are there conditions or persons that might impede the success of the intervention?
(6) If carried out, would the actions involved in the intervention be likely to have adverse side effects for the client or others?
(7) Is the intended intervention sufficiently potent to achieve the intended outcome, yet not overly strong?
(8) If there are mediators involved, do they have the willingness and capability to engage in the requisite mediating behaviors?
(9) Is the proposed intervention ethically suitable?

When appropriate, individualized interventions have been identified, they provide a firm foundation for extending the contributions to cases having similar or related problems.

SUMMARY

1. Among the practice techniques that have application in D&D are neutral interviewing, the determination of probable controlling conditions, the assessment experiment, and individualized, data-based intervention planning.

2. To reduce bias and unwanted influence, neutral interviewing involves asking questions in an unbiased fashion to attempt to obtain accurate information from the client or others.

3. Controlling conditions are those contemporary, environmental, or personal factors that serve to maintain problem behavior or conditions at their existing level.

4. There are four different types of controlling conditions: repertoire deficit, setting events, stimulus antecedents, and stimulus consequences. These may operate singly or in combination for individuals taken separately or for individuals in interaction with others in family or other systems.

5. Individualized, empirically based assessment is recommended as the way to obtain the information essential to isolate controlling conditions.

6. The functional hypothesis expresses a possible causal relationship between a controlling condition and a problem or other behavior.

7. In the process of formulating and testing functional hypotheses, fresh empirical data are gathered that serve as the basis for the corroboration or noncorroboration of the hypotheses.

8. The plan for individualized intervention is based on the functional hypotheses as well as other assessment data.

9. The assessment experiment is an experiment in which selected variables or conditions are manipulated systematically prior to beginning intervention to obtain assessment information that would not otherwise be readily available.

10. Among the objectives of the assessment experiment are to learn about controlling conditions for the target behavior, to obtain information about behavioral resources that may be employed in intervention, to provide specification of target responses, and to determine response levels for alleged response deficits.

11. Like other experiments, the assessment experiment involves a design, procedure, the collection and analysis of the data, and conclusions—all of which are related to the assessment objectives.

12. An empirically based assessment is essential to providing the data needed for individualized intervention planning.

13. Individualized intervention based on empirical methods can increase the chances of success and is invaluable when working in new and difficult problem areas, such as those encountered in D&D.

NOTE

1. For example, empathic interviewing, a style that has intervention components and is generally strongly biased, would be inappropriate for obtaining accurate information

and should be used in limited and special circumstances, such as to try to convey emphatic understanding of selected unfortunate and difficult conditions that the client has experienced.

The Design Specification Chart

To move beyond the statement of the innovation objective, as discussed in Chapter 11, it is desirable to identify provisional design specifications. These specifications provide further direction and focus for subsequent effort by indicating more concretely the component areas for development and some of the special requirements that must be met.

THE CHART

A useful tool for this purpose is the Design Specification Chart (see Figure A.1 for a format for this chart). The purpose of the chart is to facilitate specification of the scope, boundaries, and requisites of the developmental effort. There are four steps in preparing the chart. Step 1 calls for the identification and enumeration of the intervention components involved in the helping strategy.

Step 2 is the determination of intervention components having fixed parameters designed in at the outset. This is done by identifying the fixed stipulations for each intervention component. These stipulations represent important restrictions, boundaries, and limitations in the developmental effort and are given at the beginning of D&D.

Component of Helping Strategy	Stipulated	Open	Special Requirements
Change Objectives			
Targets of Intervention			
Participants			
target persons			
helping persons			
Roles			
helping person roles			
target person roles			
Contexts of Helping			
helping situations			
service settings			
Adjuncts and Props			
Assessment Methods			
Method of Planning Inter-vention			
Intervention Methods			
techniques of intervention			
program format			
Implementation Procedures			
Maintenance Methods			
Termination Procedures			
Monitoring Methods			
Evaluation Methods			
Follow-Up Procedure			
Behavior Theory			
Intervention Theory			

Figure A.1: Design specification chart.

TABLE A.1

Design Specification Chart with Illustrative Entries for a Proposed Unilateral Family Therapy for Alcohol Abuse

Component of Helping Strategy	Stipulated	Open	Special Requirements
Change Objectives	Largely remediational as they involve enhancing spouse coping, strengthening family relationships, and assisting the abuser to stop drinking.	Possible secondary objectives could include education for the spouse and abuser, enhancement for the spouse, and prevention for the children.	
Targets of Intervention	Three areas: individual coping for the spouse, improvement of functioning for the family, and facilitation of sobriety for the abuser.	Other aspects to be developed.	Priority and sequence of target areas must be determined along with what the constituent target behaviors should be for each area.
Participants: Target Persons	Primarily cooperative spouses and their alcohol-abusing partners who refuse treatment.	To be developed: use of other family members as target persons.	How to use spouse as a mediator of change in the family and with the abuser.
Participants: Helping Persons	Alcohol counselors and professional helpers who work with an alcohol-abusing clientele.	To be developed: extent to which special training and experience will be required of counselors and helping persons.	
Roles: Helping Person	Primarily clinician-behavior changer and researcher-evaluator and, secondarily, the roles of consultant-educator and broker-advocate.	To be developed: details of clinician-behavior changer role and other roles that go with it.	Maintaining compatibility of the roles of clinician-behavior changer and researcher-evaluator in keeping with the objectives of intervention and the research.

(Continued)

TABLE A.1 Continued

Component of Helping Strategy	Stipulated	Open	Special Requirements
Roles: Target Person	Primarily changee and subject for spouse and abuser.	To be developed: other aspects of role of target person(s), particularly the role of spouse as mediator.	Development of appropriate human subjects protections for spouse and abuser.
Contexts of Helping: Helping Situations	Primarily office-based intervention with the spouse and spouse-mediated intervention with the abuser in the home and with the abuser's family.	To be developed: other aspects of context.	
Contexts of Helping: Service Settings	Open community agencies serving individuals and families, including agencies specializing in working with alcohol and substance abuse.		
Adjuncts and Props		Primarily to be developed.	

| Assessment Methods | Primary source of assessment data to be the spouse using individualized clinical assessment and research instruments. Areas to include spouse coping for the spouse, family functioning, and alcohol-related behavior for the abuser. | Details of assessment methodology to be developed. | Need to assess the capability of spouse to mediate change in the family; need to develop assessment methods that rely on data supplied only or largely by the spouse, who may or may not provide reliable and accurate data. For present purposes of research and development, need to screen out spouses who themselves are alcohol abusers and spouses and abusers who are mentally unstable or who are prone to engage in domestic violence. |

TABLE A.1 Continued

Component of Helping Strategy	Stipulated	Open	Special Requirements
Intervention Methods	Primarily intervention to be instigative with the spouse.	Techniques and program format to be developed for the three areas of spouse coping, family functioning, and sobriety facilitation for the abuser.	Need to develop methodology to use the spouse as a mediator, including possible training and methods of handling possible domestic violence.
Implementation Procedures	To progress as far as possible toward restabilization of change, focusing mainly on one intervention area at a time, using relatively tight structure and doing so with reliance on the spouse as mediator.	Remaining aspects of implementation to be developed.	Need to assist spouse to handle possible countervailing conditions to the intervention that may arise from his or her position in the family or from reactions of the abuser or other family members.
Maintenance Methods	Program maintenance where possible.	Suitable maintenance methods to be developed.	
Termination Procedures	Intervention to be terminated at six months or earlier if by mutual consent of practitioner-researcher and spouse.	Details and termination to be developed.	
Monitoring Methods	Clinical monitoring to be carried out by interventionist and research monitoring to be carried out by an independent assessor.	Clinical and research assessment methods to be developed.	

Evaluation Methods	Clinical assessment to focus primarily on effectiveness in attaining individualized treatment objectives and research evaluation to focus on a broad-band spectrum of effectiveness for the three areas of individual coping for the spouse, family functioning, and drinking behavior for the abuser. Whereas the method of clinical evaluation will be largely nonexperimental in the early phases of the development, the research evaluation will be carried out with a delayed treatment design in which one spouse in a yoked dyad is assigned at random to receive unilateral treatment first with no treatment for the other spouse in the dyad until the first had finished treatment. Research assessment to be carried out before and during intervention and at follow-up.	Details of and research evaluation to be determined in the development prior to assignment of spouses to experimental conditions and the details of clinical evaluation to be developed, as appropriate, for each case.	Use of spouse as the primary source of data, except when the abuser also agrees to participate in the research assessment.
Follow-Up Procedure	All spouses and abusers to be followed up at six months and one year following termination of intervention.	Procedures of follow-up to be based on research assessment methods used in evaluation.	Again, use of spouse as the primary source of data, except when the abuser agrees to participate in the research assessment.

(Continued)

TABLE A.1 Continued

Component of Helping Strategy	Stipulated	Open	Special Requirements
Behavior Theory	Particularly relevant would be behavior theory and research dealing with the causes and effects of excessive alcohol consumption for abusers, spouses of abusers, and other family members; and material on family functioning, spouse coping and marital stability and discord.	Other relevant areas are to be determined.	
Intervention Theory	Intervention theory applicable to providing differential intervention for improved individual coping of the spouse, improved family functioning, and facilitation of sobriety for the abuser.	Intervention theory to be developed applicable to spouse coping, strengthening family functioning, and increasing sobriety for the abuser, with emphasis on conditions under which the unilateral approach would be appropriate.	Human subjects protections that avert infringement on client rights need to be evolved.

Step 3 entails the determination of intervention components that are open. If a component is open, most, if not all, aspects of the component are subject to specification through subsequent D&D. Open components correspond to the domain of design as discussed in Chapter 11 and relate to the scope of development discussed in Chapter 12. The components open for development may range from the broad to the narrow, as indicated in Figure 11.1.

Step 4 is designation of special requirements that may be applicable for each component. A special requirement is one that needs to be highlighted because it is a particularly important focus for D&D. It is important to recognize, however, that many other requirements necessitating D&D would not necessarily be noted in a Design Specification Chart other than that development is open for that component.

Not all design problems can be identified and specified early on and at once. Although some aspects lend themselves to early specification, others are not capable of further specification until development has progressed further. It is advantageous, however, to try to specify design problems so that further work is made possible.

A CASE IN POINT

A case in point are the design specifications evolved in the early stages of D&D in unilateral family therapy for alcohol abuse. As indicated earlier, the innovation objective was to develop a treatment approach to assist the cooperative spouses of uncooperative alcohol abusers to moderate the drinking of the abuser and, where appropriate, to strengthen family relationships and to assist the spouse to cope more effectively with the distress caused by excessive drinking. The plan was to engage a team of specially trained practitioner-researchers to carry out developmentally oriented intervention with the cooperative spouses of alcohol-abusing partners who refused treatment.

As is presented in Table A.1, illustrative stipulations and special requirements for the components of the helping strategy were specified for the unilateral approach. As may be seen, there was a core of eight fixed parameters—the first eight components listed up to assessment methods—that served to pin down critical factors that needed to be established before beginning the clinical work. This left a broad domain of design within which to work and evolve innovations in developmental practice with the spouses. Although all the remaining open components were important, to provide additional focus in the development these components were ordered in priority as follows: Assessment methods, intervention methods, and intervention theory were designated as having first priority along with monitoring and evaluation methods, which were integral parts of the research; implementation, maintenance, and monitoring were second priority; and the remaining components were third priority. The special requirements highlighted challenges that would have to be met and resolved if innovation in this area were to be successful. Although preliminary and provisional, these specifications provided a basis for progressing to subsequent steps of D&D in this area.

References

Abel, G. G., Blanchard, E. B., Barlow, D. H., & Mavissakalian, M. (1978). Identifying specific erotic cues in sexual deviations by audio tape descriptions. *Journal of Applied Behavior Analysis, 8*, 247-260.

American Psychiatric Association. (1980). *Diagnostic and statistical manual of mental disorders* (3rd ed.). Washington, DC: American Psychiatric Association.

Angle, H. B., Ray, L. R., Hay, W. M. & Ellinwood, E. H. (1977). Computer assisted behavioral assessment. In J. Cone & R. P. Hawkins (Eds.), *Behavioral assessment: New directions in clinical psychology.* New York: Brunner/Mazel.

Antler, S. (1978). Child abuse: An emerging priority. *Social Work, 23*, 58-62.

Argyris, C. (1970). *Intervention theory and method.* Reading, MA: Addison-Wesley.

Association for the Advancement of Behavior Therapy. (1977). Ethical issues for human service. *Behavior Therapy, 8*, 763-764.

Azrin, N. H. (1977). A strategy for applied research: Learning based but outcome oriented. *American Psychologist, 32*, 140-149.

Azrin, N. H. (1979). The present state and future trends of behavior therapy. In P. J. Sjoden, S. Bates, & W. S. Dockens (Eds.), *Trends in behavior therapy.* New York: Academic Press.

Baer, D. M. (1977). Perhaps it would be better not to know everything. *Journal of Applied Behavioral Analysis, 10*, 167-172.

Baer, D. M. (1982). The role of current pragmatics in the future analysis of generalization technology. In R. B. Stuart (Ed.), *Adherence, compliance and generalization in behavioral medicine.* New York: Brunner/Mazel.

Baer, D. M., Wolf, M. M., & Risley, T. R. (1968). Some current dimensions of applied behavior analysis. *Journal of Applied Behaviors Analysis, 1*, 91-97.

Bandura, A. (1969). *Principles of behavior modification.* New York: Holt, Rinehart & Winston.

Barlow, D. H. (Ed.), (1981a). *Behavioral assessment of adult disorders.* New York: Guilford Press.

Barlow, D. H. (1981b). On the relation of clinical research to clinical practice: Current issues, new directions. *Journal of Consulting and Clinical Psychology, 49*, 147-156.

Barlow, D. H., Hayes, S. C., & Nelson, R. O. (1984). *The scientist practitioner: Research and accountability in clinical and education settings.* New York: Pergamon.

Bastien, J. S. (1979). *Technological transfer: A process for the generation of social technology.* Unpublished manuscript, University of Michigan School of Social Work.

Begelman, D. A. (1975). Ethical and legal issues of behavior modification. In M. Hersen, R. M. Eisler & P. M. Miller (Eds.), *Progress in behavior modification* (Vol. 1). New York: Academic Press.

Bell, R. A., Njuyen, T. D., Warheit, G. J., & Buhl, J. M. (1978). In C. Attkisson, W. A. Hargreaves, M. J. Horowitz, & J. E. Sorensen (Eds.), *Evaluation of human service programs.* New York: Academic Press.

Benn, C. (1977). *A study of the development of consumer participation in the family centre project: A demonstration antipoverty program of the Brotherhood of St. Laurence.* Master's thesis, University of Melbourne, Melbourne, Australia.

Benn, C. (1981) *Attacking poverty through participation.* Melbourne, Australia: Preston Institute of Technology Press.

Bergin, A. E. (1980). Psychotherapy and religious values. *Journal of Consulting and Clinical Psychology, 48,* 95-106.

Bijou S. W., & Baer, D. M. (1966). Operant methods in child behavior and development. In W. K. Honig (Ed.), *Operant behavior: Areas of research and application.* New York: Appleton-Century-Crofts.

Billingsley, F., White, O. R., & Munson, R. (1980). Procedural reliability: A rationale and an example. *Behavioral Assessment, 2,* 229-241.

Birnbrauer, J. S. (1979). Applied behavioral analysis, service and the acquisition of knowledge. *The Behavior Analyst, 2,* 15-22.

Bloom, M. (1975). *The paradox of helping: Introduction of the philosophy of scientific practice.* New York: John Wiley.

Bloom, M., & Block, S. (1977). Evaluating one's own effectiveness and efficiency. *Social Work, 22,* 130-137.

Bloom, M., Butch, P., & Walker, D. (1979). Evaluation of single interventions. *Journal of Social Service Research, 2,* 301-310.

Bloom, M., & Fischer, J. (1982). *Evaluating practice: Guidelines for the accountable professional.* Englewood Cliffs, NJ: Prentice-Hall.

Borkevec, T. D., Weerts, T. C., & Bernstein, D. A. (1977). Assessment of anxiety. In A. R. Ciminero, K. S. Calhoun, & H. E. Adams (Eds.), *Handbook of behavioral assessment.* New York: John Wiley.

Borkman, T. (1976). Experiential knowledge: A new concept for the analysis of self-help groups. *Social Service Review,* 445-455.

Briar, S. (1973). Effective social work intervention in direct practice: Implications for education. In *Facing the challenge.* New York: Council on Social Work Education.

Bronson, D. (1979). *The "creativity transition" in developmental research.* Unpublished manuscript, University of Michigan School of Social Work.

Brooks, H. (1968). *The government of science.* Cambridge, MA: MIT Press.

Browning, R. M., & Stover, D. O. (1971). *Behavior modification in child treatment: An experimental and clinical approach.* Chicago: Aldine-Atherton.

Butcher, J. N., Koss, M. P. (1978). Research on brief and crisis-oriented therapies. In S. L. Garfield & A. E. Bergin (Eds.), *Handbook of psychotherapy and behavior change: An empirical analysis* (2nd ed.). New York: John Wiley.

Campbell, T. D. (1969). Reforms as experiments. *American Psychologist, 24,* 409-429.

Campbell, D. T., & Fiske, D. W. (1959). A convergent and discriminate validity by the multitrait-multimethod matrix. *Psychological Bulletin, 56,* 81-105.

Campbell, D. T., & Stanley, J. C. (1966). *Experimental and quasi-experimental designs for research.* Chicago: Rand McNally.

Chassan, J. B. (1979). *Research design in clinical psychology and psychiatry* (2nd ed., rev. and enlarged). New York: Irvington.

Ciminero, A. R., Calhoun, K. S., & Adams, H. E. (1977). *Handbook of behavioral assessment.* New York: John Wiley.

Community Research Associates. (1953). *The prevention of dependency in Winona County* New York: Author.

Cone, J. D., & Hawkins, R. P. (1977). *Behavioral assessment: New directions in clinical psychology.* New York: Brunner/Mazel.

Congdon, R. J. (Ed.). (1977). *Introduction to appropriate technology.* Emmaus, PA: Rodale Press.

Cook, T. D., & Campbell, D. T. (Eds.). (1979). *Quasi-Experimentation: Decision and analysis issues for field settings.* Chicago: Rand McNally.

Corey, S. M. (1954). *Action research to improve school services.* New York: Columbia University Press.

Corsini, F. J. (Ed.). (1981). *Handbook of innovative psychotherapies.* New York: John Wiley.

Davidson, P. O., Clark, F. W., & Hamerlynck, L. A. (Eds.). (1974). *Evaluation of behavioral programs in community, residential and school settings.* Champaign, IL: Research Press.

Davison, G. C., & Stuart, R. B. (1975). Behavior therapy and civil liberties. *American Psychologist, 30,* 755-764.

Davis, H., & Salasin, S. (1975). The utilization of evaluation. In E. Struening & M. Guttentag (eds.), *Handbook of evaluation research* (Vol. 1). Beverly Hills, CA: Sage.

deBono, E. (1977). *Lateral thinking: A textbook of creativity.* Middlesex, England: Pelican.

Deitz, S. M. (1978). Current status of applied behavior analysis: Science versus technology. *American Psychologist, 33,* 805-813.

Doctors, S. I. (1969). *The role of federal agencies in technology transfer.* Cambridge, MA: MIT Press.

Dukes, W. F. (1965). N-1 *Psychological Bulletin, 1964,* 74-79.

D'Zurilla, T. J., & Goldfried, M. R. (1971). Problem solving and behavior modification. *Journal of Abnormal Psychology, 78,* 107-126.

Elstein, A. S., Shulman, L. S., & Sprafka, S. A. (1978). *Medical problem solving: An analysis of clinical reasoning.* Cambridge, MA: Harvard University Press.

Epstein, S. (1980). The stability of behavior: II. Implications for psychological research. *American Psychologist, 35,* 790-807.

Eveland J. D., Rogers, E. M., & Klipper, C. M. (1977). *The innovative process in public organizations: Some elements of a preliminary model.* Final Report, NSF Grant RDA75-17952. Ann Arbor: Department of Journalism, University of Michigan.

Epstein, I., & Tripodi, T. (1977). *Research techniques for program planning: Monitoring and evaluation.* New York: Columbia University Press.

Fairweather, G. (1967). *Methods for experimental social innovation.* New York: John Wiley.

Fawcett, S. B., Matthews, R. M., & Fletcher, R. K. (1980). Some promising dimensions for behavioral community technology. *Journal of Applied Behavior Analysis, 13,* 505-518.

Federal Register. (1974, May 30). Protection of human subjects: Policies and procedures. Washington, DC: Department of Health, Education and Welfare. Vol. *39,* 105, Pt. 2.

Fischer, J. (1978). *Effective casework practice: An eclectic approach.* New York: McGraw-Hill.

Fiske, D. W. (1983). The meta-analytic revolution and outcome research. *Journal of Consulting and Clinical Psychology, 51,* 65-71.

Fitts, P. M., & Jones, R. E. (1947). Psychological aspects of instrument display. I: Analysis of 270 "pilot error" experiences in reading and interpreting aircraft instruments. Dayton, OH: U.S. Air Force, Air Materiel Command, Wright-Patterson Base (*Mem. Rep.* TSEAA-694-12A).

Flanagan, J. C. (1954). The critical incident technique. *Psychology Bulletin, 51,* 327-357.

Foster, R. W. (1978). *The use of systems technology in developing education and therapy systems.* Lawrence, KS: Camelot Behavioral Systems.

Franks, C. M., & Wilson, G. T. (Eds.). (1976). *Annual review of behavior therapy: Theory and practice.* New York: Brunner/Mazel.

French, J. R. P. (1953). Experiments in field settings. In L. Festinger & D. Katz (Eds.), *Research methods in the behavioral sciences.* New York: Dryden.

French, W. L., & Bell, C. H. (1973). *Organization development.* Englewood Cliffs, NJ: Prentice-Hall.

Friedman, P. R. (1975). Legal regulation of applied behavioral analysis in mental institutions and prisons. *Arizona Law Review, 17,* 39-104.

Galton, F. (1869). *Hereditary genius: An inquiry into its laws and consequences.* London: Macmillan.

Gambrill, E. D., Thomas, E. J., & Carter, R. G. (1971). Procedure for socio-behavioral practice in open settings. *Social Work, 16,* 51-62.

Garbarino, J. (1980). Meeting the needs of mistreated youths. *Social Work, 25,* 122-128.

Gardiner, W. L. (1970). *Psychology: A story of a search.* Belmont, CA: Brooks/Cole.

Gelfand, D. M., & Hartmann, D. P. (1975). *Child behavior analysis and therapy.* New York: Pergamon.

Glaser, E. M. (1981). Durability of innovations in human service organizations: A case-study analysis. *Knowledge, 3,* 167-185.

Glass, G. D., & Kliegl, R. M. (1983). An apology for research integration in the study of psychotherapy. *Journal of Consulting and Clinical Psychology, 51,* 28-44.

Glass, G. V., Willson, V. L., & Gottman, J. M. (1975). *Design and analysis of time-series experiments.* Boulder: Colorado Associated University Press.

Goode, W. J. (1960). A theory of role strain. *American Sociological Review, 25,* 483-496.

Gottman, J. M., & Clasen, R. E. (1972). *Evaluation in education: A practitioner's guide.* Itasca, IL: F.E. Peacock.

Gottman, J. M., & Markman, H. J. (1978). Experimental designs in psychotherapy research. In S. L. Garfield & A. E. Bergin (Eds.), *Handbook of psychotherapy and behavior change* (2nd ed.). New York: John Wiley.

Gouldner, A. W. (1957). Theoretical requirements of the applied social sciences. *American Sociological Review, 22,* 92-103.

Greenwood, E. (1955). Social science and social work: A theory of their relationship. *Social Service Review, 29,* 20-28.

Grinnell, R. M. (Ed.). (1981). *Social work research and evaluation.* Itasca, IL: F.E. Peacock.

Gruber, W. H., & Marguis, D. G. (1969). *Factors in transfer of technology.* Cambridge, MA: MIT Press.

Hansen, K. E., Johnson, J. H. & Williams, T. A. (1977). Development of an on-line management information system for community mental health centers. *Behavior Research Methods and Instrumentation, 9,* 139-143.

Hartmann, D. P., & Atkinson, C. (1973). Having your cake and eating it too: A note on some apparent contradictions between therapeutic achievements and design requirements in N = 1 studies. *Behavior Therapy, 4,* 589-592.

Havelock, R. G. (1973). *Planning for innovations through dissemination and utilization of knowledge.* Ann Arbor: Institute for Social Research, University of Michigan.

Hayes, S. C. (1978). Theory and technology in behavioral analysis. *Behavior Analyst, 1,* 25-34.

Hayes, S. C. (1981). Single-case experimental design and empirical clinical practice. *Journal of Consulting and Clinical Psychology, 49,* 193-212.

Haynes, S. N. (1978). *Principles of behavioral assessment.* New York: Gardiner Press.

Herman, J. A., de Montes, A. I., Dominques, B., Montes, F., & Hopkins, B. L. (1973). Effects of bonuses for punctuality on the tardiness of industrial workers. *Journal of Applied Behavior Analysis, 6,* 563-570.

Hersen, M., & Barlow, D. H. (1976). *Single-case experimental designs: Strategies for studying behavior change.* New York: Pergamon Press.

Hersen, M., & Bellack, A. S. (1976). *Behavioral assessment: A practical handbook.* New York: Pergamon Press.

Hobbs, N. (1948). The development of a code of ethical standards for psychology. *American Psychologist, 3,* 80-84.

Hodgson, R., & Rackman, S. (1974). Desynchrony in measures of fear. *Behavioral Research and Therapy, 2,* 319-326.

Horner, R. D., & Keilitz, I. (1975). Training mentally retarded adolescents to brush their teeth. *Journal of Applied Behavioral Analysis, 8,* 301-309.

Howe, M. W. (1974). Casework self evaluation: A single-subject approach. *Social Service Review, 48,* 1-24.

Hunt, G. M., & Azrin, N. H. (1973). A community reinforcement approach to alcoholism. *Behaviour Research and Therapy, 11,* 91-104.

Hussain, K. M. (1973). *Development of information systems for education.* Englewood Cliffs, NJ: Prentice-Hall.

Jacobson, N. S. (1977). Problem solving and contingency contracting in the treatment of marital discord. *Journal of Consulting and Clinical Psychology, 45,* 92-100.

Janis, I. L., & Mann, L. (1977). *Decision making: A psychological analysis of conflict, choice and commitment.* New York: Free Press.

Jayaratne, S., & Levy, R. L. (1979). *Empirical clinical practice.* New York: Columbia University Press.

Jayaratne, S., Stuart, R. B., & Tripodi, T. (1974). Methodological issues and problems in evaluating treatment outcomes in the Family and School Consultation Project, 1970-1973. In P. O. Davidson, F. W. Clark, & L. A. Hamerlynch (Eds.), *Evaluation of behavioral programs in community, residential and school settings.* Champaign, IL: Research Press.

Johnson, F. M. (1975). Court decisions and the social services. *Social Work, 20,* 343-347.

Johnson, J. H., & Williams, T. A. (1975). The use of on-line computer technology in a mental health admitting system. *American Psychologist, 30,* 388-391.

Johnson, V. E. (1973). *I'll quit tomorrow.* New York: Harper.

Jones, R. R., Vaught, R. S., & Weinrott, N. (1977). A time-series analysis in operant research. *Journal of Applied Behavior Analysis, 10,* 151-167.

Kane, R. A. (1974). Look to the record. *Social Work, 19,* 412-419.

Katz, D. (1975). Videotape programming for social agencies. *Social Casework, 56,* 44-51.

Katzan, H. (1979). *Introduction to computers and data processing.* New York: D. Van Nostrand.

Kazdin, A. E. (1973). Methodological and assessment considerations in evaluating reinforcement programs in applied settings. *Journal of Applied Behavior Analysis, 6,* 517-532.

Kazdin, A. E. (1976). Statistical analyses for single-case experimental designs. In M. Hersen & D. H. Barlow (Eds.), *Single case experimental designs: Strategies for studying behavior change.* New York: Pergamon Press.

Kazdin, A. E. (1977). *The token economy: A review and evaluation.* New York: Plenum.

Kazdin, A. E. (1978a). Methodological and interpretive problems of single-case experimental designs. *Journal of Consulting and Clinical Psychology, 46,* 629-643.

Kazdin, A. E. (1978b). Evaluating the generality of findings in analogue therapy research. *Journal of Consulting and Clinical Psychology, 46,* 673-686.

Kazdin, A. E. (1980). *Research design in clinical psychology.* New York: Harper & Row.

Kazdin, A. (1982). *Single-case research designs: Methods for clinical and applied research.* New York: Oxford University Press.

Kazdin, A. E., & Kopel, S. A. (1975). On resolving ambiguities of the multiple baseline design: Problems and recommendations. *Behavior Therapy, 6,* 601-609.

Keefe, F. J., Kopel, S. A., & Gordon, S. B. (1978). *A practical guide to behavioral assessment.* New York: Springer.

Kendall, P. C., & Butcher, J. N. (Eds.). (1982). *A handbook of research methods in clinical psychology.* New York: John Wiley.

Kendall, P. C., & Norton-Ford, J. D. (1982). Therapy outcome research methods. In P. C. Kendall & J. N. Butcher (Eds.), *Handbook of research methods in clinical psychology.* New York: John Wiley.

Kiesler, D. J. (1971). Experimental design in psychotherapy research. In A. E. Bergin & S. L. Garfield (Eds.), *Psychotherapy and behavior change.* New York: John Wiley.

Killilea, M. (1976). Mutual help in organizations: Interpretations in the literature. In G. Caplan & M. Killilea (Eds.), *Support systems and mutual help: Multi-disciplinary explorations.* New York: Grune & Stratton.

King, W. R., & Cleland, D. I. (1975). The design of management information systems: An information analysis approach. *Management Science, 22,* 286-297.

Kiresuk, T. J., & Sherman, R. E. (1968). Goal attainment scaling: A general method for evaluating comprehensive mental health programs. *Community Mental Health Journal, 4,* 443-453.

Kraener, H. C. (1981). Coping strategies in psychiatric clinical research. *Journal of Consulting and Clinical Psychology, 49,* 309-319.

Kratochwill, T. R. (1978). Foundations of time-series research. In T. R. Kratochwill (Ed.), *Single subject research: Strategies for evaluating change.* New York: Academic Press.

Kratochwill, T. R., & Piersel, W. C. (1983). Time-series research: Contributions to empirical clinical practice. *Behavioral Assessment, 5,* 165-176.

Lang, P. J. (1968). Fear reduction and fear behavior: Problems in treating a construct. In J. M. Shlien (Ed.), *Research in psychotherapy.* Washington, DC: American Psychological Association.

Leitenberg, H. (1973). The use of single-case methodology in psychotherapy research. *Journal of Abnormal Psychology, 82,* 87-102.

Leitenberg, H. (Ed.). (1976). *Handbook of behavioral modification and behavior theory.* Englewood Cliffs, NJ: Prentice-Hall.

Lewin, K. (1946). Action research in minority problems. *Journal of Social Issues, 2,* 34-46.

Lewis, B. N., Horabin, I. S., & Gane, C. P. (1967). *Flow charts, logical trees and algorithms for rules and regulations.* Her Majesty's Stationery Office: Civil Service College. Occasional Paper No. 2.

Lindsley, O. R. (1964). Geriatric behavioral prosthetics. In R. Kastenbaum (Ed.), *New thoughts on old age.* New York: Springer.

Local Government Training Board. (1969). *Algorithms for the social services: Children and Young Persons Act 1969, sect. 1; Mental Health Act, 1959, sects. 5, 25, 26, 29 & 33.* London, England.

Lohmann, R. A. (1976). Break-even analysis: Tool for budget planning. *Social Work, 21,* 300-307.

Mahoney, M. J. (1978). Experimental methods and outcome evaluation. *Journal of Consulting and Clinical Psychology, 46,* 660-672.

Marks, I. M. (1982). Toward an empirical practice: Behavioral psychotherapy in the 1980s. *Behavioral Therapy, 13,* 63-82.

Martin, R. (1975). *Legal challenges to behavior modification: Trends in schools, corrections and mental health.* Champaign, IL: Research Press.

Martins, W. M., & Holmstrup, E. (1974). Problem oriented recording. *Social Casework, 55,* 554-561.

Mash, E. J., & Terdall, L. G. (Eds.). (1976). *Behavior therapy assessment: Diagnosis, design, and evaluation.* New York: Springer.

McCain, L. J., & McCleary, R. (1979). The statistical analysis of the simple interrupted time-series quasi-experiment. In T. D. Cook & T. C. Campbell (Eds.), *Quasi-experimentation: Design and analysis issues for field settings.* Chicago: Rand McNally.

McFall, R. M. (1977). Analogue methods in behavioral assessment: Issues and prospectus. In J. D. Cone & R. P. Hawkins (Eds.), *Behavioral assessment: New directions in clinical psychology.* New York: Brunner/Mazel.

McFall, R. M., & Lillesand, D. B. (1971). Behavioral rehearsal with modeling and coaching in assertion training. *Journal of Abnormal Psychology, 77,* 313-323.

McReynolds, B. (Ed.). (1975). *Advances in psychological assessment* (Vol. 3). San Francisco, CA: Jossey-Bass.

McShane, C. (1979). Community services for battered women. *Social Work, 24,* 34-39.

Miller, D. C. (1977). *Research design and social measurement* (3rd ed.). New York: David McKay.

Miller, G. A. (1973). Assessment of psychotechnology. In R. K. Schwitzgebel & R. K. Schwitzgebel (Eds.), *Psychotechnology: Electronic control of mind and behavior.* New York: Holt, Rinehart & Winston.

Miller, W. H. (1975). *Systematic parent training: Procedures, cases and issues.* Champaign, IL: Research Press.

Mintz, J. (1983). Integrating research evidence: Commentary on meta-analysis. *Journal of Consulting and Clinical Psychology, 51,* 71-76.

Minzberg, H., Raisinghaui, D., & Théorèt, A. The structure of "unstructured" decision processes. *Administrative Science Quarterly, 21,* 246-275.

Moore, A. D. (1969). *Invention, discovery, and creativity.* New York: Doubleday.

Mullen, E. J. (1978). The construction of personal models for effective practice: A method for utilizing research findings to guide social interventions. *Journal of Social Service Research, 2,* 45-65.

Mullen, E. J. (1981). Development of personal intervention models. In R. M. Grinnell, Jr. (Ed.), *Social work research and evaluation.* Itasca, IL: F. E. Peacock.

Nay, W. R. (1979). *Multimethod clinical assessment.* New York: Gardiner Press.

Nelson, R. O. (1981). Realistic dependent measures for clinical use. *Journal of Consulting and Clinical Psychology, 49,* 168-182.

Neuber, K. A., Atkins, W. T., Jacobson, J. A., & Reuterman, N. A. (1980). *Needs assessment: A Model for community planning.* Beverly Hills, CA: Sage.

Newell, A., & Simon, H. A. (1972). *Human problem solving.* Englewood Cliffs, NJ: Prentice Hall.

Ostrofsky, B. (1977). *Design, planning and development methodology.* Englewood Cliffs, NJ: Prentice-Hall.

Page, T. J., Iwata, B. A., & Neef, N. A. (1976). Teaching pedestrian skills to retarded persons: Generalizations from the classroom to the natural environment. *Journal of Applied Behavioral Analysis, 9,* 433-444.

Parsonson, B. S., & Baer, D. M. (1978). The analysis and presentation of graphic data. In T. R. Kratochwill (Ed.), *Single subject research: Strategies for evaluating change.* New York: Academic Press.

Patti, R. J. (1981). The prospects for social R&D: An essay review. *Social Work Research & Abstracts, 17,* 38-45.

Pelz, D. C., & Munson, F. C. (1982). Originality level and the innovating process in organizations. *Human Systems Management, 3,* 173-187.

Poertner, J., & Rapp, C. A. (1980). Information system design in foster care. *Social Work, 25,* 114-122.

Porter, A. L., Rossini, F. A., Carpenter, S. R., Roper, A. T., Larson, R. W., & Tiller, J. S. (1980). *A guidebook for technology assessment and impact analysis* (Vol. 4). New York: North Holland.

Prigmore, C. S., & Davis, P. R. (1973). Wyatt *v.* Stickney: Rights of the committed. *Social Work, 18,* 10-19.

Resnick, L. B., & Ford, W. W. (1978). The analysis of tasks for instruction: An information-processing approach. In A. C. Catania & T. A. Brigham (Eds.), *Handbook of applied behavioral analysis: Social and instructional processes.* New York: Irvington Publishers.

Rice, R. E., & Rogers, E. M. (1980). Re-invention in the innovation process. *Knowledge: Creation, Diffusion, Utilization, 1,* 449-515.

Rimm, D. C., & Lefebvre, R. C. (1981). Phobic disorders. In S. M. Turner, K. S. Calhoun, & H. E. Adams (Eds.), *Handbook of clinical behavior therapy.* New York: John Wiley.

Risley, T. R. (1969). Behavior modification: An experimental-therapeutic endeavour. In L. A. Hamerlynck, P. O. Davidson, & L. E. Acker (Eds.), *Behavior modification and ideal mental health services.* Calgary, Canada: University of Calgary Press.

Risley, T. (1982). *Behavioral design for residential programs.* Paper presented at the annual convention of the Australian Behavior Modification Association, Surfers Paradise, Australia, May.

Rogers, C. (1970). *On encounter groups.* New York: Harper & Row.

Rogers, E. M., & Shoemaker, F. F. (1971) *Communication of innovations: A cross-cultural approach.* New York: Free Press.

Rosen, A. (1972). The treatment relationship: A conceptualization. *Journal of Consulting and Clinical Psychology, 38,* 329-337.

Rosove, P. E. (1967). *Developing a computer based information system.* New York: John Wiley.

Rotherberg, A., & Hausman, C. R. (Eds.). (1976). *The creativity question.* Durham, NC: Duke University Press.

Rothman, J. (1974). *Planning and organizing for social change: Action principles from social science research.* New York: Columbia University Press.

Rothman, J. (1980). *Social R&D: Research and development in the human services.* Englewood Cliffs, NJ: Prentice-Hall.

Schinke, S. P. (1983). Data-based practice. In A. Rosenblatt & D. Waldfogel (Eds.), *Handbook of clinical social work.* San Francisco, CA: Jossey-Bass.

Schon, D. (1967). *Technology and change.* New York: Delcorte Press.

Schwartz, R. M., & Gottman, J. M. (1976). Toward a task analysis of assertive behavior. *Journal of Consulting and Clinical Psychology, 44,* 910-920.

Schwitzgebel, R. L. (1976). Behavioral technology. In H. Leitenberg (Ed.), *Handbook of behavior modification and behavior therapy.* Englewood Cliffs, NJ: Prentice-Hall.

Shapiro, D. A., & Shapiro, D. (1983). Comparative therapy outcome research: Methodological implications of meta-analysis. *Journal of Consulting and Clinical Psychology, 51,* 42-54.

Sidman, M. (1960). *Tactics of scientific research.* New York: Basic Books.

Specht, H. (1968). Casework practice in social policy formulation. *Social Work, 13,* 42-53.

Spencer, D. L. (1970). *Technology gap in perspective.* New York: Spartan Books.

Steinman, W. M. (1977). Generalized imitation and the setting event concept. In B. C. Etzel, J. M. LeBlanc, & D. M. Baer (Eds.), *New developments in behavioral research: Theory, method and application.* Hillsdale, NJ: Lawrence Erlbaum.

Stokes, T. F., & Baer, D. M. (1977). An implicit technology of generalization. *Journal of Applied Behavior Analysis, 10,* 349-367.

Stolz, S. B. (1978). Ethics of social and educational interventions: Historical context and a behavioral analysis. In T. A. Brigham & A. C. Catania (Eds.), *Handbook of applied behavior research: Social and instructional processes.* New York: Irvington-Nielburg/Wiley.

Stolz, S. B. (1981). Adoption of innovations from applied behavioral research: "Does anybody care?" *Journal of Applied Behavior Analysis, 14,* 491-505.

Stolz, S. B., Wienckowsky, L. A., & Brown, B. S. (1975). Behavior modification: A perspective on critical issues. *American Psychologist, 30,* 1027-1049.

Strube, M. J., & Hartmann, D. P. (1983). Meta-analysis: Techniques, applications and functions. *Journal of Consulting and Clinical Psychology, 51,* 14-28.

Struening, E., & Guttentag, M. (1975). *Handbook of evaluation research.* Beverly Hills, CA: Sage.

Strupp, H. H. (1978). Psychotherapy research and practice: An overview. In S. L. Garfield & A. E. Bergin (Eds.), *Handbook of psychotherapy and behavior change: An empirical analysis* (2nd ed.). New York: John Wiley.

Stuart, R. B. (1971). Research in social work: Social casework and social group work. In *Encyclopedia of social work.* New York: National Association of Social Workers.

Suchman, E. A. (1967). *Evaluation research: Principles and practice in public service and social action programs.* New York: Russell Sage.

Szasz, T. (1960). The myth of mental illness. *American Psychologist, 15,* 113-118.

Thomas, E. J. (1960). Field experiments and demonstrations. In A. Polansky (Ed.), *Social work research.* Chicago: University of Chicago Press.

Thomas, E. J. (1964). Selecting knowledge from behavioral science. In *Building social work knowledge: Report of a conference.* New York: National Association of Social Workers.

Thomas, E. J. (1973). Bias and therapist influence in behavioral assessment. *Journal of Behavior Therapy and Experimental Psychiatry, 4,* 107-111.

Thomas, E. J. (1975). Uses of research methods in interpersonal practice. In N. A. Polansky (Ed.), *Social work research: Methods for the helping professions* (rev. ed.). Chicago: University of Chicago Press.

Thomas, E. J. (1977a). *Marital communication and decision making: Analysis, assessment, and change.* New York: Free Press.

Thomas, E. J. (1977b). The BESDAS Model for effective practice. *Social Work Research & Abstracts, 13,* 12-16.

Thomas, E. J. (1978a). Generating innovation and social work: The paradigm of developmental research. *Journal of Social Service Research, 2,* 95-115.

Thomas, E. J. (1978b). Mousetraps, developmental research, and social work education. *Social Service Review, 52,* 468-483.

Thomas, E. J. (1978c). Research and service in single-case experimentation: Conflicts and choices. *Social Work Research & Abstracts, 14,* 20-32.

Thomas, E. J. (1980). Beyond knowledge utilization in generating human service technology. In D. Fanshel (Ed.), *Future of social research.* Washington, DC: National Association of Social Workers.

Thomas, E. J. (1983). Problems and issues in single-case experimentation. In A. Rosenblatt, and D. Waldfogel (Eds.), *Handbook of clinical social work.* San Francisco, CA: Jossey-Bass.

Thomas, E. J., Abrams, K. S., & Johnson, J. B. (1971). Self monitoring and reciprocal inhibition in the modification of multiple tics of Gilles de la Tourette's Syndrome. *Journal of Behavior Therapy and Experimental Psychiatry, 2,* 159-171.

Thomas, E. J., Bastien, J., Stuebe, D., Bronson, D., & Yaffe, J. (1982). The critical incident technique: A method of assessing procedural adequacy. Unpublished manuscript, University of Michigan School of Social Work.

Thomas, E. J., & Biddle, B. J. (1966). Basic concepts for the properties of role phenomena. In B. J. Biddle & E. J. Thomas (Eds.), *Role theory: Concepts and research.* New York: John Wiley.

Thomas, E. J., & Carter, R. D. (1971). Instigative modification with a multi-problem family. *Social Casework, 52,* 444-445.

Thomas, E. J., & McLeod, D. (1960). *In-service training and reduced workloads-experiments in a state welfare department.* New York: Russell Sage.

Thomas, E. J., O'Flaherty, K., & Borkin, J. (1976). Coaching marital partners in family decision making. In J. D. Krumboltz & C. E. Thoresen (Eds.), *Counseling methods.* New York: Holt, Rinehart & Winston.

Thomas, E. J., & Santa, C. A. (1982). Unilateral family therapy for alcohol abuse: A working conception. *American Journal of Family Therapy, 10,* 49-58.

Thomas, E. J., & Walter, C. L. (1973). Guidelines for behavioral practice in the open community agency: Procedure and evaluation. *Behavior Research and Therapy, 11,* 93-205.

Thomas, E. J., Walter, C. L., & O'Flaherty, K. (1974). Computer assisted assessment and modification: Possibilities and illustrative data. *Social Service Review, 48,* 170-183.

Tornatzky, L. G., Fergus, E. O., Avellar, J. W., Fairweather, G. W., & Fleischer, M. (1980). *Innovation and social process: A national experiment in implementing social technology.* New York: Pergamon Press.

Tribe, L. H. (1973). *Channeling technology through law.* Chicago, IL: Bracton Press.

Tripodi, T. (1974). *Uses and abuses of social research in social work.* New York: Columbia University Press.

Tripodi, T., & Epstein, I. (1978). Incorporating knowledge of research methodology into social work practice. *Journal of Social Service Research, 2,* 65-79.

Tripodi, T., & Epstein, I. (1980). *Research techniques for clinical social workers.* New York: Columbia University Press, 1980.

Tripodi, T., Fellin, P., & Epstein, I. (1971). *Social program evaluation: Guidelines for health, education, and welfare administrators.* Itasca, IL: F.E. Peacock.

Tripodi, T., Fellin, P., & Meyer, H. J. (1969). *The assessment of social research: Guidelines for the use of research in social work and social science.* Itasca, IL: F.E. Peacock.

Truax, C. B., & Carkhuff, R. R. (1967). *Toward effective counseling and psychotherapy.* Chicago: Aldine.

Truax, C. B., & Mitchell, K. M. (1971). Research on certain therapists' interpersonal skills in relation to process and outcome. In A. E. Bergin & S. L. Garfield (Eds.),

Handbook of psychotherapy and behavior change: An empirical analysis. New York: John Wiley.

Vondracek, F. W., Urban, H. B., & Parsonage, W. H. (1974). Feasibility of an automated intake procedure for human services. *Social Service Review, 48,* 271-278.

Walz, T., Willenbring, G., & Demoll, L. (1974). Environmental design. *Social Work, 19,* 38-47.

Warfel, D. J., Maloney, D. M., & Blase, K. (1981). Consumer feedback in human service programs. *Social Work, 26,* 151-157.

Webb, E. J., Campbell, D. T., Schwartz, R. D., & Sechrest, L. (1966). *Unobtrusive measures: Nonreactive research in the social sciences.* Chicago: Rand McNally.

Weeks, H. A. (1958). *Youthful offenders at Highfields: An evaluation of the effectiveness of the short-term treatment of delinquent boys.* Ann Arbor: University of Michigan Press.

Weiss, C. (1972). *Evaluation research.* Englewood Cliffs, NJ: 'rentice-Hall.

Wexler, D. B. (1973). Token and tabu: Behavior modification, token economies, and the law. *California Law Review, 61,* 81-109.

White, C. (1973). *Sources of information in the social sciences.* Chicago: American Library Association.

Wilson, G. T., & Rachman, S. J. (1983). Meta-analysis and the evaluation of psychotherapy outcome: Limitations and liabilities. *Journal of Consulting and Clinical Psychology, 51,* 54-65.

Winner, L. (1977) *Autonomous technology: Technics out-of-control as a theme in political thought.* Cambridge, MA: MIT Press.

Wyatt *v.* Stickney. 344 f. suppl. 281 (MD Ala. 1972) (Bryce and Searcy Hospitals).

Young, D. W. (1974). Management information systems in child care: An agency experience. *Child Welfare, 53,* 102-111.

Zetterberg, H. L. (1965). *On theory and verification in sociology* (3rd rev. ed.). Totowa, NJ: Bedminister Press.

Zifferblatt, S. N., (1973). Behavior systems. In C. E. Thoresen (Ed.) *Behavior modification in education: The 72nd Year Book of the National Society for the Study of Education,* Pt. 1. Chicago: University of Chicago Press.

About the Author

Edwin J. Thomas is Professor in the School of Social Work and in the Department of Psychology at the University of Michigan. After receiving the M.S.W. degree from Wayne State University in 1953, he took his Ph.D in social psychology from the University of Michigan in 1956. He has published over 100 articles and some 12 books, mostly in selected areas of behavior theory, behavior and marital therapy, and research methodology. Professor Thomas is also currently Director of the Marital Treatment Project at the University of Michigan, in which unilateral family therapy for alcohol abuse is being developed and evaluated.